of **Psy**

M000229810

Everything you need to know to administer, sco

I'd like to order the following *Essentials of Psychological Assessment:*

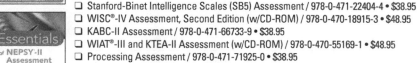

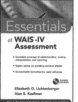

Please complete the order form on the back.
To order by phone, call toll free 1-877-762-2974
To order online: www.wiley.com/essentials
To order by mail: refer to order form on next page

Essentials
of **Psychological Assessment** Series

ORDER FORM

Please send this order form with your payment (credit card or check) to:
John Wiley & Sons, Attn: J. Knott, 111 River Street, Hoboken, NJ 07030-5774

QUANTITY	TITLE	ISBN	PRICE
_____	_____	_____	_____
_____	_____	_____	_____
_____	_____	_____	_____
_____	_____	_____	_____
_____	_____	_____	_____

Shipping Charges:	Surface	2-Day	1-Day
First item	$5.00	$10.50	$17.50
Each additional item	$3.00	$3.00	$4.00

For orders greater than 15 items,
please contact Customer Care at 1-877-762-2974.

ORDER AMOUNT _____
SHIPPING CHARGES _____
SALES TAX _____
TOTAL ENCLOSED _____

NAME_____

AFFILIATION_____

ADDRESS_____

CITY/STATE/ZIP _____

TELEPHONE _____

EMAIL_____

❏ Please add me to your e-mailing list

PAYMENT METHOD:

❏ Check/Money Order   ❏ Visa   ❏ Mastercard   ❏ AmEx

Card Number _____ Exp. Date _____

Cardholder Name *(Please print)* _____

Signature _____

*Make checks payable to **John Wiley & Sons**. Credit card orders invalid if not signed.*
All orders subject to credit approval. • Prices subject to change.

To order by phone, call toll free 1-877-762-2974
To order online: www.wiley.com/essentials

Essentials of
IDEA for Assessment Professionals

Essentials of Psychological Assessment Series
Series Editors, Alan S. Kaufman and Nadeen L. Kaufman

Essentials

of IDEA for Assessment
Professionals

Guy McBride,

Ron Dumont, and

John O. Willis

John Wiley & Sons, Inc.

Published by John Wiley & Sons, Inc., Hoboken, New Jersey.
Published simultaneously in Canada.

For general information on our other products and services please contact our Customer Care Department within the U.S. at (800) 762-2974, outside the United States at (317) 572-3993 or fax (317) 572-4002.

Wiley also publishes its books in a variety of electronic formats. Some content that appears in print may not be available in electronic books. For more information about Wiley products, visit our website at www.wiley.com.

Library of Congress Cataloging-in-Publication Data:
McBride, Guy Madara, 1944-
  Essentials of IDEA for assessment professionals / Guy McBride, Ron Dumont, and John O. Willis.
    p. cm. — (Essentials of psychological assessment ; 86)
  Includes bibliographical references and index.
  ISBN 978-0-470-87392-2 (pbk.)
  ISBN 978-1-118-04169-7 (ebk)
  ISBN 978-1-118-04170-3 (ebk)
  ISBN 978-1-118-04168-0 (ebk)
  1. Children with disabilities—Services for—United States.   2. Children with disabilities—Education—United States.   I. Dumont, Ron.   II. Willis, John Osgood.   III. Title.
HV888.5.M24 2011
371.90973—dc22
                                                                        2010051399

Printed in the United States of America

10 9 8 7 6 5

To Peggy, my wonderful wife,
and the only person as happy as
I am that I never got sued.
Also to my daughter, Lori Muse, and my grandson,
Tyler Muse, who taught me
the meaning of unconditional love . . .
and that it really is all about the children.
—GMM

To my beloved wife and partner Marybeth,
who has been forever supportive in my projects,
thank you. I will try to find another project for a cruise.
To my daughter Kate, for whom everything in my
life has been dedicated, I love you.
—RPD

To Ursula with all my love forever,
deep gratitude for your loving and patient support,
heartfelt thanks for four wonderful decades,
and joyful hopes for more to come.
You still make everything possible and worthwhile.
To Janet, Doug, Bernie, Amy, Bob, and Anna with great
love and deep appreciation.
—JOW

Table of Contents

Series Preface

I n the *Essentials of Psychological Assessment* series, we have attempted to provide the reader with books that will deliver key practical information in the most efficient and accessible style. The series features instruments in a variety of domains, such as cognition, personality, education, and neuropsychology. For the experienced clinician, books in the series will offer a concise yet thorough way to master utilization of the continuously evolving supply of new and revised instruments, as well as a convenient method for keeping up to date on the tried-and-tree measures. The novice will find here a prioritized assembly of all the information and techniques that must be at one's fingertips to begin the complicated process of individual psychological diagnosis.

Wherever feasible, visual shortcuts to highlight key points are utilized alongside systematic, step-by-step guidelines. Chapters are focused and succinct. Topics are targeted for an easy understanding of the essentials of administration, scoring, interpretation, and clinical application. Theory and research are continually woven into the fabric of each book, but always to enhance clinical inference, never to sidetrack or overwhelm. We have long been advocates of "intelligent" testing—the notion that a profile of test scores is meaningless unless it is brought to life by the clinical observations and astute detective work of knowledgeable examiners. Test profiles must be used to make a difference in the child's or adult's life, or why bother to test? We want this series to help our readers become the best intelligent testers they can be.

The *Essentials of IDEA for Assessment Professionals* is written by experienced *assessment* professionals, not by attorneys or government officials. It is designed to be a practical reference for psychologists and special education professionals trying to meet mandates of the IDEA, Section 504, and the Family Educational Rights and Privacy Act (FERPA) in the assessment of public school children ages three through 21 years. The book is also intended for students, interns, and professionals responsible for supervising or collaborating with assessment professionals in schools. The authors weave expert guidance throughout to help the reader avoid common legal errors; they also offer insightful guidance, particularly with regard to evaluations, assessment, classifications, and eligibility. The accompanying CD-ROM contains Microsoft Word™ documents and Adobe PDF™ files that the authors reference throughout the book to permit the reader to study and evaluate primary source documents rather than blindly accepting the authors' interpretations or the interpretations of other professionals. Even before Section 504 and the IDEA gave parents every due process right known to man (and woman), and then invented a few more, the assessment professional's life was governed by rules. However, the rules have grown ever more complicated since P. L. 94-142 (Education for All Handicapped Children Act, in effect the first "IDEA") was passed in the mid-1970s.

This book will also assist the prudent practitioner in identifying and avoiding those landmines and pitfalls while protecting children's civil and educational rights. This assistance is given in an appropriate and legally defensible manner under laws enforced by the Office of Special Education Programs (OSEP), the Office for Civil Rights (OCR), and the Family Policy Compliance Office (FPCO) in the United States Department of Education, including the FERPA, Section 1983 of the Civil Rights Act, and Title VI and Title IX. Interpretative advice from various enforcement agencies and landmark court decisions are cited to validate the authors' opinions. Written by assessment professionals for assessment professionals, this book is a highly practical guide, but not a substitute for legal advice from government officials and licensed attorneys.

Alan S. Kaufman, Ph.D., and Nadeen L. Kaufman, Ed.D., Series Editors
Yale University School of Medicine

Acknowledgments

Without the support and forbearance of our families, this book could never have been written. We give loving thanks to Peggy, Marybeth, Kate, Ursula, Janet, Doug, Amy, Bernie, Anna, and Bob.

We truly appreciate Alan and Nadeen Kaufman's generosity in allowing us to make a contribution to the *Essentials of Psychological Assessment* series. This is distinguished company and we are grateful for the opportunity.

Our thanks to Isabel Pratt, former Editor for John Wiley & Sons, for her early encouragement and support with developing the idea for this book and the daunting process of beginning it. We are very grateful to Leigh Camp, Production Editor, for incredible diligence and patience as we struggled through the later stages of the process. Thanks also to Marquita Flemming, Senior Editor, who inherited this project and saw it through to completion. Credit for any indication of literacy on our part is due to Debra Manette's extremely skilled and careful copy editing. Throughout the entire process, Kara Borbely, Senior Editorial Assistant, has handled many major tasks and myriad essential details with phenomenal efficiency, tact, kindness, and extraordinary attention to all of those details.

J.O.W. owes a particular debt of gratitude to J. Philip Boucher, for whom he worked in private and public special education programs for half a decade before and more than a decade after the passage of Public Law 94-142. We joyfully celebrated the signing of that law, and Phil, who apparently memorized every word of the federal regulations and state rules, was a magnificent mentor in special education law and the delivery of special education services.

R.P.D. and J.O.W. have long been appreciative fans of G.M.M.'s generously helpful and carefully documented listserv posts on special education law, which were the inspiration for this book and the source of much of the information in it.

G.M.M., on the other hand, acknowledges the contribution of R.P.D., whose idea this book was in the first place, and who single-handedly provided the first draft copy; and of course last but not least J.O.W., whose attention to details enabled us to provide the reader with a thoroughly reviewed references list, as well as saved us from a multitude of potentially embarrassing errors.

One

OVERVIEW OF THE IDEA 2004

The Buck Stops Here
—Sign on President Truman's desk in his White House office

The buck never stops here.
—McBride, Dumont, and Willis (2004)

The federal laws affecting the rights of children with disabilities have always been, to put it tactfully, ambiguous. For many school systems, getting simple answers to simple questions has been a lengthy and costly process, sometimes analogous to seeing if a gun is loaded by staring down the barrel and pulling the trigger. After publication of the 1999 Final Regulations, (entitled "Assistance to States for the Education of Children With Disabilities and the Early Intervention Program for Infants and Toddlers With Disabilities; Final Regulations," 1999), that situation seemed to intensify. The authors, participants in a number of national listservs related to school psychology and special education, saw an increasing number of questions about the law and the burdens it imposed. Over the years, in attempting to find and share answers to those questions, the authors accumulated a substantial body of information. That body of information provided the basis for this book. We took some of the more frequently asked questions and updated our answers based on the most recent statutory and regulatory revisions (up to 2010) affecting children with disabilities. It is our hope that our readers might find herein answers to some of their questions without incurring the inconvenience or expense of litigation. Recognizing that our unsupported opinions might carry little weight in an adversarial situation, wherever possible, we have, on the accompanying CD, also provided our readers with authoritative resources (statutes, regulations, case law, federal letters, and federal topic briefs) that can be relied on.

Traditionally, when writing a book whose basis is the law, the first thing anyone does is provide a statement ensuring that the buck never stops here—a major theme of this book, as it turns out. Nailing the basics of special education law (henceforth referred to as spedlaw) is like trying to nail pudding to a post. Some wonder if it can be done at all, and anyone who does try ends up becoming exceedingly frustrated as well as running the risk of feeling incredibly stupid. It would be nice if we could say with some assurance, "If you read such and such, and adhere to the rules therein, you will be safe from harm." But it is not true. Anybody can be sued any time for any reason. Understanding the law from a layperson's perspective may help to avoid some litigations or due process procedures, but knowing the law is no guarantee that we will never be sued. A person does not have to be evil, wrong, or mistaken. He or she just has to be in the wrong place at the right time. Ambrose Bierce, writing in *The Devil's Dictionary*, defined litigation as "a machine which you go into as a pig and come out of as a sausage" (Bierce, 1911/1958, p. 78).

Let us try to start out with realistic expectations. When we are trying to comprehend the world of spedlaw, several things actually do carry the force of law: federal and state statutes (because they *are* the law) and federal regulations. Federal law trumps state law, unless it explicitly defers to the states. For example, the 2006 Final Regulations for the Individuals with Disabilities Education Act (IDEA) establish a 60-day timeline from date of testing to an entitlement decision—unless a state has another timeline.

One of the problems readers often encounter is that what the federal special education regulations say in one paragraph they can modify or even take away a page later. The same is also true with federal regulations. Additionally, basic terms in both the IDEA and in Section 504 of the Rehabilitation Act (such as "Free Appropriate Public Education," "adversely affects," or "substantially limits") remain essentially undefined in the statutes. The regulatory agencies (e.g., Office of Special Education Programs [OSEP], Office for Civil Rights [OCR]) may tell us that those terms are meant to be defined on a case-by-case basis by the group (504) or Individualized Education Program (IEP) team (IDEA) after reviewing the results of a comprehensive evaluation. Whatever the intent, these types of guidance are not really very helpful. In order to simplify matters, when we refer generically to spedlaw (or "the law"), we will be including both the statutes and their implementing federal regulations (which carry the force of law).

Office of Special Education Programs (OSEP) letters (which will be referred to often in the pages to come) help clarify the law but do not carry the force of law; still, they might be persuasive in a court of law.

Circuit court decisions carry the force of law in the states overseen by that circuit, but they are not binding on other circuit courts. (When there is a split in the circuit courts, then the issues become ripe for Supreme Court of the United States review.) See Rapid Reference 1.1 for a list of sources of information with force of law.

Circuit court decisions are binding in the states they serve, but they are also fact specific. Change the facts, and while the standards will remain the same, the outcome may differ. For example, suppose a circuit court says Johnny is only socially maladjusted, not emotionally disabled, and cites in support of that conclusion the fact that all his teachers liked him and he got all As and Bs until he made "bad choices" in high school, falling in with a bad crowd. Then suppose an eligibility group has to make a decision about Jamie, who is just like Johnny—except everybody hates him, he never got a grade above a C (in physical education, once), and who always ran with a bad crowd. Can the group count on the precedent in your circuit's decision to support a find of noneligibility due to social maladjustment? Not with the same degree of assurance, because different facts can lead to different outcomes.

The Supreme Court's decisions are binding everywhere in the country, of course, but the same problems can arise. The Supreme Court decides a deaf child who is making all Cs has received a free appropriate public education (FAPE) from her special education. Can an eligibility group infer from that that a regular education child making all Cs is, therefore, not eligible for classification? No, because the court's ruling applied *only* to children who had *already* been classified and served, not to children being considered for services.

So is there an authority school evaluators can rely on? Well . . . if you find something that is precisely "on point" with respect to a particular question in the IDEA 2004, the Final Regulations of 2006, or the Preface to the Final Regulations of 2006, you are probably on safe ground—with no need for further support, assuming of course you have interpreted and applied it appropriately.

≡ *Rapid Reference 1.1*

Authoritative (though sometimes equivocal) sources of information with force of law include:

- Current federal statutes
- Current federal regulations
- Current state statutes
- Current state board of education codes, procedures, rules, or regulations
- U.S. Supreme Court decisions (to the extent that the particular facts are applicable and the relevant law has not changed since the decision)
- Circuit court decisions (in your circuit and to the extent that the particular facts are applicable and the relevant law has not changed since the decision)

If you find something written by a spedlaw attorney or parent advocate or school psychologist or college professor or educational specialist (or us) that seems "on point," you would be wise to look for at least two other independent sources confirming that interpretation before acting on it. If, for example, you stake out a position based on something we have written in this text without finding at least two other opinions that are authoritative (or something in the regulations or from Office of Special Education and Rehabilitative Services (OSERS), OSEP, or OCR and get clobbered, we explicitly deny responsibility. This is, in part, because if you have done everything suggested in the volume but still have a real problem, then our recommendation would always be to obtain the services of a real lawyer; but mostly it is because "the buck never stops here." That is not quite as cold as it may sound, because we have provided extensive documentation—authoritative documentation—on the CD accompanying this book to support many of the assertions herein so you can validate our opinions for yourself.

DON'T FORGET

Full texts of several important statutes and regulations, excerpts from some court decisions, and other information can be found on the CD accompanying this book. Material on the CD cited in text is annotated "(on CD)."

Most of the issues addressed in this book are taken from actual questions from school professionals in various venues and forums, some private and some public. The advice "The buck never stops here" may seem particularly appropriate for psychologists who test children, write reports, and make recommendations—proposals to be disposed of by others. But it is also applicable to school special education directors who aspire to the title "Teflon™ administrator." In this context especially, being a Teflon™ administrator is a good thing, because in special education, FAPE was defined by the United States Supreme Court (paraphrasing) as receiving educational benefit within the context of due process procedures, with particular reference to the right of parents to participate. What is trivial for one child, according to the Court, might be substantial for another.

The Act's requirement of a "free appropriate public education" is satisfied when the State provides personalized instruction with sufficient support services to permit the handicapped child to benefit educationally from that instruction. Such instruction and services must be provided at public expense, must meet the State's educational standards, must approximate grade levels used in the State's regular education, and must comport with the child's IEP, as formulated in accordance with the Act's requirements. If the child is being educated in regular classrooms, as here, the IEP should be reasonably calculated to enable the child to achieve passing marks and advance from grade to grade (*Hendrick Hudson v. Rowley*, U.S. Supreme Court 1982) (on CD).

William Rehnquist (then associate justice) included this statement in his opinion in the same case.

The Act requires participating States to educate a wide spectrum of handicapped children, from the marginally hearing-impaired to the profoundly retarded and palsied. It is clear that the benefits obtainable by children at one end of the spectrum will differ dramatically from those obtainable by children at the other end, with infinite variations in between. One child may have little difficulty competing successfully in an academic setting with nonhandicapped children while another child may encounter great difficulty in acquiring even the most basic of self-maintenance skills. We do not attempt today to establish any one test for determining the adequacy of educational benefits conferred upon all children covered by the Act (*Hendrick Hudson v. Rowley*, U.S. Supreme Court 1982) (on CD).

Nowhere does it say that school administrators get to unilaterally make decisions about special education children—except possibly within the context of properly convened IEP team meetings wherein they are serving as local education agency (LEA) representatives. Another maxim of sped-law is, or should be, as Clare Boothe Luce quipped, "No good deed goes unpunished" (Dickson, 1978, p. 109). Special education administrators who go beyond the scope of their authority (e.g., by giving parents a heads-up on the outcome he or she expects from an eligibility or IEP team meeting) outside the context of duly constituted meetings expose themselves and their schools to litigation, however well intentioned their motivations.

Be nice to parents. Always be nice. When the time comes not to be nice, that is why we have board attorneys.

Being nice does not mean rolling over like an old dog to be petted. But neither does it mean ceding the role of advocate to the child's parents and advocates, or "engaging" parents as if we were two locomotives converging at full speed on the same spot on the same track. It does mean ensuring that every child and every parent is made to feel welcome; it means disagreeing, if necessary, without being disagreeable; and it means ensuring that every child and every parent is provided with the rights accorded to them (whether we agree or not) by Congress and our respective state legislatures.

It is a basic tenet of this book that nobody really wins in a due process lawsuit. Staff is stressed, time that could be spent on other matters is lost, and, most important, the only ones who are guaranteed to profit are the attorneys. Generally, parents have to be awfully angry to go to due process. It costs them a lot of money, and while they are oftimes literally betting the family farm, school administrators are almost always playing with someone else's money. Still, there is always a cost-benefit analysis to be made—whether it would be better to spend a little more money serving a child with a disability than (strictly speaking) would be legally required for him or her to receive FAPE or whether it would be better to spend a lot of money subsidizing the board attorney's condo in Cancun over a trivial issue. For example, the school evaluates the child. The parents want an independent evaluation at district expense. The school can (1) pay for the evaluation or (2) go to due process, fighting the case up to the circuit court. In that kind

≡ Rapid Reference 1.2

Before deciding to pursue a due process hearing, consider all the costs: time, energy, stress on staff, damaged relationships with parents, and attorneys' fees.

of scenario (not an imaginary one by the way), if it goes to court, the district almost certainly spends more than it would have originally cost for the independent educational evaluation (IEE), whatever the judges decide. It is simply a matter of degree. (We discuss IEEs in Chapter 2 and in even more depth in Chapter 3.) See Rapid Reference 1.2.

Schools, perhaps even more than other organizations, fear "precedents." To some extent,

DON'T FORGET

Acronyms and Abbreviations

As in most specialized disciplines, special education comes complete with its own jargon. While we have made every effort to spell them out at least once in each chapter, a list of common acronyms and abbreviations used in this book and elsewhere is included in Appendix A at the end of this book for the reader's convenience.

there might be a legitimate concern that acceding to one parent's demand for services beyond FAPE (as interpreted by the school) might open the floodgates of parental demands for the same services for many other children. This fear must be evaluated from two viewpoints:

1. Would the extra services really be all that expensive (compared to the true total costs of due process hearings)?
2. Would there really be a large number of children whose circumstances were identical to this one?

A precedent is a precedent only if the relevant facts are the same.

STATUTES AND REGULATIONS

When Congress writes a statute, it often mandates that the department under which enforcement will fall write regulations that operationalize and enforce that law.

Various agencies within the Department of Education (ED) write and/ or enforce regulations for the Individuals with Disabilities Education Act, the Family Educational Rights and Privacy Act (FERPA), the Americans with Disabilities Act (ADA) and the Americans with Disabilities Act Amendments Act (2008) (ADAAA), Section 504 of the Rehabilitation Act, Title VI of the Civil Rights Act, Title IX of the Education Amendments of 1972, and the Protection of Pupil Rights Amendment (PPRA).

More specifically, the IDEA Statute and Regulations are the responsibility of the Office of Special Education and Rehabilitative Services/ Office of Special Education Programs (OSERS/OSEP), a division of ED, which among other things is responsible for assisting the states in implementation. Section 504 regulations are administered by the ED's Office for Civil Rights (OCR). The Family Policy Compliance Office (FPCO), also a division of the ED, interprets and enforces regulations and issues advisory information on the Family Educational Rights and Privacy Act (FERPA) as well a less familiar law, the Protection of Pupil Rights Amendment (PPRA).

Office of Special Education and Rehabilitative Services

OSERS is the lead agency in writing the regulations for the IDEA. It also "provides a wide array of supports to parents and individuals, school districts and states in three main areas: special education, vocational rehabilitation and research."

Office of Special Education Programs

A subdivision of OSERS, OSEP "assists states with implementation of the Individuals with Disabilities Education Act (IDEA). As part of its mission, OSEP is charged with developing, communicating and disseminating federal policy on early intervention services to infants and toddlers with disabilities and on the provision of special education and related services for children with disabilities."

OSERS provides a wide array of supports to parents and individuals, school districts and states in three main areas: special education, vocational rehabilitation, and research.

OSEP Letters

OSEP letters do not carry the force of law but continue a long-standing tradition of providing additional nonregulatory interpretations of the implementing regulations for the IDEA. The Pennsylvania Training and Technical Assistance Network (more commonly known as PaTTAN) maintains a searchable database of OSEP letters that can be easily searched by date or by general topic. (OSEP maintains its own database, arranged chronologically and by topic. Using Google's advanced search engine, the OSEP database, like PaTTAN, can be searched for specific phrases.)

Communications from State Departments of Education

Some state special education offices disseminate occasional memos and instructions. Like OSEP letters, these communications do not carry the force of law. They might have more influence in a due process hearing than in court, especially at the federal level, but that would depend on the hearing officers or judges. Oral and written advice from state education department personnel sometimes can be very helpful but are not determinative in a legal proceeding.

Office for Civil Rights

OCR is responsible for interpreting and enforcing implementation of the ADA/504 and Title VI in the schools. On its web page, it writes:

> An important responsibility is resolving complaints of discrimination. Agency-initiated cases, typically called compliance reviews, permit OCR to target resources on compliance problems that appear particularly acute. OCR also provides technical assistance to help institutions achieve voluntary compliance with the civil rights laws that OCR enforces. An important part of OCR's technical assistance is partnerships designed to develop creative approaches to preventing and addressing discrimination. (www2.ed.gov/about/offices/list/ocr/index.html)

Family Policy Compliance Office

FPCO is responsible for monitoring compliance with FERPA and the PPRA.

Although monitoring compliance with FERPA and addressing non-compliance issues is the responsibility of FPCO, OSERS also asserts its authority to monitor and address compliance issues regarding confidentiality as required by the statute and 2006 Final Regulations (Preface, 2006 Final Regulations, p. 46672).

Links to OSERS, OSEP, OCR, and FPCO are included on the accompanying CD.

Other sources of information and opinions regarding spedlaw include Sattler (2008, Chapter 3) and several books available on Wrightslaw (www.wrightslaw.com). Perry Zirkel (www.lehigh.edu/~ineduc/assets/vitas/zirkel_051209.pdf) has published many articles on special education law.

Typically within this book we reference specific regulations; those regulations carry the force of law and may be referenced in their entirety, for example, 34 CFR 300.8, or just by their section number (300.8). Attorneys, however, often reference the statutes themselves (e.g., USC § 1414(a)(1)(D)(i)(I)), which use an entirely different notation. We will not be referencing the statutes in this text. (If a reader wants to know the statutory justification for an IDEA regulation, all she or he needs to do is look up the section in question in the regulations, identify the statutory referents provided therein, and then look at the statute itself. We have provided both the statute and the implementing regulations on the accompanying CD, but they can also be easily found on the Internet.)

At certain points throughout this book we will be referring to specific sections and specific wording from IDEA itself.

How can one decipher this legalistic shorthand?

DON'T FORGET

Some important federal spedlaw agencies include:

- Office of Special Education and Rehabilitative Services (OSERS)
- Office of Special Education Programs (OSEP)
- Office for Civil Rights (OCR)
- Family Policy Compliance Office (FPCO)

STATUTES

Statutes are laws passed by federal, state, and local legislatures. Congress publishes laws, calling each an "Act," in the Statutes at Large, and then organizes laws by subject in the United States Code (USC or U.S.C.). The United States Code has subject classifications called "Titles," with Title 20 being the one designated for education. Within each title, laws are indexed and assigned section numbers. The symbol § often is used as the abbreviation for "section" (plural §§). Statutes published in the Statutes at Large have sections (section 1, 2, 3, 4, etc.) and the sections themselves may have multiple levels of subsections ((a), (b), (c), (d), etc.). See Rapid Reference 1.3.

So, back to deciphering our original mystery: What does 20 USC § 1414(a)(1)(D)(i)(I) mean? 20 USC tells us that we are dealing with a law (Act) published in the Statutes at Large and then classified as Title 20 (Education). Next, § 1414 tells us that we are referring to Section 1414 of the Title 20 Act. The subsection designations take us to a specific provision within that section. Confusingly, amendments and revisions are assigned the same titles and more or less the same sections as the statutes they replaced, so current and obsolete versions might have the same designation. Statutes are also referred to as Public Laws (PL or P.L.) with a hyphenated number, the first part referring to the Congress that passed the law and the second part a number specific to the statute. For example, the current, 2004, IDEA (20 USC 1400) is also called Public Law 108-446. (Each Congress is in session for two years, beginning in 1789–91, so the latest revision was passed in 2004 by the 108th Congress.) The 1997 version, also 20 USC 1400, was designated Public Law 105-17.

CAUTION

When researching an issue, be sure you are reading the most recent version of statutes and regulations.

REGULATIONS

In addition to the federal statutes, there are also regulations. It is to these that we will most often refer. Regulations provide clarification and explanations for the USC. Because regulations must be consistent with the USC and must be approved by Congress, they carry the same force of law. Each

State must ensure that its statutes and regulations are consistent with the *USC* as well as with the Code of Federal Regulations (CFR). Although the individual state statutes and regulations may provide more rights than federal laws, they cannot provide fewer or weaker rights than guaranteed by federal law. Some states have added more definitions to their special education regulations than are required by the USC. New Jersey, for example, is one of the few states to officially recognize "Social Maladjustment" as an educationally handicapping condition that would make a child eligible for special education services. (See Chapter 5 for additional discussion.) States may provide parents with more rights than the federal act; they may not restrict those rights. Similarly, they can increase the burdens on their LEAs; they cannot decrease them. If a state law or regulation is in conflict with a federal law, the federal law prevails, because of the "Supremacy Clause" of the U.S. Constitution (Article VI, Clause 2).

The Department of Education was responsible for developing and then publishing the federal special education regulations. Before the ED published those regulations, it published the proposed regulations in the Federal Register (FR) and solicited comments from citizens about the proposed regulations. The final special education regulations were published in Volume 34, Part 300 of the CFR, making the legal citation for the IDEA regulations 34 CFR § 300. Regulations in the CFR follow very similar notations to those of the USC, with sections (§§) and subsections. So, 34 CFR § 300.300(a)(1)(i) would refer to IDEA Federal Regulations (34 CFR § 300) subsection "300 (Parental consent) (a) Parental consent for initial evaluation (1)(i). The public agency proposing to conduct an initial evaluation to determine if a child qualifies as a child with a disability under § 300.8 must, after providing notice consistent with §§ 300.503 and 300.504, obtain informed consent, consistent with § 300.9, from the parent of the child before conducting the evaluation." While written consent is required on the occasions noted earlier, it is *not* necessary to obtain a parent signature on every occasion when their participation is required. For example, a parent may agree to sign consent for placement but refuse to sign an IEP. As long as the school documents parental participation in the IEP process (e.g., by recording that the parent was in attendance but declined to sign), it has met its legal obligation. (Assuming, of course, that the parent does not pursue his or her other avenues of appeal!)

≡ Rapid Reference 1.3

USC = United States Code (federal statute)
CFR = Code of Federal Regulations
§ = section (plural §§)
(a)(1)(A)(i)(I) = successive subsections

Unless noted otherwise, all references with the section symbol, §, refer to the federal regulations for IDEA 2004, 34 CFR Parts 300 and 301, Assistance to States for the Education of Children With Disabilities and Preschool Grants for Children With Disabilities; Final Rule, published in the Federal Register, Vol. 71, No. 156, August 14, 2006, pp. 46540–46845. The actual regulations begin on p. 46753. The commentary in the preface to the IDEA Regulations is referenced herein as "Preface, 2006 Final Regulations." Similarly, the 1999 Regulations for the 1997 law are cited as "1999 Final Regulations."

See how easy it is!

A COMMENT ON SPEDLAW

For all their complexity, omissions, and apparent arbitrariness, IDEA and state laws and regulations were written in a sincere attempt to rectify a terrible injustice. In the 1960s, when one of the authors (J.O.W.) was volunteering at a private special education school, the local superintendent of schools told a group of people that there were no handicapped children in the public schools because there were none in the town. It was probably rude to retort loudly "Then I sure [expletive deleted] away my time building a wheelchair ramp this weekend!" Until Public Law 94-142 was passed in 1975, loud, rude rejoinders and relentless, dedicated activism by parents, advocates, and teachers were about all that could be done to assert rights for children with disabilities. School districts and states were free to offer as much or as little education as they wished to children with disabilities. Many offered little or nothing. The law can indeed make our lives more difficult and can be cynically misused, but those of us who were involved in special education before the advent of spedlaw would never want to go back to the bad old days.

A VERY BRIEF HISTORY OF IDEA

Less than 40 years ago, schools in the United States educated only about one in five children with disabilities. Also at that time, many states had laws excluding from its schools students who were deaf or blind or who had emotional disturbance or intellectual disabilities. In 1975, the United States Congress enacted Public Law 94-142, the Education for All Handicapped Children Act (EAHCA or, more simply, EHA) to protect the rights of infants, toddlers, children, and youth with disabilities and to assure the right to a free appropriate public education (FAPE) for all children with disabilities. In return for federal funding, each state had to ensure, among other things, that the students with disabilities received nondiscriminatory testing, evaluation, and placement; the right to due process; and education in the least restrictive environment (LRE). Under EAHCA, students with identified disabilities were to receive an Individualized Education Program (IEP) that would clearly spell out the child's "unique" educational needs and how the school would address those needs. The IEP would contain relevant instructional goals and objectives, a statement about the determination of the most appropriate educational placement, and descriptions of criteria to be used in evaluation and measurement.

As mentioned previously, in 1982, the U.S. Supreme Court, in the *Board of Education of the Hendrick Hudson Central School District v. Rowley* case, provided some clarification regarding the level of services to be afforded to students with special needs and ruled that special education services need only provide some "educational benefit" to students—public schools were not required to maximize the educational progress of students with disabilities. Hence the now-old cliché that schools need only provide the Ford, not the Cadillac. (That still does not mean a 20-year-old Ford would suffice.)

In 1990, Congress updated Public Law 94-142 and changed its name to the Individuals with Disabilities Education Act (IDEA; Public Law 101-476). The updates to the law included the addition of new classification categories for students with autism and traumatic brain injury and required transition plans within IEPs for students age 14 or older. In 1997, the IDEA was reauthorized and amended (Public Law 105-17; referred to as IDEA '97). IDEA '97 required, among other things, the inclusion of students with disabilities in statewide and district-wide assessments, measurable IEP goals and objectives, and functional behavioral assessment and behavior intervention plans for students with emotional or behavioral needs. In 2004, the IDEA was again reauthorized by the Individuals with Disabilities Education Improvement Act (IDEIA) (Public Law 108-446). See Rapid Reference 1.4 for a quick reference list of special education statutes.

Part C

"Part B" refers to those regulations affecting school-age children with a disability who, as a result of their disability, need special education, and those children are for the most part the subject of this book. "Part C" refers to those statutes and regulations regarding children with a disability from birth through age 3 who, as a result, need special education. This book does not address Part C responsibilities in any detail. Part C was revised in 2004 as a part of the revisions made to the IDEA. Draft regulations for Part C were issued in 2007, but they were withdrawn by OSERS in January 2009. At the time this book was written, no final regulations for Part C had been issued based on the 2004 revisions. Pending the issuance of final regulations, OSEP has posted no current Topic Briefs on the subject. Therefore, the 1999 Final Regulations for Part C continue to carry the force of law (except insofar as they conflict with the IDEIA passed in 2004). For reference purposes only, some select Part C references (the 1999 Final Part C regulations, a listing of changes in the IDEIA 2004 affecting Part C, and a few OSEP Part C letters), are included on the CD.

The most significant changes, from our perspective, were the addition of mediation as another dispute resolution mechanism under Part C and the changes in their requirements for an Individualized Family Services Plan (IFSP)—specifically, the requirements that the IFSP include "[a] statement of specific early intervention services based on peer-reviewed research, to the extent practicable . . . and a statement of the measurable results or outcomes." Those changes should not in and of themselves significantly impact how evaluators conduct their business, but the requirement that to the extent practicable interventions be based on scientifically based research could affect how evaluators frame some of their recommendations (OSERS, n.d.b).

≡ *Rapid Reference 1.4*

Federal special education statutes include:

1975: Public Law 94-142, the Education for all Handicapped Children Act (EAHCA or EHA)

1990: Public Law 101-476, Individuals with Disabilities Education Act (IDEA)

1997: Public Law 105-17, Individuals with Disabilities Education Act (IDEA '97)

2004: Public Law 108-446, Individuals with Disabilities Education Act or Individuals with Disabilities Education Improvement Act of 2004 (IDEA or IDEA 2004 or IDEIA)

SOME GENERAL GUIDANCE

Like most things, spedlaw changes. Even some of the bedrock standards we discuss here may change with revisions in the IDEA, ADA, or Section 504. They change with circuit court decisions. They may, when there has been a split in the circuit, be overruled by a Supreme Court decision. The IDEA 2004 was itself amended in 2008 giving parents the right to unilaterally withdraw their child from special education. The ADA was also amended in 2008, broadening the definition of a disability by providing more examples of potentially entitling disabilities and by forbidding the consideration of mitigating measures (except for eyeglasses) in determining eligibility, thereby substantially reversing a decision by the United States Supreme Court in *Sutton v. United Airlines* in 1999. (See the regulatory amendments to the 2006 Final Regulations, effective December 31, 2008, on the accompanying CD. Also see the ADAAA amendments from December 2008 on the accompanying CD.)

Sometimes changes occur not in the law but in our understanding of the law. How does anyone keep up?

We recommend downloading key documents for easy reference. We have included among other documents searchable copies of the IDEA 2004, the 2006 Final Regulations for the 2004 IDEA, and 2008 Final Regulations for the 2004 IDEA, along with a searchable copy of the most recently posted copy of federal regulations for Section 504. An understanding of procedural requirements will never be complete without reference to state regulations, procedures, code, or policies governing a state's programs for exceptional children. We recommend anyone with a serious interest in spedlaw download an electronic, searchable copy of their state regulations onto their computer. Many of the issues addressed in this book arising out of questions posed in various forums could be (and ofttimes were) answered just by searching that database using key words in the search engine.

> ## DON'T FORGET
>
> Downloading copies of federal and state regulations to your laptop allows you to search quickly for relevant information before or during a meeting.

Thus far, we have only touched on the legislative and quasi-legislative side of spedlaw. Because the IDEA is so vague with respect to defining key terms and phrases (such key words and phrases as "free appropriate public education" [FAPE], "specially designed instruction," "adversely affects educational performance," "least restrictive environment," "determinant factor," and . . . the list goes on [see Chapter 2]), people spend incredible sums of money to get answers from hearing officers and judges to seemingly simple questions. Staying current with spedlaw in the courts is easy . . . if you have deep pockets and can afford to attend national conferences on the topic. LRP probably puts on the best conferences on spedlaw; information on its currently scheduled conferences can be obtained from www.lrpconferences.com/. LRP provides another source of free information regarding developments in spedlaw: *Special Ed e-news*: Go to www.specialedconnection.com/ and click on "Free e-news." It provides updates on important letters from OCR and OSEP as well as significant court decisions.

The best free information on the influence of the courts on a variety of issues can, in our opinion, be obtained from Peter and Pam Wright at Wrightslaw.com (www.wrightslaw.com). Their Web site is supported by their advertisements and sale of various products.

The Wrights maintain a searchable database running the gamut of special educational issues. Two caveats. First, because it is a free public service, it is not always up to date. Second, the opinion pieces, even when written by attorneys (even those who, like Peter Wright, have won U.S. Supreme Court cases), do not provide information that is necessarily determinative in deciding matters of law. That is up to courts and Congress.

A number of other agencies such as the Council for Exceptional Children, NICHCY at www.nichcy.org and www.Edweek.org offer free emailed newsletters that are dedicated to the service of special education children and which also occasionally offer updates on matters of interest to special educators. However, spedlaw is not their primary focus. See Rapid Reference 1.5 for a list of sources of information about spedlaw.

If you want to thoroughly research a question for your school system that is not answered in the chapters that follow (or if you want to find confirmation of opinions you have found here or elsewhere), we recommend that you take these steps:

1. Do a word search on the Final Federal Regulations (2006).
2. Do a word search on your state code/regulations/procedure/ policies. Federal regulations supersede state policies and regulations except where the federal statute explicitly defers to state law or state special education regulations. As another example, the IDEA regulations defer to the state with respect to using foster parents as parents (Section 300.30(a), p. 46760 of the 2006 Regulations). Also, while states cannot limit the federal rights given to parents, they can expand on them. For example, a state may make transition planning mandatory from age 14, not 16, as the 2004 IDEIA amendment requires, require functional behavioral assessments in a wider range of situations than mandated by the 2006 federal regulations, or require written parental consent when federal law does not.
3. After that, we recommend checking out OSEP's letters on the topic (paying particular attention to the dates; some OSEP letters before 2006 are no longer authoritative.)
4. OCR has always held that if an LEA meets the IDEA requirements, it has also met the Section 504 requirements regarding the same issue. However, if a child is identified as Section 504 eligible only, then we recommend doing a search for answers to your questions in the federal regulations for Section

DON'T FORGET

State laws and regulations may offer more and broader rights and services than federal laws and regulations. They must not offer fewer or narrower ones. If state laws or regulations afford parents and their children a lesser right than the federal law or standard, then the federal laws and regulations prevail.

504, articles in the OCR Reading Room, and the OCR Frequently Asked Questions for 504. All are included on the CD.

5. If the issues you are researching involve an adversarial relationship with parents, doing a preliminary search on Wrightslaw for key cases (followed by a search for the cases themselves) on the point(s) in question is recommended. Pay particular attention to decisions made by the circuit court for your state. Supreme Court decisions supersede both federal and state court decisions. Again, our warning about making sure that the decision still reflects current law still applies. In some cases, Congress has overturned landmark case decisions in its various amendments to the IDEA and ADA.

> ## CAUTION
>
> Court opinions and policy guidance letters from federal and state agencies may not always be applicable if the law or regulations have changed since they were published or if a federal court decision has altered the interpretation of a law.

Summary: "The buck never stops here." "Always be nice to parents." "In spedlaw, no good deed goes unpunished."

If you have a question that is not addressed in any of the letters found at OSEP or PaTTAN (e.g., is my state violating the regulations by not

≡ Rapid Reference 1.5

Other sources of information about spedlaw include:

- OSEP Letters
- Advisory memos from your state department of education
- U.S. Department of Education Web sites
- State departments of education Web sites
- Pennsylvania Training and Technical Assistance Network (PaTTAN)
- Wrightslaw.com
- Googling the IDELR identifier (e.g., 17 IDELR 950) listed with a court decision in the references to this book. You will get law articles and citations in other cases

allowing parents and schools to extend testing timelines for an SLD evaluation?), you can write to OSEP and OSERS directly at:

Office of Special Education Programs
Office of Special Education and Rehabilitative Services
U.S. Department of Education
400 Maryland Ave., S.W.
Washington, DC 20202-7100
Telephone: (202) 245-7459

Don't hold your breath waiting for a response. We have known turnover time to take from six months to up to a year.

You can also call the office at the number listed. The thing is, nobody is going to take your word that OSEP said such and such, and sometimes you do not get the same information via telephone that the office sends you in writing. G. M. M. was once told in no uncertain terms over the telephone that retention was a change of placement under the IDEA; but the written response said just as unequivocally that it was not!

How to Obtain Copies of Older Letters from OSEP Not in Their Online Data Bank under the Freedom of Information Act without Paying

Beg.

Anyone can contact the office at the address listed.

Actually, at the time this book was written, OSEP policy was to charge educational institutions, representatives of the news media, and noncommercial scientific institution requesters for duplication only, and even then (if a person requesting that information meets one of those qualifications) he or she would not be charged for the first 100 pages. However, we suggest you ask what the current fee policy is or specify a maximum amount you are willing to pay if there is a charge before submitting a request that could generate thousands of pages of documentation.

THE 46753 TRICK: COMMENTARY VERSUS REGULATIONS

If you do download a version of IDEA 2006 Final Regulations (on CD) in PDF format (this trick does not work if you have it in Word format), finding what you want may be time consuming if you are not exactly sure where it is located within the regulations. The PDF version of the law is actually a copy of the Federal Register starting with a page numbered 46540. The total document is 307 pages long. Of that, over 200 pages consist of commentary that provides wonderful discussions of issues and questions raised by concerned parties during the reauthorization process. Some commentators raised substantive issues that resulted in equally substantive changes to the final law. These 200 pages are chock full of interesting examples that in many cases demonstrate the government's rationale for its decision making. That being said, if you want to go directly to the actual law, skipping over all the commentary, you must go to page 46753 of the Federal Register. The 2008 amendments to the IDEA began on page 73006 of the Federal Register. The 1999 Final Regulations for the IDEA 1997 are referred as "1999 Final Regulations."

Unless noted otherwise, all of the text references that use the section symbol, §, refer to the federal regulations.

Conferences or Workshops on Spedlaw

School attorneys would never let their clients go into expensive litigation if they knew they were going to lose. (Not ethical ones, anyway.) But lose schools do, more than 40% of the time. You can help improve the odds for your school system by learning to be proactive, but nobody offers a foolproof away to protect a school system against all possible lawsuits.

Local law firms, local parent advocacy groups, and national parent advocates, such as Wrightslaw (www.wrightslaw.com/) offer less expensive workshops. Workshops by local firms and groups will vary in quality, and law firms and advocacy groups may have strong points of view biasing their interpretation of the law.

FINAL THOUGHTS

Throughout the chapters to come, we attempt to address, in layperson's terms but supported by citation and references to the law, common concerns raised by those who are responsible for following the special education laws and regulations. What follow are questions that have been asked over and over again by inexperienced and experienced professionals in the special education field. Each one seems on its face to be relatively simple to answer, but you may be surprised by what the "correct, legal" answer is.

✎ TEST YOURSELF ✎

1. **When determining special education eligibility, academic achievement must be measured by test scores.**
   True or False

2. **When it comes to learning disability classification under the IDEA, children are required to demonstrate at least average intelligence.**
   True or False

3. **When using ability/achievement discrepancies for the determination of eligibility for Specific Learning Disability, the IDEA says that the IQ score is equal to the expected achievement score.**
   True or False

4. **Ability/achievement discrepancy is important when determining disabilities other than Specific Learning Disability.**
   True or False

5. **If the school decides to utilize an ability/achievement discrepancy, the discrepancy must be determined by a numerical formula.**
   True or False

6. **A Full Scale IQ score must be used if the school decides to utilize an ability/achievement discrepancy calculation.**
   True or False

7. **Once testing is completed and eligibility determinations are made, record forms (protocols) should be destroyed.**
   True or False

8. **Students without disabilities may not have individual tutoring.**
   True or False

9. **Special education services are permitted only in area(s) of the child's identified disabilities.**
   True or False

Note: All of the answers to this short quiz are False.

Two

IDEA TERMINOLOGY

Lawyer, n. One skilled in circumvention of the law.
— Ambrose Bierce, *Devil's Dictionary*

When reviewing a library as massive and complex as special education law, one will inevitably encounter terms, legal or descriptive, that raise questions about intent. Throughout the Individuals with Disabilities Act (IDEA), terms are used that may or may not have clear intended meaning. This chapter reviews several of the terms used in IDEA and attempts to provide clarification, when it is available, about what Congress actually may have meant when it created the terms within the law. To demonstrate the problem associated with the terms presented in IDEA, consider the next hypothetical discussion:

> Parent 1: My child was just evaluated by the school and found to be a child with a *specific learning disability*. Because of the disability, the school says he is now eligible for *special education* and *related services* and for something called *FAPE*. The school also says that he will be provided with an *IEP* and placed in a program that is in the *least restrictive environment*.

> Parent 2: Wow, my child was just evaluated by the school and found not to have a specific learning disability because she was found to have a *cultural disadvantage*.

Trying to understand the terms set forth in IDEA sometimes reminds us of the famous Tea Party scene in Lewis Carroll's *Alice's Adventures in Wonderland* in which Alice, the March Hare, Mad Hatter, and Dormouse made these observations:

> "Come, we shall have some fun now!" thought Alice. "I'm glad they've begun asking riddles.—I believe I can guess that," she added aloud.

"Do you mean that you think you can find out the answer to it?" said the March Hare.

"Exactly so," said Alice.

"Then you should say what you mean," the March Hare went on.

"I do," Alice hastily replied; "at least—at least I mean what I say— that's the same thing, you know."

"Not the same thing a bit!" said the Hatter. "You might just as well say that 'I see what I eat' is the same thing as 'I eat what I see'!"

"You might just as well say," added the March Hare, "that 'I like what I get' is the same thing as "I get what I like'!"

"You might just as well say," added the Dormouse, who seemed to be talking in his sleep, "that 'I breathe when I sleep' is the same thing as 'I sleep when I breathe'!"

"It is the same thing with you," said the Hatter, and here the conversation dropped, and the party sat silent for a minute, while Alice thought over all she could remember about ravens and writing-desks, which wasn't much.

—Lewis Carroll, 1865/1962, pp. 104–105

The language of special education law (spedlaw) can be as logically illogical as Alice's conversations in Wonderland. See Rapid Reference 2.1.

This chapter presents issues and answers about some of the most common terms used in the IDEA. One problem with definitions related to

≡ *Rapid Reference 2.1*

In the practice of law, one question always generates other questions and then more questions. (See the 1973 film *The Paper Chase*.) That is why we have courts of law—to answer seemingly simple questions generated by unique sets of facts when the rule of law is applied to them. If lawyers already knew the answers beforehand, nobody would go to court.

IDEA is that, as Alice discovered, the words often do not mean what we thought they meant; or that the government never did make it crystal clear what it intended when it wrote the law; or that having said something on one page that appears clear, in the next page or paragraph the government introduces qualifications that change the meaning entirely. Anyone involved with special education will quickly learn that they must deal with these ambiguities.

Key Terms Defined Ambiguously or Incompletely in Section 504, IDEA 2004, and Their Implementing Regulations

In alphabetical order, here are a few terms that come to mind as undefined or defined ambiguously or incompletely in the statutes or regulations:

Adversely affects
Comprehensive evaluation
Day (school day, calendar day)*
Educational performance
Environmental, cultural, or economic disadvantage
Free appropriate public education
Highly qualified*
Intellectual development
Least restrictive environment
Native language*
Pattern of strengths and weaknesses
Peer reviewed*
Performance and achievement
Qualified professional*
Response to intervention
Scientific research-based intervention*
Special education
Specially designed instruction
Substantially limits

*These terms are defined at some length either in the Elementary and Secondary Education Act (ESEA) or in the Individuals with Disabilities Education Improvement Act of 2004 (IDEIA).

Definitions for "Environmental, Cultural, or Economic Disadvantage"

In the 2006 Final Regulations, the Office of Special Education and Rehabilitative Services (OSERS) simply said that the team decided whether environmental, cultural, or economic factors were sufficiently important to be exclusionary only after the evaluation was completed. The relative impact of any cultural factor, environmental, or economic disadvantage can be assessed only within the context of a comprehensive evaluation that also takes into account what reasonable expectations might have been for such a child who received (or did not receive) appropriate instruction in reading and math.

In the preface to the 2006 Final Regulations, OSERS noted:

> We believe the term "cultural" is generally understood and do not see a need for further clarification. We also do not believe that it is necessary to clarify that language cannot be the basis for determining whether a child has a specific learning disability. Section 300.306(b) (1)(iii), consistent with section 614(b)(5)(C) of the Act, clearly states that limited English proficiency cannot be the basis for determining a child to be a child with a disability under any of the disability categories in § 300.8. (p. 46551)

Later in the preface, in reference to all of this definition, OSERS wrote:

> The eligibility group makes the determination after the evaluation of the child is completed. Therefore, we believe that there is minimal risk that a child who is underachieving due to these factors will be identified as having an SLD. (p. 46654)

Sometimes we just wish OSERS would say "We don't have a clue. The courts will have to decide."

Exclusionary Factors as the "Determinant" Factor for a Child's Learning Disability

Potentially exclusionary factors are a lack of instruction in reading and math (applicable to all categories) and environmental, cultural, or environmental factors. If a school team determined that speaking English as a second language is the determinant factor for a child's deficiencies in educational performance, that too would be exclusionary. However, in all cases in which a team is deciding on exclusionary factors, it must use a two-pronged test: (1) Is a potentially exclusionary factor present? and (2) Does the team conclude that factor was the determinant factor in explaining the child's problems? OSERS has never been much help, saying even as far back as 1999 that, with regard to 34 Code of Federal Regulations (CFR) 300.534 of the 1999 Final Regulations for the Individuals with Disabilities Education Act (IDEA) 97, the standards and procedures were "appropriately left to State and local discretion" (p. 12633). There is a similar lack of clarity in the 2006 Final Regulations, where OSERS added:

> Whether a child has received "appropriate instruction" is appropriately left to State and local officials to determine. While information regarding the quality of instruction a child received in the past may be helpful in determining whether a child is eligible for special education services, it is not essential." (p. 46646)

It does seem clear, however, that OSERS' expectation at least was that those decisions not be made until a comprehensive evaluation had been completed—that the decision not be made a priori, for example, simply because a student came from the wrong side of town, spoke English as a second language, had been home-schooled for several years, or had been homeless as a result of poverty.

Also, exclusions do not exclude children. They only require eligibility groups to exclude from consideration low achievement when that low achievement is primarily the result of one of the exclusionary factors. "Specific learning disability does not include learning problems that are primarily the result of visual, hearing, or motor disabilities, of mental retardation, of emotional disturbance, or of environmental, cultural, or economic disadvantage" (§ 300.8(c)(10)(ii)). "The group determines that its findings under paragraphs (a)(1) and (2) of this section are not primarily the result of—(i) A visual, hearing, or motor disability; (ii) Mental retardation; (iii) Emotional disturbance; (iv) Cultural factors; (v) Environmental or economic disadvantage; or (vi) Limited English proficiency" (§ 300.309(a)(3) p. 46787).

The key word is "primarily." A child with one or more of the disabilities or disadvantages listed still might also have a specific learning disability. More in Chapter 4.

IEP and a Child's "Unique Needs"

The only guidance in determining a child's unique needs given by OSERS in the Final 2006 Regulations was procedural, that is, that it is up to the Individualized Education Program (IEP) team to determine what special educational and related services are needed in order to meet each child's unique needs and provide him or her with free appropriate public education (FAPE) (2006 Final Regulations, p. 46668).

DISABILITIES

Definition of What Constitutes a "Disability" (Educational or Otherwise)

Although there are many definitions of a disability, evaluators of children in public schools operate within a legal context wherein their responsibility is to ensure children are provided the rights guaranteed by Congress. Therefore, we rely not on the professional literature but on the statutory definitions, federal and state regulatory definitions, federal agency interpretations, and court precedents defining key terms to base our understanding of what constitutes a disability. Given that there are several laws focusing on disability (e.g., IDEA, Section 504, Americans with Disabilities Act [ADA]), as well as multiple advocacy groups, each can, and often does, have its own definition of what may or may not constitute a disability. Definitions also change with time. For example, the definition of a disability under Section 504 has been broadened as of January 2009 as a result of the Americans with Disabilities Act Amendments Act of 2008 (ADAAA), included on the supplementary CD.

The definition of what constitutes a disability is also broader now that Congress has decreed that in determining whether someone has a disability, 504 groups/committees may not consider mitigating factors such as the use of prescription drugs (although the ameliorative impact of eyeglasses still can be considered as the sole exception). (While mitigating factors generally cannot be considered when determining a child's eligibility for protection under Section 504, they still can be considered in determining what accommodations, if any, that child might need.) (See Chapter 5.)

Definition of What Constitutes a "Substantial Limitation" as It Is Used in Section 504

OCR has never given much guidance to teams in defining what constitutes "substantial limitation." OCR has always said that what constitutes a "substantial limitation" must be decided on a case-by-case basis by the team. This leaves everyone hanging from a limb and twisting in the wind. Courts, however, have generally compared a person with a disability to an "average person" in determining whether his or her limitations are substantial under 504. Under 504, in order to qualify as a person with a disability, a child need only be limited in a basic life function (in schools, usually learning, but not always). Under IDEA, the disability must adversely affect a child's educational performance to such a degree that special education is needed to meet those needs arising out of that disability.

Eligibility for Services

If a student does not need special education but does need extended time accommodations on high-stakes tests, would he or she be eligible for services if the team believed that the redefinition of specific learning disability was synonymous with any educational deficit? Could he or she be eligible for consideration as having a moderate learning disability (small "l," small "d") and eligible for extended time?

Not without a diagnosis from a qualified professional. Of course, if attention deficit hyperactivity disorder (ADHD) was suspected, the Office of Special Education Programs (OSEP) has long held that a medical doctor is not required to diagnose ADHD as long as an appropriately trained qualified professional has made the diagnosis (OSEP Letter to Michel Williams, 1994; OSEP letter from Riley to redacted, 2000 [on CD]). While states might require a medical evaluation for classification under "Other Health Impaired" (OHI) under the IDEA, a psychologist's diagnosis of ADHD could stand alone if accepted by the 504 group. In fact, even in states requiring a medical evaluation, unless the state explicitly requires a medical diagnosis (and at least one state does), there is nothing in the Individuals with Disabilities Education Improvement Act of 2004 (IDEIA 2004), the 2006 Final Regulations, or Section 504 to prohibit an eligibility group from basing an OHI classification on a psychological diagnosis and a medical ruling out medical conditions coexisting with or mimicking ADHD. (The 504 group could also require a medical evaluation to rule out other disabilities, but then the school would have to pay for it.)

FREE APPROPRIATE PUBLIC EDUCATION

Differences between FAPE under Section 504 and IDEA

The main difference between 504 and the IDEA in defining FAPE is that under 504, FAPE consists of the special education, related services, *or* related aids and services a student receives in order to meet those needs arising out of his or her disability. Under the IDEA, "FAPE" refers to the special education, related services, *and* related aids and services a student receives in order to meet those unique needs arising out of his or her disability. The key distinction is that under IDEA, FAPE is defined as special education *and* anything else the child needs. Under 504, FAPE is defined as special education *or* anything else he needs. Under the IDEA, a child cannot be entitled if he or she needs related services and/or related aids and services but not special education. Under 504, he or she can. For a complete definition, see Section 34 CFR 104.33 for the 504 definition; and 34 CFR 300.101 (p. 46762) of the 2006 Final Regulations for the IDEA on the accompanying CD.

Defining "Special Education" by IDEA

Special education means specially designed instruction, at no cost to the parents, to meet the unique needs of a child with a disability, including—(i) Instruction conducted in the classroom, in the home, in hospitals and institutions, and in other settings; and (ii) Instruction in physical education. (§ 300.39, p. 46761)

This section also lists as part of "special education" travel training, vocational education, and related services (but only "if the [related] service is considered special education rather than a related service under State standards"). Please see the complete text of this definition in the IDEA 2006 Regulations on the CD accompanying this book (or on the copy of the Regulations you have downloaded to your computer).

Defining "Specially Designed Instruction"

Specially designed instruction means adapting, as appropriate to the needs of an eligible child under this part, the content, methodology, or delivery of instruction—(i) To address the unique needs of the child that result from the child's disability; and (ii) To ensure access of the child to the general curriculum, so that the child can meet the educational standards within the jurisdiction of the public agency that apply to all children. (§ 300.39, excerpt, p. 46761)

The "or" is important; *special education is not a place*. It is the adapting of content, methodology, *or* delivery of instruction to meet a child's needs.

There is *no set standard* defining FAPE. What is an appropriate and meaningful benefit for one child may for another child be trivial and unimportant. The more recent iterations of the IDEA, requiring schools to provide services with a reasonable expectation of progress in the general curriculum, may have raised bar from the 1982 *Rowley* Supreme Court decision, but school systems are still not required to maximize each child's potential in order to have met its burden of providing a free appropriate public education (FAPE), and the *Rowley* standard still prevails.

Defining "Non-Trivial Benefit"

FAPE consists of special education delivered in accordance with the procedural requirements that provides the child with a reasonable expectation of non-trivial benefit. Determining what is non-trivial is not a comparative process between competing methodologies; and just because a progress is measureable does not mean it is not trivial. It is hard to pin down precisely because what is trivial for one child might be miraculous for another. For some it will be academic; but for others it might be social/self-help skills. If non-trivial benefit meant only that the student had made measurable progress, then almost all special education children would be doing that. As we noted in Chapter 1, the Supreme Court in 1984 established a foundation for determining whether a school system had provided a child with FAPE that included documentation of a reasonable expectation of benefit provided within the context of due process procedures (*Hendrick Hudson v. Rowley*, U.S. Supreme Court 1982) (on CD).

However, as early as 1985, the circuit courts were expanding on the Supreme Court decision. The Fourth Circuit in 1985 said, "Clearly, Congress did not intend that a school system could discharge its duty under the EAHCA [Education for All Handicapped Children Act] by providing a program that produces some minimal academic advancement, no matter how trivial" (*Hall v. Vance*, 1985; decision on CD).

Peter Wright made use of that argument in his arguments before the same court in 1991 in *Florence v. Carter*. The Fourth Circuit said in part (ultimately ruling in Shannon Carter's favor):

> The school district drafted the IEP to apply to a learning disabled tenth-grade student whose reading and mathematics skills were at a fifth and sixth grade level, respectively. Although the amount of appropriate advancement will necessarily vary depending on the abilities of individual students, see *In re Conklin*, 946 F.2d 306, 315–16 (4th Cir. 1991), the district court did not err in finding that a goal of four months' progress over a period of more than one year was rather modest for a student such as Shannon and was unlikely to permit her to advance from grade to grade with passing marks. Thus, it was proper for the district court to conclude that the itinerant program failed to satisfy the Act's requirement of more than minimal or trivial progress." (*Carter v. Florence Cty*, 1991) (on CD)

However, it may not even be necessary for a child to continue learning at the same rate as before placement for a court to conclude he or she has received FAPE. In 2000, in the *Caius* case (*HISD v. Caius*, 2000) (on CD), the Fifth Circuit asserted as its principle:

> An IEP need not be the best possible one, nor one that will maximize the child's educational potential; rather, it need only be an education that is specifically designed to meet the child's unique needs, supported by services that will permit him "to benefit" from the instruction. In other words, the IDEA guarantees only a "basic floor of opportunity" for every disabled child, consisting of "specialized instruction and related services which are individually designed to provide educational benefit." Nevertheless, the educational benefit to which the Act refers and to which an IEP must be geared cannot

be a mere modicum or de minimis; rather, an IEP must be "likely to produce progress, not regression or trivial educational advancement." In short, the educational benefit that an IEP is designed to achieve must be "meaningful."

In applying that standard, the court found that

the argument that Caius should not experience declining percentile scores may be an unrealistic goal, and it is a goal not mandated by the IDEA. Instead, the district court was correct to focus on the fact that Caius's test scores and grade levels in math, written language, passage comprehension, calculation, applied problems, dictation, writing, word identification, broad reading, basis reading cluster and proofing improved during his years in HISD. These improvements are not trivial, and we cannot say that the district court committed "clear error" in its factual determination that Caius received an educational benefit from his IEP (*Houston v. Caius*, 2000).

Still feeling a little confused? If you're looking for crystal clear clarity in the law, spedlaw should not be your field.

Determining How and What Is "Appropriate"

The IEP team has the final say on what is "appropriate"—unless, of course, the parent appeals and requests state assistance in developing a directed IEP, goes to mediation, or invokes the child's due process rights for an impartial hearing.

Defining "the Unique Needs" of a Student

Both the IDEA and Section 504 provide procedural standards with respect to what the teams must consider and how those teams should go about determining those unique needs. But there are no objective standards, and "unique" is not defined; that (and it is the feds who are repetitious, not us) is to be decided by each team on a case-by-case basis. See the previous discussion for some of the options parents have if they disagree with the IEP team's conclusion.

Proving "Educational Benefit"

Hearing officers and judges will look at measurements of progress in meeting IEP goals and objectives as well as standardized test scores. The IDEA requires that the IEP contain measureable goals; failure to do so could be fatal to any school system trying to argue that it had provided a child with FAPE. The kind of data collected would of course vary based on the goals (and the kinds of measurements needed to measure the child's progress). Goals measured with such scientific precision as "teacher observation" and "report cards" are often the downfall of otherwise adequate IEPs.

School systems regularly failed to win due process lawsuits when autism was involved (at least until they started collecting hard data documenting progress), even though the Supreme Court cautioned lower courts to give deference to schools when methodology was at issue. The Supreme Court, however, did not require blind deference, and when lower courts were confronted with parent advocates bringing reams of data and school systems relying solely on teacher testimony, schools lost because they could not show the IEP had been reasonably calculated to provide the child with benefit.

Generally, when we are assessing children, standard scores are the most accurate estimates of progress. Grade equivalents are not statistically defensible in most situations, a topic we address in more detail later on. However, when standard scores and percentiles have decreased over time, sometimes grade equivalents are all a school has to document that a child is plateauing but has not regressed.

In the *Caius* ruling (discussed earlier), the court established four factors that serve as an indication that an IEP is reasonably calculated to provide a meaningful educational benefit. These factors are whether

1. The program is individualized on the basis of the student's assessment and performance.
2. The program is administered in the least restrictive environment.
3. The services are provided in a coordinated and collaborative manner by the key "stakeholders."
4. Positive academic and nonacademic benefits are demonstrated.

Defining "Adversely Affects Educational Progress"

If a child is advancing from grade to grade and making reasonable progress, schools often claim that he or she is not eligible for special education services since reasonable progress is already being made. OSERS/OSEP has begged off when asked to provide some sort of comprehensible standard for "adversely affects educational progress," but it has been crystal clear in saying that

> LEAs [local education agencies] must ensure that FAPE is available to any child with a disability who needs special education and related services, *even though the child is advancing from grade to grade* ... [and that] the determination that a child [who is advancing from grade to grade] is eligible under this part, must be made on an individual basis by the group within the child's LEA responsible for making eligibility determinations. (§ 300.101(c) p. 46762, emphasis added)

However, it is important to understand that just because a child is advancing from grade to grade, that in and of itself does not necessarily mean an otherwise qualified student with a disability is ineligible. The *Rowley* standard can be applied with confidence *only* to students already identified and already being served.

CAUTION

Although both the IDEA and Section 504 provide procedural standards with respect to what the teams must consider and how those teams should go about determining unique needs, there are no objective standards. Eligibility decisions regarding children suspected of having a disability must be made by each team or group on a case-by-case basis based on the results of a comprehensive evaluation.

LEAST RESTRICTIVE ENVIRONMENT

Defining "Least Restrictive Environment"

Before we cite the relevant reference, we think it important to point out that FAPE and LRE (least restrictive environment) go together like a horse and carriage. Every child with a disability eligible for services under either the IDEA or Section 504 is entitled to FAPE in the least restrictive environment. The relevant IDEA reference (§ 300.114, p. 46764) states that:

> Each public agency shall ensure—(1) That to the maximum extent appropriate, children with disabilities, including children in public or private institutions or other care facilities, are educated with children who are nondisabled; and (2) That special classes, separate schooling or other removal of children with disabilities from the regular educational environment occurs only if the nature or severity of the disability is such that education in regular classes with the use of supplementary aids and services cannot be achieved satisfactorily.

That means, cutting to the chase, if a child can receive FAPE in a regular classroom, it does not really matter if being shipped off to a residential school in Timbuktu would provide an educational opportunity to maximize potential. Placement in the LRE is a right, not a preference, and not an option.

Determining What Is the Least Restrictive Environment

The IEP team makes that decision after consideration of all available relevant information and placement options. The criteria to be applied are (1) what is the setting that will afford the child maximum interaction with peers while (2) affording him or her with a reasonable expectation of receiving non-trivial benefit from his or her education. The decision by the team or group is of course subject to appeal by the parent.

Differences between 504 and IDEA with Respect to FAPE in the LRE

The differences are not substantial. See Section 104.34 of the Section 504 regulations on the accompanying CD for the regulatory definition of a student's right to placement in the LRE and Section 300.114 for the IDEA listing of LRE requirements.

Children who are entitled to services under the IDEA would be entitled to any additional due process rights affirmed by the statute; however, a comparison between the IDEA and 504 shows that, while the language differs, the right to a free appropriate education in the LRE is basically the same (including the right to a residential placement at district expense if needed) under both laws.

Continuum of Placements

Since the requirement for educating a child in the least restrictive environment implies that there are a variety of services available, schools often feel that they must apply some sort of continuum of placements that a child must actually go through, one step at a time. While in most cases it would make sense to increase a child's resource room support services before contemplating a self-contained or residential placement, there is nothing in the federal regulations that would require a school system to start a child with a nonverbal IQ of 26 and no measureable expressive or receptive language skills in a mainstreamed setting with an itinerant special education teacher. However, schools should *not* assume that just because a 5-year-old child has an IQ in the 40s, he or she could not be appropriately served in an inclusive setting. Sacramento made that mistake in 1994 with respect to a child named Rachel Holland; the fight that ensued with the child's parents ended up costing the school system in excess of $1 million in legal fees alone. A significant win for parents, a substantial loss for the school system (*Sacramento v. Rachel H.*, 1994, on CD).

Specific Criteria for Determining Least Restrictive Environment

We should consider several specific factors in making a determination of the appropriateness of an LRE. Not all circuits have adopted the same list of factors, however. In *Sacramento v. Rachel H.,* the court considered four factors:

1. The educational benefits available to Rachel in a regular classroom, supplemented with appropriate aids and services, as compared with the educational benefits of a special education classroom.
2. The nonacademic benefits of interaction with children who were not disabled.

3. The effect of Rachel's presence on the teacher and other children in the classroom.

4. The cost of mainstreaming Rachel in a regular classroom. (With respect to the latter, the court found that the district had fudged its numbers—not the kind of finding one wants when more than $1 million is at stake.)

For a more detailed description of the analysis done by that court, see *Sacramento v. Rachel H.*, 1994, on the accompanying CD.

Defining "Highly Qualified"

The only legal requirement for meeting the criteria of "highly qualified" is that an individual be licensed or certified by the state education agency (SEA) or licensed by the state to perform the functions being questioned. For a complete definition of the term "highly qualified," see p. 46553 in the Final 2006 Regulations on the CD. Assessors should, however, be sensitive to the fact that what parents may really be saying is that they do not believe you are personally qualified to be assessing their child; and that is really an entirely different issue. Parents are always anxious about putting their child in the hands of a stranger; their skepticism should never be taken personally.

Additionally, when assessing high-risk, low-incidence children, evaluators should be aware that those who meet the legal standard might not always meet the ethical burden to offer services based on their boundaries of competence based on training/experience. . . . or satisfy a judge that a highly qualified professional based on state credentials actually qualifies as someone with expertise in a specific area, such as autism. The examiner's actual experience and level of training in a specific area under review will routinely be questioned in any adversarial judicial or quasi-judicial process. Just as psychologists licensed by the state could be censured for engaging in practices for which they were not specifically trained, so too should all school evaluators be careful to practice within the limits of their actual competency. (The ethical burden placed upon professionals is to always practice within the boundaries of our competence, e.g., National Association of School Psychologists, 2010, Principle II.1, p. 6.)

Defining "Scientific, Research-Based Intervention"

The definition of a "scientific, research-based intervention" is taken from the Elementary and Secondary Education Act (ESEA), and it is quite detailed. Very briefly, "scientifically based research" means research that involves the application of rigorous, systematic, and objective procedures to obtain reliable and valid knowledge relevant to education activities and programs. The complete 201-word definition from the ESEA can be found in its entirety in the 2006 Final Regulations on p. 46576 (on CD).

Defining "Days" in Special Education Timelines

"Days," by itself, always refers to calendar days in the federal regulations for the IDEA. "School days" refers to days that the school is in session for students. The length of the day that students were actually attending is irrelevant; if they were there, it was a school day. (However, days that only exceptional children are in school for extended school year services would *not* count as school days within the context of the federal regulations. § 300.311.) "Business days" includes the days Monday through Friday, excluding days that are federal and state holidays, unless those days are specifically included. (It does *not* refer to days that school teachers or administrators are actually working; § 300.311.)

The term "school day" is generally used only regarding disciplinary procedures with respect to the number of days a child may be suspended without triggering due process rights.

"Business days" is used in a number of contexts, ranging from the authority of school administrators to discipline exceptional children, to the timing of events leading up to a due process hearing (see § 300.512 for details), to the amount of notice parents must give (10 business days) before placing their child unilaterally in a private school when FAPE is at issue (§ 300.148).

Defining "Stay Put"

"Stay put" applies whenever a district has recommended a change of placement, including some disciplinary change of placement and the parent disagrees and requests a due process hearing. What it means is that the child must be continued in his or her current placement while the matter is being resolved through due process.

However, it is important to note that there are exceptions. When a child has been unilaterally placed for 45 days in an alternative educational setting because of a weapons violation, drug violation, or serious personal injury to another person, the "stay put" setting would be the alternative setting, not the previous setting. Also, "stay put" would not apply to Part C children (children with disabilities being served who are less than 3 years of age) who are aging out of Part C but who have not yet been identified under Part B, which covers children age 3 and above. Or in the more stilted language of the regulations, "during the pendency of any administrative or judicial proceeding regarding a due process complaint notice requesting a due process hearing, . . . unless the State or local agency and the parents of the child agree otherwise, the child involved in the complaint must remain in his or her current educational placement."

Defining "Peer Reviewed"

A teacher mentions that she had discussed her interventions with her peers (other teachers in her school), and they all thought what she was doing was best practice. Does that meet the standard of "peer reviewed"?

Absolutely not. While the phrase is vaguely defined in the statutes, "peer reviewed" generally refers to research that has been reviewed by peers in a journal or through a comparably rigorous, objective, and scientific review. Additionally, the fact that someone, some group, or some group of intellectuals considered something "best practice" would not meet the standard for scientifically based research as summarized in the answer just preceding.

CHILD FIND

Defining "Child Find"

"Child Find" refers to the procedures established by each state and LEA to ensure that all children with disabilities residing in the LEA, including homeless children, children who are wards of the state, and children who have been parentally placed in a private school located in the LEA, are identified, located, and evaluated. Although they are subject to OSERS/ OSEP monitoring, Child Find procedures vary from state to state and from LEA to LEA. (Office of Special Education Programs, n.d.).

Responsibility for Child Find

SEAs are responsible for ensuring LEAs have Child Find procedures; LEAs are responsible for implementing them. In some states, the SEA may mandate Child Find procedures, while in other states it may delegate responsibility to each LEA for developing its own Child Find procedures.

> **DON'T FORGET**
>
> The IDEA regulations leave some issues for individual states to determine, and states may impose additional regulations on schools regarding their Child Find obligations as long as those regulations do not deprive students of their rights under federal law.

Finding Children Who May Have Disabilities

The way in which schools go about "finding" children with learning disabilities varies from state to state and LEA to LEA. However, each LEA is individually responsible for having procedures in place to identify every child with a disability between the ages of 3 and 21, whether they are homeless, whether they are wards of the state, or if they are in private schools, regardless of the severity of their disability (34 CFR 300.111 and 34 CFR 300.131).

In states where LEAs have been assigned lead agency responsibility for Part C (children birth to 3), they would also be responsible for identifying those children. Some states may have extended the age; in North Carolina, for example, children with disabilities are eligible for services through age 22 if they have not graduated from school with a regular diploma.

Children Attending Private Schools or Who Are Home Schooled

If a child does not attend public school, is the school still responsible for that child's education?

It depends on why the child does not attend public school. If it was for reasons unrelated to receiving FAPE (i.e., the child does not attend public school by parent choice), the LEA's only obligation is to extend Child Find procedures to the private schools, evaluating children suspected of having a disability, and offering to provide an IEP if the child enrolls in public school *or* offering a services plan of special education and related services (§ 300.37) *if that is what the school has elected, after consulting with the private schools, to provide.* If the school placed the child in the private school, however, then it is responsible for seeing that the child receives a free appropriate public education in the private school setting. A third possibility is that the parents, having met their due process obligations to provide the schools with prior notice, assert that they are placing the child in a private setting because the school failed to offer an IEP that was reasonably calculated to provide the child with more than trivial benefit (FAPE). In that case, if the school disagreed with the parents' assertion, a hearing officer or judge would decide who was responsible (*Carter v. Florence County*, 1991).

Home-schooled children fall within a special category. In states that regard home-schooled students as being in the same class as private school students, Child Find rights apply; in states that do *not* regard home-schooled children as being in the same class as private school students, those rights may not apply.

Along similar lines, schools often encounter students from another district or state who come to enroll in a school. The question arises as to who is responsible for the child's education.

If it was simply a case of parents wanting to put their child in a school or school system where they thought the child was going to get a better education, if residency could not be established, then the school or school system could deny admittance to the student. However, things are usually not that simple. Here are a variety of scenarios:

1. *Out-of-district child with a disability enrolled in private school.* The local LEA is responsible for evaluation and a services plan (if district services meet the child's needs). If the child's parents wanted to enroll the child in public school for an IEP or Section 504 plan, they would need to return to their home district. Parentally placed children with disabilities in private schools do not have an individual entitlement to FAPE.

2. *Out-of-district child with a disability enrolled in a group home for disabled children.* The local LEA is responsible for evaluation, services plan (if in private school), or IEP or Section 504 plan if the child is enrolled in one of the LEA's public schools.

3. *Homeless child with a disability enrolls in district.* The local district is responsible for evaluation, IEP, or Section 504 plan. The child has a right to FAPE and to select the school of choice irrespective of his or her entitlement as disabled based on the McKinney-Vento Homeless Assistance Act of 1987, and reauthorized in 2002.

4. *A child with a disability is in custody of the Department of Social Services (DSS).* The local district is responsible for evaluation, IEP, or Section 504 plan.

5. *A child with a disability under the guardianship of relative or other individual.* The local district is responsible for evaluation, IEP, or Section 504 plan. *The local district may, if their state allows, require the guardians to provide documentation from a court or the child's biological parents giving them (the relative or other individual) legal guardianship.*

6. *Parents paid tuition for their child to attend the public school.* LEA assumes responsibility for everything.

Defining "Pattern of Strengths and Weakness," "Performance," "Achievement," "State Approved Grade Level Standards," and "Intellectual Development"

Briefly, while OSERS provided some guidance in the preface to the 2006 Final Regulations (e.g., pp. 46646–46661), absent state clarifications, eligibility groups and IEP teams have a considerable amount of flexibility in interpreting those regulations. We discuss this in depth in Chapter 4, but, in general, most (not all) states are still allowing two basic methodologies: the discrepancy methodology and an RTI methodology.

OSERS intended to allow both historical and response to intervention (RTI) methodologies to coexist. Many teams in most states still determine eligibility based on intra-individual achievement/ability differences. In schools or states that have adopted RTI within a multitiered problem-solving model, the standard against which student performance is measured is that of the average peer, a standard not inconsistent with what would be required under Section 504. "Performance" is essentially undefined; some states are making a distinction between classroom performance as measured by nonstandardized instruments and achievement as measured by normed assessments. Assessments of cognitive performance, however, would also be allowed but not required. (OSERS was explicit, however, in saying that using intra-individual patterns of strengths and weaknesses in cognitive performance would not be an appropriate marker for SLD; p. 46654, 2006 Final Regulations).

PROCEDURAL SAFEGUARDS

Due Process

"Due process" does not just refer to a parent's right to file a due process complaint or to an impartial hearing but to all the procedural burdens placed upon school systems in Sections 300.500 through 300.536 of the 2006 Final Regulations (see CD). They include the prior notices that must be given before referring, evaluating, identifying, or placing a child in special education; the right to participate in various meetings; the right to an independent educational evaluation (IEE) if they disagree with the school system's evaluation; and the right to prior notice before the district changes or decides not to change just about anything (see below). Each of those decisions and actions must be documented, with copies of the documentation regarding prior notice being given to the parents as part of the due process requirements.

Due process safeguards must be provided in writing to a parent. Most if not all states have model parent handbooks that are to be copied and distributed. We recommend handing them out like candy, because if the LEA cannot document that the parents got their rights, it loses out on a lot of protections. For example, if the parent rights handbook says that appeals must be made within 6 months of a district decision, and the parents never got the handbook, courts may not hold them to the 6-month deadline.

The IDEA 2006 Final Regulations are specific, however, in saying that parent rights must be given each time that the LEA:

1. Proposes to initiate or change the identification, evaluation, or educational placement of the child or the provision of FAPE to the child; or

2. Refuses to initiate or change the identification, evaluation, or educational placement of the child or the provision of FAPE to the child (from Section 300.503 of the 2006 Final Regulations).

FERPA

The Family Educational Rights and Privacy Act (FERPA) (20 U.S.C. § 1232g; 34 CFR Part 99, on CD) is a federal law (sometimes known as "the Buckley amendment") that protects the privacy of student education records. The law applies to all schools that

DON'T FORGET

"Due process" does not refer just to a parent's right to file a due process complaint but to all the procedural burdens placed on school systems.

receive funds from the U.S. Department of Education (ED). The Family Policy Compliance Office (FPCO) in ED is responsible for monitoring compliance and enforcing the regulations nationwide.

FERPA gives parents the right to inspect all of their child's education records. These rights transfer to the student when he or she reaches the age of 18 or attends a school beyond the high school level. (See Chapter 9 for a more in-depth discussion of FERPA.)

INFORMED WRITTEN CONSENT

Defining "Informed Written Consent"

Section 300.9 of the 2006 Final Regulations for the IDEA 2004 requires written parental consent before a number of activities are undertaken by the school system when the public school suspects their child has a disability. In order for that consent to be valid, the parents must be informed specifically as to:

- What actions will be undertaken as a result of their giving that consent.
- That their consent is voluntary.

- Their rights under the law to appeal any decisions made as a result of the school's action (e.g., testing or special educational placement).
- Their right to withdraw that consent at any time.
- That the withdrawal of consent cannot be applied retroactively with respect to any action taken before their consent was withdrawn.

All of these elements must be present for the consent to be legal, and the requirement for schools to get that written consent is triggered *only* in the specific situations just listed when the school suspects or has determined the child to be disabled.

NATIVE LANGUAGE

If a child was born in Mexico and moved here when he was 3 years old, do we have to conduct his evaluation entirely in Spanish, even though he has always been taught in English? And do we need an interpreter for his parents?

These really are two separate questions. With respect to the parents, "native language" is the language normally used by that individual. Sometimes if the parents use both (seem proficient in English in everyday conversations but speak their first language at home), the school's contact

≡ Rapid Reference 2.2

§ 300.29 Native language

(a) *Native language*, when used with respect to an individual who is limited English proficient, means the following: (1) The language normally used by that individual, or, in the case of a child, the language normally used by the parents of the child, except as provided in paragraph (a)(2) of this section. (2) In all direct contact with a child (including evaluation of the child), the language normally used by the child in the home or learning environment. (b) For an individual with deafness or blindness, or for an individual with no written language, the mode of communication is that normally used by the individual (such as sign language, Braille, or oral communication).

person will just have to ask what language they prefer. With respect to the child, the school has to make a choice—whether to use in the assessment process the language used by the child at home or whether to use the language used by the child in the learning environment (assuming it is different). See Rapid Reference 2.2 for the legal definition of "native language." For more on the assessment of English as a Second Language/ Limited English Proficient (ESL/LEP) students, see Chapter 3 (§ 300.29; Lee, 2004; OCR, 2000b on CD).

INDEPENDENT EDUCATION EVALUATIONS

Defining "Independent Education Evaluation"

Parents have the right to obtain an evaluation of their child at any time. That evaluation is called an independent educational evaluation (IEE) if it is conducted by a qualified examiner not employed by the school. They have the right to an IEE at public expense only if they disagree with an evaluation already conducted and completed by the district. They cannot get it at district expense if the district has not already evaluated the child. Districts can refuse to approve an IEE at district expense, but only if they take the parent to due process and prove their evaluation was adequate, a costly endeavor, especially if one party or the other appeals a hearing officer's decision to the court system. Schools must consider the parents' IEE if it meets agency criteria (and it must tell the parents what those criteria are) (§ 300.502, p. 46791; Office of Special Education Programs, n.d.).

"SHOULD," "SHALL," "MAY," AND "MUST"

Words are particularly important in understanding statutory and regulatory language. When the regulatory language is expressed as a "shall" or a "must," failure to provide the rights or services indicated would trigger a finding of noncompliance by any independent auditor. When, however, something is expressed as a moral or ethical imperative or is expressed as something that is permitted ("may"), the indication usually is that it would be best practice to do it, but a school system would not be in violation of a parent's procedural rights if it failed to do so. Not all "musts" or "shalls" necessarily carry equal weight in the eyes of a court, however.

For example, failure to complete an evaluation within federally mandated timelines would not necessarily be fatal in and of itself to a school's case. Failure to allow for mandated parental participation in an IEP team meeting would, however, almost always be fatal to a school system's case.

TEST YOURSELF

1. **Section 504 and the IDEA both guarantee a child with a disability the right to special educational services if needed to receive FAPE.**

   True or False

2. **Most of the terms used in special education have very clear definitions located somewhere within the respective laws or regulations.**

   True or False

3. **In order to be considered "highly qualified" a person must**

   (a) have a doctorate degree.

   (b) have a specific certification attesting to being "highly qualified."

   (c) be licensed or certified by the SEA or state to perform the functions being questioned.

   (d) possess a teaching certificate.

4. **Parents can review only those educational records that the school deems necessary.**

   True or False

5. **Which of the following laws apply both to disabled and general education children?**

   (a) FERPA

   (b) IDEA

   (c) Section 504

   (d) No Child Left Behind

Answers: 1. True; 2. False; 3. c; 4. False; 5. a and d

Three

IDEA AND EVALUATIONS/ ASSESSMENTS

Experience is the worst teacher. It always gives the test first and the instruction afterward.

—Benjamin Franklin

In examinations those who do not wish to know ask questions of those who cannot tell.

—Sir Walter Raleigh

We are defining "assessment" as data-gathering strategies, analyses, and reporting processes that provide relevant information that can be used to make decisions about a person. There are many types of assessments (e.g., screening, focused, diagnostic), and there are many ways to conduct an assessment. Testing, formal or informal, criteria referenced or norm referenced, is only one form of assessment. Sattler (2008, p. 8) "advocates a multimethod assessment" that involves gathering relevant data from several sources, the use of several different assessment methods, and the assessment of multiple areas (e.g., cognition, perception, personality).

Evaluation uses the information gathered through assessments and strategies to support decisions on eligibility as well as in establishing present levels of performance for initiating, maintaining, changing, or discarding instructional or programmatic practices in the Individualized Education Program (IEP). (See Rapid Reference 3.1 for the legal definition of "evaluation.") Given the vast number of evaluations and assessments that are performed each year by school personnel following the guidelines presented in the Individuals with Disabilities Education Act (IDEA), one might think that the process would be a simple, straightforward one. Unfortunately, it is anything but that. At every step along the way, school

≡ Rapid Reference 3.1

§ 300.15 Evaluation

Evaluation means the use of assessment tools and strategies used in accordance with §§ 300.304 through 300.311 to determine whether a child has a disability and the nature and extent of the special education and related services that the child needs.

personnel, parents, and evaluators are confronted by legal guidelines (often unclear), rigorous obligations, and expectations, which, if not followed, can result in legal repercussions.

ANNUAL REVIEWS AND ELIGIBILITY SECTION 300.324 DEVELOPMENT, REVIEW, AND REVISION OF IEP

This information is related to students who *already have qualified* for special education services and/or programs.

Annual Review versus a Reevaluation

Typically, an annual review is less intensive than a reevaluation under the IDEA, but we have always held that an appropriately documented annual review updating a child's strengths, needs, and success in meeting IEP goals would meet the minimum regulatory requirements of Section 504 for a reevaluation prior to any change in placement (not a requirement under the IDEA).

Basically, the purpose of an annual review is to determine whether the annual goals in the IEP are being achieved and to revise the IEP to address any unexpected lack of progress. It may include reviewing the results of a reevaluation if one was recently conducted. Written parental consent is not required (§ 300.324, p. 46790) for an annual review. A reevaluation is conducted under the IDEA whenever the team determines it is necessary in order to ascertain whether the child continues to have a disability and/or to determine whether any changes are needed in the child's special education or related services. Written consent is required only if the team decides new testing is needed in addition to the review specified in § 300.304 of the 2006 Final Regulations to determine the child's continued eligibility or current levels of performance (§ 300.304, p. 46785).

Specific Requirements for Annual Review

The list in § 300.324 regarding requirements for annual reviews is extensive, and the reader is referred to the Federal Regulations on CD. In brief, the team must consider the child's strengths; parent concerns; the results of the most recent evaluation; and the academic, functional, and developmental needs of the child. Special factors to be considered include behavioral needs as well as needs arising out of speaking English as a second language (having limited English proficiency), being classified as blind, or being classified as deaf. Assistive technology needs must be considered as appropriate. Best practice would dictate review of the assessment data that have been collected at frequent, regular intervals throughout the year (a requirement if reclassification to specific learning disability [SLD] eligibility is being considered). Vision and hearing can change quickly and dramatically, so it is always prudent to review current vision and hearing testing/screening for all children with disabilities at least every three years, not just those classified as deaf, blind, or deaf-blind.

Reevaluations: Annually or Every Three Years

There is no obligation to conduct a reevaluation annually unless a parent or teacher requests it, and the school system is not obliged to conduct a reevaluation more than once annually unless both parties agree. Based on federal statute, local education agencies (LEAs) and parents may also agree in writing that no three-year reevaluation is required either. States may impose a higher standard (e.g., a state may mandate three-year reevaluations with no option to "opt out" even if the parents agree).

DON'T FORGET

Each state may impose requirements above and beyond those mandated by federal regulation. These opinions should always be read within the context of your state regulations.

Meeting Goals or Objectives at an Annual Review

If at the annual review it is determined that a student has not met all of her or his goals or objectives, does that automatically qualify the student as eligible for continuation of special education services?

Nothing is ever "automatic" (although unmet goals might suggest that the goals were unrealistic, that the program was not working as well as had been hoped, and/or that the student was still eligible). The question that must be answered in determining eligibility is not whether a child with a disability has unmet needs but whether he or she requires specially designed instruction in order for those needs to be met. It is worth repeating here that the definition of "special education" does not necessarily mean a child needs the content of instruction altered. "Special education" is defined as "specially designed instruction," which is defined as

> adapting, as appropriate to the needs of an eligible child under this part, the content, methodology, or delivery of instruction—(i) To address the unique needs of the child that result from the child's disability; and (ii) To ensure access of the child to the general curriculum, so that the child can meet the educational standards within the jurisdiction of the public agency that apply to all children. (§ 300.39, 2006 Final Regulations, p. 46762)

So even if a child is being taught on the same page out of the same book on the same day as classmates, if the child needs additional preparation before the lesson and more reinforcement through direct instruction after the lesson, and that service cannot in the opinion of the eligibility group realistically be provided long term through regular education, that could be considered "specially designed instruction" or "special education." Special education and regular classroom remediation may be qualitatively the same, the difference being in the intensity and duration of the intervention.

Review Team Members

Annual reviews are conducted by IEP teams, including the parent. However, state requirements regarding required participants may in some situations expand on the required federal membership requirements. For example, a January 2010 New York State (NYS) list of NY requirements

≣ *Rapid Reference 3.2*

IDEA addresses evaluations primarily at § 300.301 Initial Evaluations, § 300.304 Evaluation Procedures, and § 300.305 Additional Requirements for Evaluations and Reevaluations.

not required by federal regulation includes: "the school psychologist is a required member whenever a new psychological evaluation is reviewed or a change to a program option with a more intensive staff-to-student ratio is recommended" (New York State Education Department, 2010, p. 4).

The inclusion of a school psychologist is not a requirement imposed by federal regulations either at IEP team meetings or, for that matter, at eligibility group meetings. Many states simply echo the federal language in their regulations. While federal regulations do require someone to be on the team who is qualified to interpret the educational implications of the testing, that person, according to the Office of Special Education and Rehabilitative Services (OSERS), does not necessarily have to be a school psychologist (Preface, 2006 Final Regulations, p. 46670). So, although federal regulations require having someone on the team who is qualified to interpret the instructional implications of the test results, that person need not also be qualified to give the tests—unless state regulations or policies specify otherwise.

EVALUATIONS

Timelines Related to Evaluations

Until 2004, the federal regulations imposed no timeline for initial evaluations, leaving it up to the states. Now, however, if a state has failed to set a

≣ *Rapid Reference 3.3*

Section 614(a)(1)(C) of the Act requires that an initial evaluation be conducted within 60 days of receiving parental consent for the evaluation, or within the time frame established by the state.

specific timeline, the child must be evaluated within 60 days of the date the parent consented. If the state has set a timeline, state rules apply. See Rapid Reference 3.2 and 3.3.

TESTING ON OR OFF MEDICATIONS

A situation arises in which an initial evaluation is being planned and the parents are insisting that they want to take their child off prescribed medications during the testing. The parents' rationale is that the first time the child was tested, the examiner wanted the child off medications, so they are convinced this is the way it is supposed to be. What should the school do?

School personnel do not have the professional qualifications to tell parents to put their child on medications or to tell parents to take their child off medications. It is a decision to be made between the parents and their physician. If an evaluator other than the child's physician in the past said "Take your children off meds or I'm not testing him," the evaluator would have exceeded his or her professional boundaries. What you really need to know when you test, however, is whether the child is or is not on the prescribed medications—and if he or she has been taken off, how long that has been. That means building a trusting relationship with the parents so they will tell you the truth.

If they want to take the child off meds, it is their decision to make, no matter what anyone in the school thinks; and there is in an abundance of evidence suggesting that when schools start trying to influence parents into giving (or continuing to give) their children psychotropic medications, bad things happen.

Parents will sometimes do a blind study, taking their child off meds just to see if the teacher can tell a difference. We do not encourage that, and we recommend that parents consult with their child's doctor before unilaterally discontinuing prescribed medications even for weekends (giving their children a "drug holiday").

Even if your intentions were honorable, given that the IDEA explicitly prohibits schools from requiring parents to administer psychotropic drugs to their children as a condition for receiving an evaluation, you would be on very shaky ground if you tried to force this issue. The relevant section in IDEA is found at § 300.174 (p. 46775), *Prohibition on mandatory medication*. See Rapid Reference 3.4.

≡ *Rapid Reference 3.4*

§ 300.174 Prohibition on mandatory medication

(a) *General.* The SEA [state education agency] must prohibit State and LEA personnel from requiring parents to obtain a prescription for substances identified under schedules I, II, III, IV, or V in § 202(c) of the Controlled Substances Act (21 U.S.C. 812(c)) for a child as a condition of attending school, receiving an evaluation . . . or receiving services under this Part.

Regardless, any evaluation must (to be comprehensive) be based not just on the test results on a single day but reference all the data the eligibility group has from the classroom, teacher reports, school disciplinary records, and end-of-grade group scores (assuming there are any). If in the evaluator's or eligibility group's opinion they prove to be better indicators of the child's present levels of performance, then it would be appropriate to say so.

The preface to IDEA 2004 Final Regulations (2006) states:

> We believe that § 300.174 provides sufficient guidance on what school personnel can and cannot communicate to parents regarding a child's medication. Paragraph (a) clarifies that school personnel cannot require parents to obtain a prescription for medication for a child as a condition of attending school, receiving an evaluation to determine if a child is eligible for special education services, or receiving special education and related services under the Act. (p. 46622)

INDEPENDENT EDUCATIONAL EVALUATION

Here is a common scenario encountered by school special education teams. A parent requests an independent educational evaluation (IEE) (see Rapid Reference 3.5) at public expense after the school has already performed the child's three-year reevaluation. The parents say they are not disagreeing with the evaluation; they just want an evaluation to get a medical diagnosis. Must the school go to due process in order to reject this request?

In order to trigger their right to an IEE at public expense (parents can always get one at their own expense), parents must disagree with the school's evaluation. However, nothing is ever quite what it seems in special education law (spedlaw).

Disagreement might come in the form of their belief that the initial evaluation was not sufficiently comprehensive to identify all of the child's needs. The fly in the ointment is that parents are not required under past or present regulations to be any more (or even as) specific than that— which can leave a district guessing as to the nature of their complaint and, therefore, uncertain what an effective district defense might be in refuting it.

If the parents request an IEE and if the school system determines that its evaluation was adequate, it can go to due process to prove that was the case. While all special education litigation involves a roll of the dice, taking on the parents here could be particularly dicey. If, for example. they proceeded with the evaluation at their own expense, the IEP team would inevitably be required to consider it in the development of the child's IEP. If it adopted any significant recommendations from the outside evaluator, the school's case would be weakened. If it did not adopt any significant recommendations, the parents' attorney could argue that the school's review was perfunctory and the outcome predetermined. The thing is, it really would not matter how the hearing officer or judge finally ruled; the school would lose. It is just the extent of the loss that would change. Win, and the school would have to pay only its own legal fees (generally much

≡ Rapid Reference 3.5

§ 300.502(b)(4) Independent educational evaluation

If a parent requests an independent educational evaluation, the public agency may ask for the parent's reason why he or she objects to the public evaluation. However, the public agency may not require the parent to provide an explanation and may not unreasonably delay either providing the independent educational evaluation at public expense or filing a due process complaint to request a due process hearing to defend the public evaluation.

higher than the cost of the evaluation itself). Lose, and the school would have to pay for both its fees and the parents' legal fees. And, of course, for the IEE.

In the words of George Herbert, "A lean compromise is better than a fat lawsuit."

REEVALUATIONS FOR POSTSECONDARY INSTITUTIONS

Reevaluation for College Documentation

Public schools are not responsible for assessing students to meet a post-secondary institution's requirements. However, parents may request a reevaluation before the next IEP comes due, saying they want to update their child's present levels of performance in order to determine need for special education or related services. Even if they also wanted it for college, it really does not matter how many irrelevant reasons or motives they had as long as at least one of them was legally relevant.

We recognize that, in this era of economic stress, some school personnel may want to "help" children with postsecondary aspirations get 504 accommodations, and some school psychologists, anxious about their job security, might be willing to go the extra mile to help. However, we would strongly recommend not being "nice" on the district's dime without prior consent from one's administrator. In situations where IEP teams are writing testing for postsecondary purposes into children's transition plans, we would also recommend informing the appropriate administrator that district resources might not have been allocated appropriately.

"Going the extra mile" by doing an early reevaluation to determine entitlement or current levels of performance would not necessarily meet the requirements of the receiving institution anyway. Typically, postsecondary institutions require a specific diagnosis, that recommendations for accommodations be based on specific assessment data, and that the recommendations be more specific than school psychologists typically make (e.g., not just that a child be given extended time but how much). See, for example, the publication from the Educational Testing Service (ETS) on Documenting a Learning Disability (2007) at www.ets.org/disabilities/. Colleges often use the same criteria that ETS uses. School psychologists often do not diagnose a specific disability because (1) their evaluations are intended to assist in determining (not predetermining!) eligibility; (2) a formal diagnosis is neither sufficient, nor required, for a determination of eligibility; and (3) only IEP teams have the authority to determine eligibility (to classify students). For a sample of a state policy statement on that issue, see Lowell Harris (2001), in the Miscellaneous folder on CD.

OSERS has said:

> We do not believe that the regulations should require public agencies to conduct evaluations for children to meet the entrance or eligibility requirements of another institution or agency because to do so would impose a significant cost on public agencies that is not required by the Act. While the requirements for secondary transition are intended to help parents and schools assist children with disabilities transition beyond high school, § 614(c)(5) in the Act does not require a public agency to assess a child with a disability to determine the child's eligibility to be considered a child with a disability in another agency, such as a vocational rehabilitation program, or a college or other postsecondary setting. (Preface, 2006 Final Regulations, p. 46664)

The Office for Civil Rights (OCR) (2007), in a document included on CD, has said pretty much the same thing. Its suggestion was that if a child was eligible for vocational rehabilitation, he or she be directed to the Vocational Rehabilitation office to see if help was available.

It wrote in part:

8. Who is responsible for obtaining necessary testing to document the existence of a disability?

The student. Institutions of postsecondary education are not required to conduct or pay for an evaluation to document a student's disability and need for an academic adjustment, although some institutions do so. If a student with a disability is eligible for services through the state VR [Vocational Rehabilitation] Services program, he or she may qualify for an evaluation at no cost. High school educators can assist students with disabilities in locating their state VR agency at: www.ed.gov/about/offices/list/ocr/transitionguide.html. If students with disabilities are unable to find other funding sources to pay for necessary evaluation or testing for postsecondary education, they are responsible for paying for it themselves.

At the elementary and secondary school levels, a school district's duty to provide a free appropriate public education (FAPE) encompasses the responsibility to provide, at no cost to the parents, an evaluation of suspected areas of disability for any of the district's students who is believed to be in need of special education or related aids and services. School districts are not required under Section 504 or Title II to conduct evaluations that are for the purpose of obtaining academic adjustments once a student graduates and goes on to postsecondary education. (OCR, 2007)

There are, of course, situations where more frequent evaluations may be warranted and both parties may agree—for example, both parents and teachers want to know if a recently brain-injured child is plateauing in skill development after his recent injury, or parents and teachers of a child with a degenerative disease want to know if her IEP objectives need to be revised.

Providing Explicit Reasons for a Reevaluation

Parents do not have to provide reasons for requesting a reevaluation. The preface of the 2006 Regulations states:

§ 300.303(b), consistent with § 614(a)(2)(A)(ii) of the Act, states that a reevaluation may occur if the child's parent or teacher requests a reevaluation. There is no requirement that a reason for the reevaluation be given and we agree that a reevaluation cannot be conditioned on the parent providing a reason for requesting a reevaluation." (p. 46640)

Change of Educational Placement

Whenever there is a significant change of placement, a reevaluation is required because Section 504 demands it. Section 504 protections form an umbrella of protections that include all children with disabilities in the public school system, including those identified as disabled under the IDEA. In general, meeting the requirements under the IDEA will also meet OCR's requirements under 504. Exiting a child identified as disabled under the IDEA requires a reevaluation because the Final Regulations (§ 300.305 Additional requirements for evaluations and reevaluations [also see Rapid Reference 3.6]) say

CAUTION

Section 504 protections apply to *all* children with disabilities in the public school system, including those identified as disabled under the IDEA. In general, meeting the requirements under the IDEA will also meet OCR's requirements under 504, but when it does not, a child identified under IDEA also has any additional 504 protections.

exiting a child requires a reevaluation. However, an exception applies when eligibility terminates because of "graduation from secondary school with a regular diploma, or due to exceeding the age eligibility for FAPE under State law."

IDEA has never required a reevaluation before a change of placement. It has required prior notice. Section 504, however, does require reevaluation before a change of placement. Those regulations are enforced by the OCR, but the burden could be met by updating the child's strengths and needs based on classroom tests and documented teacher observations.

The 2006 Final Regulations say the IEP team must give prior notice before exiting a child with a regular diploma because it is a change of placement, but the school does not have to reevaluate that child. However, if the school gives the child something other than a regular diploma, the child's right to continuing services does not change, so there is also no change of placement requiring prior notice.

Change of Placement because of Discipline Issues

When there is a disciplinary change of placement, the IDEA (and Section 504) requires that there be a hearing to determine whether the behavior was a manifestation of the child's disability.

≡ *Rapid Reference 3.6*

§ 300.305 (e) Evaluations before change in eligibility

(1) Except as provided in paragraph (e)(2) of this section, a public agency must evaluate a child with a disability in accordance with §§ 300.304 through 300.311 before determining that the child is no longer a child with a disability.

According to OCR, the process that must be followed in holding a manifestation determination hearing under the IDEA would also meet the OCR requirements for a reevaluation. A reevaluation consists of reviewing not only previous evaluations but also current classroom-based assessments, teacher observations, and parent reports. If the IEP team determines that information is sufficient to determine the child's continuing eligibility, current levels of performance, special educational needs, and need for additional related services, it need not obtain additional data.

In making a manifestation determination, the team has to review the student's file, including the IEP, any teacher observations, and any relevant information provided by the parents (§ 300.530, p. 46798).

Therefore, while ordinarily previous testing would be reviewed, the team's decision (regarding exiting) or determination (regarding manifestation) would of necessity be based on current data, not old information. While there are extensive requirements regarding the tests we do use, neither the IDEA nor Section 504 mandates that we use any tests at all or do any testing as part of a reevaluation procedure, if (paraphrasing) the classroom assessments, parent reports, and teacher observations are sufficient for the team to determine the child's continued eligibility and to identify the child's strengths and needs.

REEVALUATION TIMELINES

Parental Request for Early Reevaluation

When a parent requests an early reevaluation with formal testing, there are really no specific timelines as to when the reevaluation must be completed, as long as the reevaluation is completed within 3 years of the previous evaluation. In general, the expectation is that the reevaluation would be completed in a timely manner, but there is no explicit time frame attached to that. See Rapid Reference 3.7.

Both OSERS comments and the IDEA speak to the congressional intent and to OSERS' intent to allow parents to seek at least one reevaluation per year. Johnny, identified with a disability and provided with an IEP, is referred by Mom for a reevaluation and tested 13 months later; absent state regulation, an auditor probably would not find the folder out of compliance as long as the reevaluation was completed before the 3-year timeline expired.

That does not mean a hearing officer would be as complacent about it. If parents request an early evaluation, it is clearly the school's responsibility to tell them that it has decided not to reevaluate the child as per their request and to give the parents their rights, not just to wait them out.

The lack of a specific timeline may appear to provide schools with a loophole; it has, however, always been our experience that enticing "loopholes" more often than not ended up being a seductive noose, beckoning the unwary to put their necks therein.

≡ Rapid Reference 3.7

Excerpt from the Preface to the 2006 Final Regulations

If a parent requests a reevaluation and the public agency disagrees that a reevaluation is needed, the public agency must provide prior written notice to the parent, consistent with § 300.503, that explains, among other things, why the agency refuses to conduct the reevaluation and the parent's right to contest the agency's decision through mediation or a due process hearing. (Preface, 2006 Regulations, p. 46640)

CONSENT TO EVALUATE

Parental Consent

Section 300.300 (p. 46783) of IDEA contains regulations regarding parent consent. There are actually three parts (a, b, and c) to this section, with the first related to parental permission for initial evaluations, the second related to parental consent for services, and the third related to consent for reevaluations. As noted, the requirements for (a) and (c) (initial and reevaluation) are differently defined in the federal regulations.

Basically, if a child is to be tested at any time for special educational purposes, the LEA must (with one exception for children in group homes on initial evaluations) have previously obtained prior informed written consent from the parent or legal guardian in the format prescribed by the state after the parents or guardians were provided with their rights as outlined in the IDEA 2004. (In the case of children in group homes, the head of the group home may sign for an initial evaluation, but a surrogate parent or legal guardian must sign for everything else.) Various states have added their own state-specific requirements for the content of a testing consent form. One state may present the parent with a general form that lists all the areas that may be tested; another state may require the team to check and get permission for specific areas to be assessed; and still another may require the team to get permission from the parents for each specific test to be administered. Therefore, in this area more than in most, it is critically important to be familiar with your own state's policies and recommended forms.

Parents Decline to Provide Consent

If the parents decline the testing, federal regulations allow the LEAs to take them to due process; however, if an LEA does not do so, it would not be deemed to have violated its obligations under the IDEA (p. 46784 of the 2006 Final Regulations). Given that parents have the unilateral right to reject any placement offerings (ibid.), and given that the 2008 amendments gave parents the unilateral right to withdraw their child from special education with no appeal from the school system possible (p. 73027 of the 2008 Amendment), we see little point in trying

> **DON'T FORGET**
>
> "Testing" and "evaluation" are not synonymous in IDEA.

to make a point by invoking due process if parents do not want their child tested. Also, parents can withdraw their consent at any time, except for actions that the school has already completed.

We need prior written consent only for testing that is being done to determine eligibility or to determine the strengths and needs of a child suspected of having a disability. The 2006 Final Regulations explicitly exclude educational screenings (§ 300.302) that are being done to monitor progress in the regular classroom. A school would not, therefore, be required to get parental consent for progress monitoring using curriculum-based measurements as part of a multi-tiered response to intervention process. Written consents before engaging in interventions, obtained without giving parents their rights as outlined in the IDEA, would have no weight in an adversarial proceeding; and a legal consent for special education testing would start the state-approved timeline for completion of an initial evaluation.

Written consent would also be required if a child were being evaluated for specific learning disabilities and the school and parent wanted to extend the testing timelines. That right exists only where SLD is suspected; and it exists irrespective of whether the state has its own timelines (§ 300.309, p. 46786 of the 2006 Final Regulations).

Within the broader context, written consent from parents is of course required before sharing confidential records with persons not specifically referenced in the list of exceptions; and it is required each time a school attempts to access a parent's health insurance, unless (as with Medicaid) there would be no immediate or long-term cost to the parent (e.g., with respect to diminished lifetime benefits). Last, OCR says that consent is required before testing a child under Section 504, but it does not specify that the consent must be written. Nevertheless, age-old dicta suggest that if it is not in writing, it did not happen; getting written consent is always best practice (*if* consent is required at all).

Although some states may require written consent before a change of placement (e.g., New Hampshire), that is *not* a burden imposed by the federal regulations. Again, always check your state regulations!

WHO IS A PARENT?

For initial evaluations, if the parent has not asserted his or her right to be involved, a relative with whom the child is living, a foster parent, a legal guardian, or a surrogate parent properly appointed by the school system may sign. See Rapid Reference 3.8. In cases where the child is in the custody of a Department of Social Services but assigned to a group home, the individual in charge of the group home may sign a testing consent for initial testing but not a consent to identify and place a child. Guardians ad litem (GALs) are not automatically entitled to sign consents for testing (or placement) unless the court has explicitly given them that right. Nothing prevents a school, using the procedures approved by their state, from appointing a GAL (if he or she is willing) to serve as a surrogate parent. *In no instance or circumstance may an employee of a Department of Social Services sign*

≣ *Rapid Reference 3.8*

§ 300.30 Parent

(a) Parent means—

(1) A biological or adoptive parent of a child;

(2) A foster parent, unless State law, regulations, or contractual obligations with a State or local entity prohibit a foster parent from acting as a parent;

(3) A guardian generally authorized to act as the child's parent, or authorized to make educational decisions for the child (but not the State if the child is a ward of the State).

a consent for special education testing or placement if the child is a ward of the State (Preface, 2006 Final Regulations, p. 46711).

Written Notice to Parents (Excerpt from §300.503 of the 2006 Final Regulations)

Written notice that meets the requirements of paragraph (b) of this section must be given to the parents of a child with a disability a reasonable time before the LEA—

(1) Proposes to initiate or change the identification, evaluation, or educational placement of the child or the provision of FAPE to the child; or

(2) Refuses to initiate or change the identification, evaluation, or educational placement of the child or the provision of FAPE to the child. (p. 46792)

Probably the quickest and easiest way to get a handle on parental rights would be to review the model handbook OSERS posted on its Web site. (We have provided a copy on CD in the OSERS OSEP Guidance folder entitled "OSERS Model Forms.") (See p. 5, paragraph 4, regarding parents' right to take their kid out of special education.) For rights specific to your state, however, you would need to obtain a copy of your state's model parent rights booklet. Usually that can be obtained from any special education teacher or the special education program director's office or downloaded from the state Web site.

PARENTAL CONSENT TO SCREEN (§ 300.302 SCREENING FOR INSTRUCTIONAL PURPOSES IS NOT EVALUATION)

Screening and Consent

If professionals in the school are doing screenings to develop appropriate instructional strategies, they are not considered evaluations, and written parental consent is not required by federal law. See Rapid Reference 3.9. Whether someone thinks the child might have a disability or not is irrelevant. The student support team is not providing interventions to determine eligibility. The respective staff members are doing interventions that are specifically designed to address the child's needs and keep him or her out of special education. The fact that the data the support team accumulates could play a preeminent role in an eligibility group's eligibility determination is also, as the law currently is written, irrelevant (§ 300.302, p. 46785). Although consent is not required and therefore should not be solicited—What do you do if the parents refuse?—it is prudent to inform the parents. If the team ever gets to the point of considering special education eligibility, a previously hidden file full of little surprises will not foster cooperative communication.

Extending the Boundaries of "Screening"

If team members decide to extend the boundaries of its "screening" to include instruments typically regarded as evaluations, claiming with a straight face "We're using them as screenings to develop appropriate instructional strategies for these children," they must be cautious. Although they could hypothetically administer a Woodcock Johnson Cognitive, a Rorschach, and a battery of neuropsychological tests without giving parents their rights and without even getting parental consent, the school might "get away with it" *if* the purpose was to use these assessments as a screening to help develop appropriate instructional strategies. (We cannot imagine a convincing scenario wherein a school alleged Rorschach results were being used to develop an appropriate instructional strategy.)

However, according to OSERS in the Preface to the 2006 Final Regulations, "*Screening is typically a relatively simple and quick process that can be used with groups of children* [emphasis added], and because such screening is not considered an evaluation to determine eligibility for special education services, parental consent is not required" (p. 46639). We have italicized one of the clauses, but the key word is "typically." We have consistently interpreted this section to allow us to use curriculum-based measurement (CBM) with individual children to help us determine appropriate instructional strategies without getting parental consent.

According to IDEA, an "evaluation" refers to an individual assessment to determine eligibility for special education and related services, consistent with the evaluation procedures in §§ 300.301 through 300.311.

Another danger in conducting a full battery of tests as part of the screening process would be that entitlement decisions would be made informally and without parents being given their rights to challenge. That is not an automatic blessing for the schools, because while parents' right to sue is time limited when they have been informed of those limitations, their right to challenge is generally *not* time limited if they were not given those rights. The team would also be deprived of valuable parental input, and the damage to the relationship with the parents potentially would be severe. We have, however, heard of at least one instance where parents requested a Woodcock Johnson Achievement Test as part of Tier III monitoring, and the school agreed.

Written Consent and Response to Intervention

Some school systems persist in getting written consents even when not required. We can only point out that if a school as a matter of administrative policy solicits parental consent to screen or provide interventions, the clear implication is that the parents can refuse regular education services designed to boost achievement and help the LEAs meet their federal and state mandates under No Child Left Behind (The Elementary and Secondary Education Act as reauthorized by the No Child Left Behind Act of 2001). Tier III interventions are a regular education responsibility. Rejecting those services is not a power given to parents under any law. Additionally, under the IDEA, if consent has been given, but the rights have not

≣ Rapid Reference 3.9

§ 300.302 Screening for instructional purposes is not evaluation

The screening of a student by a teacher or specialist to determine appropriate instructional strategies for curriculum implementation shall not be considered to be an evaluation for eligibility for special education and related services. (Authority: 20 U.S.C. 1414(a)(1)(E))

been received by the parents, then the burdens under the IDEA still would not have been met.

It is generally unwise to solicit unnecessary permission for something the school needs to do anyhow. What if permission is denied? Discussing activities with parents is not the same as asking permission. Interventions are not assessments, and prior written consent has never been required for interventions. The measurements being used to monitor progress may of course become part of an eligibility report later on. However, the problem-solving model was never intended to be a "prereferral" machine or just another way to get children entitled: It was intended to ensure that every child, with or without a disability, received the help he or she needed when it was needed. For example, even children whose deficits are clearly the result of a lack of appropriate instruction or who are limited English proficient (LEP) may be served through the student support team (SST) process. No child, not even the child whose background included potentially exclusionary life experiences, gets left behind in the problem-solving (response to intervention) model.

SECOND-LANGUAGE LEARNERS

Time "in the Country"

We have heard the argument that students with English as a Second Language (ESL) or who are English language learners (ELLs) have to be "in the country" for 3 years before they could be referred for learning or communication delays. This is a base canard. We also know some people who have said two years is necessary. This is also an error. So is 23 months.

We have never understood the underlying logic of that myth. While in two years, a typical ESL child will have developed adequate basic inter-personal communication skills (BICS), he or she probably will not have the necessary cognitive academic language proficiency (CALP) (Cummins, 1979) necessary to compete on an equal footing academically for 6 to 8 years. If an LEP child cannot participate meaningfully in the educational process only because he or she does not have the language skills, the federal burden on the school system is to provide the child with language instruc-tion outside the special education framework that is reasonably calculated to teach him or her English under Title VI (a right vigorously enforced by OCR). An LEA cannot substitute special education for an LEP or ESL instructional program if only because that would result in data showing disproportional representation, triggering sanctions both from the state and under the IDEA. For a more detailed discussion of that mandate, see "The Provision of an Equal Education Opportunity to Limited-English Proficient Students" in the OCR, Title VI, and Title IX folder on CD. Also see 34 CFR 300.173 and 300.600 on state responsibilities; and 300.646 of the 2006 Final Regulations, which obligates states to direct LEAs to use the maximum amount of their IDEA discretionary funds on early intervention when disproportional representation has been found for any subgroup.

An all-time favorite article of one of these authors (G.M.M.) on iden-tifying ESL children under the IDEA was written by a North Carolina school psychologist, Cecelia Lee, and adopted by the North Carolina School Psychology Association as a Best Practices paper (Lee, 2004). A key line: "These laws also prohibit the discriminatory denial of educational opportunities based upon race, color, or national origin. Thus, a student may not be denied evaluation for special education services solely due to the lack of proficiency in English."

Ethics, ESL, and Language-Based Intelligence Tests

It is not the administration of the test that determines whether some-thing is ethical; it is how the results are interpreted and used. Results from language-based testing, even when a child is both limited in English and from a cultural background where language is not emphasized, could be very useful as long as standard scores (customarily used in eligibility decisions) are not reported—and that is only because teachers have been known to take the reported scores out of context (i.e., without reading the psychologist's caveats) and plug them into state formulas without any further investigation.

Obtaining and reporting percentile scores could serve as a check against what the ESL teachers were reporting as a result of their testing. If their tests suggest that the child has achieved cognitive academic language proficiency (CALP), and the verbal intelligence scores suggest 2nd-percentile functioning (with nonverbal scores in the normal range), that finding could serve as a basis for recommending continued or expanded ESL/LEP services.

You can, for example, get a ballpark figure regarding a child's nonverbal skills using the Perceptual Reasoning Index from the Wechsler scales, but we would not recommend anyone give the Wechsler Intelligence Scale for Children performance battery to an ESL child who lacked basic interpersonal communication skills (BICS) without an interpreter. We would even recommend an interpreter if a psychologist were giving the Comprehensive Test of Nonverbal Intelligence (CTONI-2) or the Universal Nonverbal Intelligence Test (UNIT) to a non-English-speaking child, because (frankly), if the child wanted to use the bathroom or was otherwise distressed, we would not want to miss the cues.

An eligibility group cannot rely on a nonverbal test as necessarily being culture free, either. A subtest may require no obvious receptive or expressive language skills but still require language as an intervening variable for optimal performance. See the CTONI-2, for example. Many of the pictures used in the nonverbal test are extremely specific to North American or U.S. culture. Children with visual processing problems may also be negatively impacted by guesstimating general intelligence by just using a nonverbal battery. Accurate cognitive assessment for a child with both language and visual perceptual issues is extremely challenging.

Although normally we would be disinclined to use verbal scores in guesstimating an ESL/LEP child's potential, sometimes the scores do not turn out the way we expected. There have been occasions when an LEP child's verbal cognitive scores actually turn out higher than his or her Perceptual Reasoning Index (Wechsler) or Special Nonverbal Composite

(Differential Ability Scales II); an evaluator in good conscience could not fail to report the higher scores.

For a thorough discussion of the legal and ethical ramifications, see the archived OCR paper from the Clinton administration (OCR, 2000b; on CD).

For more discussion regarding the use of language-based tests in assessing LEP children, see Lee (2004).

WHO PAYS

Paying for Specific Evaluations

Some parent attorneys are routinely recommending parents obtain neuropsychological evaluations. The school system would be responsible, for example, for a neuropsychological evaluation only if it suspects that the child has a disability that can be appropriately evaluated only by a neuropsychologist. The issue was addressed with respect to ADHD in a Joint Memorandum from OCR and OSEP and then again by OCR in a separate letter. The underlying principles are general, however. Further, as *Cedar Rapids v. Garret F.* (1999) (for text, see IDEA Court decisions on CD) made clear with respect to related services, the issue of responsibility cannot be determined by cost factors.

OCR and OSEP said in 1991:

> SEAs and LEAs have an affirmative obligation to evaluate a child who is suspected of having a disability to determine the child's need for special education and related services. Under Part B, SEAs and LEAs are required to have procedures for locating, identifying and evaluating all children who have a disability or are suspected of having a disability and are in need of special education and related services. This responsibility, known as "child find" is applicable to all children from birth through 21, regardless of the severity of their disability.
>
> Consistent with this responsibility and the obligation to make FAPE available to all eligible children with disabilities, SEAs and LEAs must ensure that evaluations of children who are suspected of needing special education and related services are conducted without undue delay. (20 U.S.C. 1412(2)) (See the entire text in the OCR Letters folder on CD.)

That 1991 clarification was clarified again in 1993 by OCR:

> To our dismay, this statement has been interpreted to mean that school districts are required to evaluate every child suspected of having ADD, based solely on parental suspicion and demand. This was not the intent of the statement. Rather, under Section 504, if parents believe their child has a disability, whether by ADD or any other impairment, and the LEA has reason to believe the child needs special education or related services, the LEA must evaluate the child to determine whether he or she is disabled as defined by Section 504. If the LEA does not believe that the child needs special education or related services, and thus refuses to evaluate the child, the LEA must notify the parents of their due process rights. (See Letter from Lim re ADD, undated, with the Subject line "Clarification of School Districts' Responsibilities to Evaluate Children with Attention Deficit Disorders (ADD)" in the OCR letters on CD.)

If a school suspects that a child needs special education or classroom accommodations because he or she has ADHD, the district must pay for his or her evaluation. As quoted, if parents believe that their child has any disability, including ADHD, and the school district has reason to believe that the child may need special education, related services, or even just 504 accommodations in order to level the playing field, the school district must evaluate the child *at no cost to the parent*—the school pays. If the school does not believe the child needs special education or related services, and therefore does not agree to provide an evaluation, the school must notify the parents of their due process rights.

USING PARENTS' INSURANCE

School's Use of Parents' Health Insurance

The current regulations allow schools to ask parents to use their health insurance to pay for medical evaluations required by state codes/regulations/policies for classification as Other Health Impaired, but schools may not require parents to let the school use their insurance. An exception would be if the child was on Medicaid, where the school's use of that insurance would involve absolutely no cost, hidden or otherwise, to the parents.

≡ *Rapid Reference 3.10*

§ 300.154 Methods of ensuring services

(e) *Children with disabilities who are covered by private insurance.* (1) With regard to services required to provide FAPE to an eligible child under this part, a public agency may access the parents' private insurance proceeds only if the parents provide consent consistent with § 300.9.

However, schools may not require parents to obtain that insurance as a condition of service.

Until (or unless) changes in the healthcare law go into effect, most insurance policies still have caps, and when parents use their insurance, there is a hidden cost, which is forbidden under IDEA. See p. 46608 of the 2006 Regulations; § 300.154 (d) and (e), pp. 46771–46772.

Note that the advice herein may change if and when changes in national healthcare laws eliminate caps and prohibit insurance companies from canceling policies when overused.

Requiring Parents to Sign Up for Public Insurance or Medicaid

Schools may not require parents to sign up for public insurance as a condition of service. The school may ask parents to allow them to use their insurance coverage for health-related evaluations needed to determine a child's eligibility or current needs and strengths, but only if parents are given their rights, including the right to refuse. That is true whether the parents are insured by public or private insurance. Again, see § 300.154 (d) of the Final 2006 Federal Regulations on CD for a more detailed (and more authoritative) answer to this question. Also see Rapid Reference 3.10.

REPORTS

Telling Students Results

The federal regulations do not address the issue of whether evaluators are required to interpret the results of assessments to the children they test. There is of course no way to stop parents from sharing whatever they deemed relevant even if we wanted to do so, and there is no regulatory or statutory burden for an evaluator to do so. The primary burden on the evaluator is to provide the team, including parents, sufficient information to address eligibility and/or present levels of performance. Some evaluators have written for their evaluations cover pages with brief summaries written as clearly as possible at relatively low reading level. The two disadvantages to this procedure are the extra time required and the risk of an attorney taking the simplified summary out of context for a hearing or court case.

Paraphrasing, the IDEA 2004 and implementing regulations (2006) say that children should be members of the IEP team when appropriate and that they must be invited whenever postsecondary goals or transition is being discussed (but do not have to come, although their preferences must be considered). There is no federal requirement that any child be a part of the eligibility group (which must be composed of qualified professionals and the parent).

Excerpt from § 300.321 (IEP Team)

§ 300.321 IEP Team. (a) *General.* The public agency must ensure that the IEP Team for each child with a disability includes—

(1) The parents of the child:

(2) Not less than one regular education teacher of the child (if the child is, or may be, participating in the regular education environment);

(3) Not less than one special education teacher of the child, or where appropriate, not less than one special education provider of the child;

(4) A representative of the public agency who—(i) Is qualified to provide, or supervise the provision of, specially designed instruction to meet the unique needs of children with disabilities; (ii) Is knowledgeable about the general education curriculum; and (iii) Is knowledgeable about the availability of resources of the public agency.

(5) An individual who can interpret the instructional implications of evaluation results, who may be a member of the team described in paragraphs (a)(2) through (a)(6) of this section;

(6) At the discretion of the parent or the agency, other individuals who have knowledge or special expertise regarding the child, including related services personnel as appropriate; and

(7) Whenever appropriate, the child with a disability. (§ 300.321)

With respect to implementing federal requirements for transition services, the regulations go on to say: "If the child does not attend the IEP team meeting, the public agency must take other steps to ensure that the child's preferences and interests are considered" (§ 300.321(b)).

While children of any age might be invited to participate in IEP team meetings, the intent of OSERS was to leave the final decision in the hands of the parent.

Generally, a child with a disability should attend the IEP Team meeting if the parent decides that it is appropriate for the child to do so. If possible, the agency and parent should discuss the appropriateness of the child's participation before a decision is made, in order to help the parent determine whether or not the child's attendance would be helpful in developing the IEP or directly beneficial to the child, or both. (Preface, 2006 Final Regulations, p. 46671)

TEST YOURSELF

1. The terms "evaluation" and "assessment" are essentially the same thing when it comes to IDEA terminology.
   True or False

2. According to the IDEA, schools can require parents to administer psychotropic drugs to their children as a condition for receiving an evaluation.
   True or False

3. According to IDEA, once a parent has consented to an initial evaluation, how many days does the school have to complete the evaluation if a state has not established its own timeline?
   (a) 40
   (b) 45
   (c) 60
   (d) 65

4. If a parent requests an independent educational evaluation at public expense because they have objections regarding the public school's evaluation, the public agency cannot require the parents to explain why they objected.
   True or False

5. If the parents provide informed written consent, a public agency may access the parents' private health insurance to provide medical evaluations required to determine eligibility.
   True or False

Answers: 1. False; 2. False; 3. c; 4. True; 5. True

Four

SPECIAL CONSIDERATIONS WHEN TESTING FOR SPECIFIC LEARNING DISABILITIES

It ain't what you don't know that gets you into trouble.
It's what you know for sure that just ain't so.

—Mark Twain

WHAT IS A SPECIFIC LEARNING DISABILITY?

Put delicately, the question is: What is a specific learning disability (SLD)? Put less delicately, the real question is: Whom do you want to include, and whom do you want to keep out? Any and all decisions made regarding criteria affect who will and who will not be served.

There is general consensus among many professionals that the definition of an SLD found in the Individuals with Disabilities Education Act (IDEA) of 2004, which is substantially the same as the definition in 1975's Public Law 94-142, adequately describes a specific learning disability. There the consensus ends, because it is about the operationalization of that general definition that arguments continue to flourish (e.g., Dumont, Willis, & McBride, 2001; Hale et al., 2010; Kavale, Kaufman, Naglieri, & Hale, 2005; Peterson & Shinn, 2002; Shinn, 2002). It is not, however, the purpose of this book to track, document, or take a position on those debates. Instead, it is our purpose to inform the school-based practitioner on how best to approach this difficult business within the context of the law. On the face of it, this should be a simple task. Section 300.307 of the 2006 Final Regulations (p. 46786) includes an additional provision that says: "(b) *Consistency with State criteria.* A public agency must use the State criteria adopted pursuant to paragraph (a) of this section in determining whether a child has a specific learning disability." So, for the question What is a specific learning disability? one might think, simplistically, that this would be correct and complete:

Within the context of federal and state law, the operational definition of a specific learning disability is whatever your state says it is.

Unfortunately, life is not that simple. Many, if not all, states have adopted at least some of the language that is in the federal regulations, language that, as we indicated in Chapter 2 was, is, and probably will be for the foreseeable future undefined. Although the IDEA 2004 allows for some flexibility in adopting other methodologies for identifying SLD, the two main methodologies continue to be one based on the historical achievement discrepancy model or a problem-solving model using response to intervention as the criterion measure. Some states have adopted regulations for only one methodology, response to intervention within the context of a multitiered problem solving model.

Irrespective of methodology, the team must be able to show that it has

(1) Data that demonstrate that prior to, or as a part of, the referral process, the child was provided appropriate instruction in regular education settings, delivered by qualified personnel; and (2) Data-based documentation of repeated assessments of achievement at reasonable intervals, reflecting formal assessment of student progress during instruction, which was provided to the child's parents. (§ 300.309(b))

Although no specific documentation is required by the regulations, the team must also collectively conclude that the deficits "are not primarily the result of—(i) A visual, hearing, or motor disability; (ii) Mental retardation; (iii) Emotional disturbance; (iv) Cultural factors; (v) Environmental or economic disadvantage; or (vi) Limited English proficiency" (§ 300.309, p. 46787).

There is, of course, a lot more in the way of documentation that is required, but (to keep it simple), the federal, state, or local education agency (LEA)—adopted forms drive the process, and special education abhors a blank space. The time-consuming part is developing all the data necessary to fill in all those spaces. The really hard part is pulling together all that information and applying the appropriate standard. The appropriate standards can be boiled down to these:

- If you are a school-based professional working in a school using a discrepancy methodology,
  (1) a child might have an SLD if he or she has an ability-achievement disparity equal to or larger than that specified in your state's formula and based on standardized discrepancy on a standardized achievement test and standardized test of intellectual development in one or more of the eight academic areas; or
  (2) a child might have an SLD if he or she has a severe discrepancy between ability and achievement based on classroom performance and an assessment of intellectual development (which may be based on a combination of factors) in one of the eight academic areas in the collective clinical judgment of the eligibility group for SLD.

- If you are in a school relying on response to intervention (RTI), the *definition* of an SLD is even simpler although the *process* is considerably more complex.

  A child in a school using RTI might have a Specific Learning Disability if, in the collective clinical opinion of the eligibility group for SLD, (1) he or she needs specially designed instruction (special education) in order to achieve adequately and/or progress satisfactorily in one or more of the eight academic areas listed in the regulation; and (2) that specially designed instruction cannot be reasonably provided long-term in a general education setting.

A few states still require documentation of a processing disorder that has been linked by research to the area of academic deficit. The Office of Special Education and Rehabilitative Services (OSERS) does not endorse the evaluation of cognitive processes as a part of the entitlement process for SLD. Nevertheless, federal regulations do not prohibit state education agencies (SEAs) from imposing that burden. In those states, the only additional burden would be to document deficits in some area of cognitive processing (whether verbal or nonverbal) related to the academic problems. Phonemic processing is the only area of psychological processing related to learning cited in the federal regulations; but documentation of any processing deficits related to one or more of the eight academic areas may suffice.

Generally, OSERS/OSEP (Office of Special Education Programs) beg off when asked to provide some sort of comprehensible standards, saying that each decision must be based on a comprehensive assessment of each individual child (e.g., "LEAs must ensure that FAPE [free appropriate public education] is available to any child with a disability who needs special education and related services, even though the child is advancing from grade to grade; and . . . that the determination that a child who is advancing from grade to grade is eligible under this part must be made on an individual basis by the group within the LEA responsible for making eligibility determinations" [Assistance to the States, 1999, Section 300.121, p. 12426].)

> ## CAUTION
> ....
> The 2006 Final Regulations pass the buck to the states on such issues as whether to permit use of a discrepancy model and how to implement RTI. In this area, state regulations rule!

SECTION 300.307–300.311 DETERMINING THE EXISTENCE OF A SPECIFIC LEARNING DISABILITY

Specific learning disability has always been a complex and disputed topic under special education law, and IDEA 2004 has only increased the complexity and disputes. See Rapid Reference 4.1.

Pattern of Strengths and Weaknesses

Determining Patterns of Strengths/Weaknesses in Achievement

Section 300.309(a)(2)(ii), states: "The child exhibits a pattern of strengths and weaknesses in performance, achievement, or both, relative to age, State-approved grade level standards, or intellectual development." Most states offer no guidance with respect to this method of determining eligibility.

OSERS did provide some interpretive dicta in the preface. The reference to age means one can compare the student's performance to that of

≡ *Rapid Reference 4.1*

§ 300.309 Determining the existence of a specific learning disability

(ii) The child exhibits a pattern of strengths and weaknesses in performance, achievement, or both, relative to age, State-approved grade level standards, or intellectual development, that is determined by the group to be relevant to the identification of a specific learning disability, using appropriate assessments, consistent with §§ 300.304 and 300.305. (§ 300.309(a)(2)(ii) p. 46786)

an average age peer; the reference to state standards means "state-approved grade-level standards"; and the reference to "intellectual development" was included so states could (optionally) allow (but not require) continued use of a discrepancy model. OSERS says the reference to "intellectual development" refers to the historical achievement/ability discrepancy criterion, which some states no longer allow.

If a school is using an RTI methodology, the eligibility group does not need to show an intra-individual difference between ability and achievement. A child who had been through the multitiered process and was still at the 10th percentile would still need a comprehensive evaluation ("comprehensive" also being a term that has generated extensive debate), but entitlement could be justified primarily by locally normed CBM data.

In section (2)(ii), when talking about intra-individual differences with respect to age or state-approved standards, OSERS was referencing the standards states developed for passing end-of-grade tests required by the Elementary and Secondary Education Act (ESEA) for grades 3 to 8. "The regulations, however, allow for the assessment of intra-individual differences in achievement as part of an identification model for SLD. The regulations also allow for the assessment of discrepancies in intellectual development and achievement" (Preface, 2006 Final Regulations, p. 46651).

Independent Evaluation Recommending Classification

Here is a hypothetical situation that school districts might run into with regard to an independent evaluator recommending a specific classification based on the independent educational evaluation (IEE):

> An independent evaluator has reported that a child he assessed had a Relative Proficiency Index (RPI) score of 75 (standard score of 91) on the Brief Reading composite score of the Woodcock-Johnson and a standard score of 75 on the Processing Speed Index of the Wechsler. The evaluator is recommending that the child be considered for classification as SLD. How should the school proceed?

In order for an independent educational evaluation to be accepted for use by a school system, the outside evaluation must meet agency criteria. The first step, if the examiner is unknown to the school system, would be to do a background check on the examiner's credentials. We believe most states provide for license checks on the respective state professional licensing board web page.

The next step would be to explain to the parents that your school uses a state-mandated methodology for identifying students and that in order for outside evaluations to be used, they must meet agency standards (34 CFR 300.502). In most instances, examiner qualifications and the tests used will meet agency standards. OSERS has said in the Preface to the 2006 Final Regulations that an evaluation must generate "information related to enabling the child to be involved in and progress in the general education curriculum (or for a preschool child to participate in appropriate activities). These requirements also apply to an IEE conducted by an independent evaluator, since these requirements will be a part of the agency's criteria" (p. 46690). Still, it is unlikely that an independent evaluation would include all the data needed to help the eligibility group determine that a lack of appropriate instruction was not the primary cause of the student's academic problems (for all disability categories); provide documentation showing that data regarding the student's progress was reported to parents on a regular basis (SLD only); and other data necessary for the consideration of other potentially exclusionary factors.

Parents should be asked if they want to complete a formal referral or for their child to be referred to your student support team (SST). Parental rights should be given regardless. The team should review the information provided to determine what additional documentation would be needed in order to actually reach an eligibility decision.

In this illustration, Brief Reading is a combination of Letter Word Identification and Passage Comprehension on the Woodcock-Johnson III Brief Battery. In North Carolina, standard achievement scores would have been required to calculate discrepancy in schools using the discrepancy model. (In schools using an RTI methodology, the evaluation would not be sufficient to meet agency criteria requiring documentation of a lack of response to research-based, scientific intervention.) The presence of a psychological processing disorder (not necessarily established in the example given) is not sufficient in and of itself in any state to establish SLD eligibility; nor is it required (in most but not all states) to support a classification of specific learning disability. In this instance, the inquiry could have ended here. For sake of the analysis, however, we will continue.

In North Carolina (as in most if not all states), children must be assessed in the discrete areas of potential entitlement (e.g., basic reading skills, reading fluency skills, and reading comprehension). Assessment results based on an amalgamation of those skills would also not have met agency criteria. (In 1994, the North Carolina Learning Disabilities Association addressed that issue in a letter to OSEP because at the time North Carolina LEAs were widely assessing for just Broad Reading and Broad Math because state regulations had compressed the seven areas to five (OSEP, Letter to Lillie/Felton, 1994; all areas must be addressed; on CD).

The 2006 Final Regulations require that the tests used be both reliable and valid for the purpose to which they are being used, so if you are not familiar with the assessments being presented, it is good practice to review their technical specifications. Purchasing a Mental Measurements Yearbook review (Buros Center for Testing, n.d.) is money well spent; individual test reviews from Buros can be purchased over the Internet for (at the time of this book's publication) $15.00 each (http://buros.unl.edu/buros/jsp/search.jsp).

A Google search often locates published test reviews. In this case, however, the Brief Battery, while part of the complete Woodcock-Johnson III Achievement Battery, according to the test publisher, was recommended only for screening, reevaluation, and progress monitoring (www. riversidepublishing.com/products/WJIIIBriefBattery/details.html).

CAUTION

Tests used by school employees and by outside evaluators must be both reliable and valid for the purposes for which they are used. See § 300.304 for more information on evaluation procedures.

If the publisher and test authors have not validated a test for the intended purpose and provided sufficient data regarding reliability and validity, the test would not meet agency criteria and would, therefore, not be usable in making an entitlement decision.

However, it is not whether we use one or two subtests that makes the difference between a good and bad decision, so the information about Brief Reading being a composite of two subtests would be irrelevant. The appropriate standard has always been reliability and validity. For example, an average composite score based on vastly superior reading decoding and nonexistent reading comprehension would not be a valid measure of anything. There appears to be a myth (we do not know how widespread, but we have come across it in different contexts in different situations) that one subtest is bad, but if you have a score based on two subtests, you are good to go. Not so. Single subtests can have adequate reliability and validity for high-stakes decision making; composite scores can have low reliability and validity and be inadequate for high-stakes decision making. The myth may also have arisen out of a long-held basic principle in spedlaw that eligibility may not be based on a single test or procedure. Indeed, that principle was reiterated in a recent 2010 California hearing (*Lassen Elementary v. Parents*), in which the hearing officer said that eligibility decisions were not to be made based on a "single test or procedure" (www.documents.dgs.ca.gov/oah/seho_decisions/2010050797.pdf).

A hearing officer's interpretation of the law is hardly dispositive, but the exact same language was used in the 1994 Lillie/Felton Letter from OSEP cited earlier. The 1999 regulations, said: "No single procedure is used as the sole criterion for determining whether a child is a child with a disability" (§ 300.532, 1999 Final Regulations, p. 12456).

That language regarding evaluation procedures was altered again in the 2006 regulations to reflect the language of the Individuals with Disabilities Education Improvement Act of 2004 (IDEIA). The current regulations now say that the schools may "[n]ot use any single measure or assessment as the sole criterion for determining whether a child is a child with a disability" (§ 300.304, 2006 Final Regulations, p. 46785). A single test score, whether from a single subtest or a composite, would still represent a single assessment.

In most cases, however, the results of an inquiry such as the one described are largely benign. The examiner is well qualified. The tests used were mainstream, reliable, and valid. While the school has the right to do its own evaluation, it usually waives that right and plugs the results from the outside evaluator's report into its own assessment. What is usually at issue is not the test results but the examiner's interpretation of those results.

That information still must be considered within the context of a comprehensive evaluation. The term "comprehensive evaluation" itself has a detailed regulatory meaning (§§ 300.304 and 305). The requirement for an individual comprehensive evaluation is not specific to IDEA; it is also embraced by Section 504 (§ 104.35; on CD).

In discussing Section 504, Office of Civil Rights (OCR), while answering the question of whether a medical diagnosis was sufficient to determine eligibility, said quite emphatically in its frequently asked questions (FAQs) on Section 504 that it is not:

> Other sources to be considered, along with the medical diagnosis, include aptitude and achievement tests, teacher recommendations, physical condition, social and cultural background, and adaptive behavior. . . . The Section 504 regulations require school districts to draw upon a variety of sources in interpreting evaluation data and making placement decisions. (OCR, 2009; on CD)

Even assuming that maximum consideration were to be given to an outside evaluation, under the IDEA, the eligibility group still must determine whether the child's disability has adversely affected the student's educational performance to such a degree that specially designed instruction and related services are needed; or the 504 committee must determine whether it has substantially affected the student in a major life function to such a degree that related services and supplementary aids are needed to level the playing field.

INTRA-INDIVIDUAL DIFFERENCES

Determine Eligibility for Special Education Based on "Intra-individual Differences" in Cognitive Function

OSERS said explicitly that intracognitive discrepancies were not reliable markers for SLD and that they did not lead to appropriate interventions. Whether one agrees or disagrees, even in the few states where testing for psychological processing disorders linked to the suspected educational deficit is a requirement, cognitive variances (e.g., a relative weakness in Processing Speed) are not sufficient for identification. (As we note previously and again later, OSERS also says that assessing for intra-individual differences in cognitive processes is permitted; but that is *not* the same as saying an eligibility group can affirm/deny eligibility as a result of that testing, unless of course your state requires documentation of psychological processing in its regulations.)

Defining "Patterns of Strengths and Weaknesses"

From OSERS, "[p]atterns of strengths and weaknesses commonly refer to the examination of profiles across different tests used historically in the identification of children with SLD. We believe that the meaning of 'pattern of strengths and weaknesses' is clear and does not need to be clarified in these regulations" (Preface, 2006 Final Regulations, p. 46654).

Although we doubt that OSERS' self-serving assumption that the meaning is clear is actually true, any additional interpretation we might make would carry the weight only of our professional opinion, which in this case probably would carry no more (or less) weight than yours in any adversarial situation.

INTELLECTUAL DEVELOPMENT

Defining "Intellectual Development": Does It Refer to IQ Scores?

From OSERS:

We believe the term "intellectual development" is the appropriate reference in this provision. § 300.309(a)(2)(ii) permits the assessment of patterns of strengths and weakness in performance, including performance in assessments of cognitive ability.

As stated previously, "intellectual development" is included as one of three methods of comparison, along with age and State-approved grade-level standards. The term "cognitive" is not the appropriate reference to performance because cognitive variation is not a reliable marker of SLD, and is usually not related to intervention. (Preface, 2006 Final Regulations, p. 46654)

Also:

> We [OSERS] do not believe it is necessary to define "intellectual development" in these regulations. Intellectual development is included in § 300.309(a)(2)(ii) as one of three standards of comparison, along with age and State-approved grade-level standards. The reference to "intellectual development" in this provision means that the child exhibits a pattern of strengths and weaknesses in performance relative to a standard of intellectual development *such as commonly measured by IQ tests* [emphasis added]. Use of the term is consistent with the discretion provided in the Act in allowing the continued use of discrepancy. (Preface, 2006 Final Regulations, p. 46651)

> **DON'T FORGET**
>
> Many terms related to identification of SLD are not defined clearly (if at all) in the 2006 Final Regulations. You must read the regulations carefully and exercise thoughtful, defensible judgment.

Again, we do not share OSERS's confidence in the clarity of its regulations.

DISCREPANCY

Guidelines for "Severe Discrepancy"

SEAs can abolish or permit the use of discrepancy in their states, or LEAs may use (but are not required to use) a discrepancy methodology if the SEA permits.

> **DON'T FORGET**
>
> If you have specific questions that have not been answered here, in most cases they should be directed to your state educational agency or to your state professional association. Be sure first to study your downloaded copy of your state regulations.

Whether to use one or the other is not to be decided on a case-by-case basis.

Because each state's procedures and standards differ, the first place to look for guidance is always your state regulations. That said, the Final Regulations still say that a public agency may "[n]ot use any single measure or assessment as the sole criterion for determining whether a child is a child with a disability and for determining an appropriate educational program for the child" (§ 300.304(b)(2)), and OSERS still says in the Preface to the 2006 Final Regulations that

> the evaluation of a child suspected of having a disability, including an SLD, must include a variety of assessment tools and strategies and cannot rely on any single procedure as the sole criterion for determining eligibility for special education and related services. This requirement applies to all children suspected of having a disability, including those suspected of having an SLD. (p. 46646)

We cannot find anywhere in the federal regulations, past or present, any specific definition or guidance to aid states or schools in determining the extent of the discrepancy that is needed for eligibility under the SLD designation. Federal regulations for IDEA and EHA have never specified numerical cut-offs for ability-achievement discrepancies for SLD; IQ or adaptive behavior scores for intellectual disability; or vision or hearing ratings—no specific score boundaries at all for any disability. An arbitrary or excessively stringent criterion might not fare well in federal court (e.g., *Riley v. Ambach*, 1981) (on CD). The existence of an ability/achievement discrepancy, regardless of how the state or (in the absence of explicit state criteria) the school district chooses to define it, is *not sufficient* in and of itself to determine eligibility as SLD. Just as all children in schools using an RTI methodology are entitled to a comprehensive evaluation, so too are children in schools using an ability/achievement discrepancy methodology so entitled.

PSYCHOLOGICAL PROCESSING DISORDER

Documenting a Processing Disorder

As we have mentioned, there is no legal requirement to document a processing disorder based on federal law or regulation (see Rapid Reference 4.2).

It is we believe important to understand the evolving nature of the debate over psychological processing and its relationship to SLD diagnosis.

Unless your state's regulations *require* documentation of a processing disorder linked to the area of educational deficit, assessment for a processing disorder might be *requested* by the individualized education program (IEP) team if it believes it would be helpful in either establishing a disabled child's educational needs or planning a remedial program.

This issue has been hotly debated in the professional literature, and a number of respected individuals advocated for inclusion of a processing component prior to passage of the IDEA in 2004. There is, however, nothing in either the 2004 IDEA or in the final 2006 Regulations for the IDEA that would prohibit an IEP team from requesting assessments of psychological processing even in states that do not specifically require them for eligibility determinations.

OSEP has long held that federal law and regulations do not require documentation of a processing disorder, although it has allowed states to impose an additional burden on eligibility groups based on the congressional definition. Some excerpts from OSEP letters over the years are presented next.

> States and local school districts may, at their option, develop criteria for defining "a disorder in one or more of the basic psychological processes," it would appear that requiring a child classified as SLD to have a "psychological processing disorder" is not an additional criterion . . . because it is already a criterion under the definition of SLD.
>
> —OSERS, 1989, Smith letter to Murphy

> It is not necessary for the multidisciplinary evaluation team to demonstrate or measure the existence of a basic disorder in psychological processing in order to determine that a child has a specific learning disability. Rather, if a psychological processing disorder exists, it could manifest itself through a variety of symptoms that can be observed, such as hyperactivity, attention problems, concept association problems, etc. . . . The end result of the effects

of these symptoms is a severe discrepancy between achievement and ability.

—OSEP, 1990, Schrag letter to Kennedy

In the 2006 Final Regulations, after having reviewed the available research at that time, OSERS wrote in the Preface:

The Department does not believe that an assessment of psychological or cognitive processing should be required in determining whether a child has an SLD. There is no current evidence that such assessments are necessary or sufficient for identifying SLD. Further, in many cases, these assessments have not been used to make appropriate intervention decisions. However, § 300.309(a)(2)(ii) permits, but does not require, consideration of a pattern of strengths or weaknesses, or both, relative to intellectual development, if the evaluation group considers that information relevant to an identification of SLD. In many cases, though, assessments of cognitive processes simply add to the testing burden and do not contribute to interventions. As summarized in the research consensus from the OSEP Learning Disability Summit (Bradley, Danielson, and Hallahan, 2002), "Although processing deficits have been linked to some SLD (e.g., phonological processing and reading), direct links with other processes have not been established. Currently, available methods for measuring many processing difficulties are inadequate. Therefore, systematically measuring processing difficulties and their link to treatment is not yet feasible. . . . Processing deficits should be eliminated from the criteria for classification. . . ." (p. 797). Concerns about the absence of evidence for relations of cognitive discrepancy and SLD for identification go back to Bijou (1942; see Kavale, 2002). Cronbach (1957) characterized the search for aptitude by treatment interactions as a "hall of mirrors," a situation that has not improved over the past few years as different approaches to assessment of cognitive processes have emerged (Fletcher et al., 2005; Reschly & Tilly, 1999).

—Preface, 2006 Final Regulations, p. 46651

≡ Rapid Reference 4.2

Although some authorities vehemently disagree, and some states may require it, the *federal* special education regulations *do not* and never did *require* assessment of "disorders in basic psychological processes" even though the term remains part of the definition of a specific learning disability.

(These references are quoted directly from the 2006 Final Regulations to the IDEA and were not independently reviewed by the authors. Full citations can be found in the references to this volume.)

With respect to an analysis of intra-individual differences, OSERS wrote in the 2006 Final Regulations, with a surprise twist:

> As indicated . . . an assessment of intra-individual differences in cognitive functions does not contribute to identification and intervention decisions for children suspected of having an SLD. The regulations, however, allow for the assessment of intra-individual differences in achievement as part of an identification model for SLD. The regulations also allow for the assessment of discrepancies in intellectual development and achievement. (Preface, 2006 Final Regulations, p. 46651)

The authors are not aware of any state formulas, however, that would operationalize the process for determining eligibility based on intra-individual differences in achievement.

Assessment of basic processes has been discussed at length (e.g., Dehn, 2006; Sattler & Hoge, 2006). However, Torgeson (2002), in his executive summary of his paper for the 2001 OSEP Learning Disabilities Summit, said that, while there are a number of possible advantages to a processing deficit model, there are two difficulties in implementing such a model. First he said we still do not completely understand what psychological processing capabilities are needed to attain good learning outcomes; and second, it is not always possible to determine with assurance that the "processing deficits" we see identified on processing tests are truly intrinsic to the child and not due to the result of a lack of appropriate instruction. For those reasons, Torgeson did *not* recommend a processing model be adopted in the next reauthorization.

Wise and Snyder (2002) said that, while research has shown that children at risk for a learning disability should improve phonological awareness, decoding, and fluency, research has not identified one best methodology, nor does the research show that transfer continues after direct instruction has been discontinued for those children. (We are just reporting, not opining here.) They also noted that double deficits in phonological awareness and naming speed seemed to be the most resistant to treatment. Hence (and here we are opining) it may not be the amount of deficit on a specific test, but the nature and the number of deficits, that would be most indicative of a learning disability.

RESPONSE TO INTERVENTION

Defining "Response to Scientific, Research-Based Intervention"

"Response to scientific, research-based intervention" is now commonly known by its abbreviation RTI. Another name for RTI is "the problem-solving model." As its name implies, its primary purpose is not to inform an eligibility decision but, instead, to bring the combined resources of a school together in an effort to resolve a child's problems in learning. Response to intervention is the measurement used by multidisciplinary teams to gauge their success in helping to enhance a child's educational progress. In a general sense, even when using an RTI methodology, low achievement is "unexpected" when a child has received direct instruction aimed at his or her identified areas of need; and even when using an RTI methodology, children are not placed unless there is a substantial discrepancy in their basic skills or fluency from an average child having received (under the federal regulations) an appropriate education. However, that seems such an obvious observation that it hardly requires a psychologist with an advanced degree to arrive at it. The promise of RTI was that every child would get the help he or she needed when it was needed, that no child would ever again "fall through the cracks," and that no child would ever again be left behind. See Rapid Reference 4.3.

The RTI (or problem solving) model represents a real paradigm shift. Answering the question "Which intervention should I use?" is not like picking out a tie: Should I wear the black one or the blue one? Implementation of RTI requires extensive preparation, a reordering of district resources,

≡ *Rapid Reference 4.3*

OSEP strongly encourages RTI; some day it might even be required. Professionals involved in special education need to develop expertise in RTI. See, for example, these references.

Brown-Chidsey, R., & Steege, M. W. (2005). *Response to intervention: Principles and strategies for effective practice.* New York, NY: Guilford Press.

VanDerHeyden, A. M., & Burns, M. K. (2010). *Essentials of response to intervention.* New York, NY: John Wiley & Sons.

Wendling, B. J., & Mather, N. (2009). *Essentials of evidence-based academic interventions.* Hoboken, NJ: John Wiley & Sons.

full commitment by regular education, a refocusing of energy on using tests to inform the educational process—not the identification process—and an investment of time and energy in using (and interpreting) an entirely different assessment strategy, most notably curriculum-based measurement. To be done well, district resources need to be brought to bear in locally norming all of those probes as well. We have just touched some of the highlights, but extensive and ongoing in-service training is required to ensure that everyone is on the same page. Change by its very nature invites resistance, and if RTI is implemented without adequate administrative buy-in, support, and leadership, teachers will not buy in, and the change agent can quickly become the scapegoat for a systemic failure (McBride, Dumont, & Willis, 2004; Zirkel & Thomas, 2010). Labeling children using a state formula has always been easy. Helping children overcome their particular impediments to learning is not. Traditionally school psychologists were taught (sometimes explicitly) that it was their job to identify a child's problems, and the teachers' job to find ways to address them. In a system where the intervention itself becomes the evaluative tool, however, those distinctions have become blurred.

COMPARISON GROUPS

Comparison to "Normal" Peers

When evaluating children for eligibility, do we always compare them to "normal" peers, or do we compare them to children who have the same disability? For example, when evaluating a child with emotional/behavioral problems who also happened to be identified as having an intellectual disability, would we compare his behavior to children with similar cognitive levels?

If a child with intellectual disability has significant behavioral problems compared to an average peer, the IEP team should be addressing that need irrespective of the child's label. If Johnny has paraplegia, we do not say "Compared to other children with paraplegia, it's normal for them not to walk, so we are not going to provide him with any accommodations."

Speech pathologists using "cognitive referencing" did that sort of thing for years. If the child's intelligence score and the child's language score were similar, they would refuse to serve the child because he or she was performing to ability. They claimed that they could not help the child, and ethically that meant they could not serve the child, which also helped control caseloads. The American Speech-Language-Hearing Association (1997–2011) has asserted for some time that it "does not support the use of cognitive referencing."

Some advocates for children who are deaf have called for achievement tests with "deaf norms." There is no requirement anywhere that a school system use norms based on any disability group. Using such norms would not only obscure the child's real needs but also would imply that below-average functioning was expected and therefore "normal" for that child.

GRADE EQUIVALENTS

Use of Grade Equivalents for Determining Eligibility

Every score has a purpose. The problems with grade equivalents (G.E.) or grade-equivalent scores have been well documented (e.g., International Reading Association, 1982; Smith, 2009).

It is not that there is something intrinsically evil with G.E.'s, but that they are often misused and easily misinterpreted. Putting G.E.'s in the hands of teachers has been compared to putting an AK-47 in the hands of a child. A fine instrument, easy to use (just pull the trigger), but generally you would want to have some control over where and when it was actually applied.

However, that said, G.E. scores have an attribute that standard scores and percentiles do not. If your school uses only standard scores to document progress, it may easily have a drop in scores from one testing to the next, even if the child passes more items. In an adversarial situation, parents will *love* those scores. Indeed, if you review the background material for *Brody v. Dare Cty* (1997), an interesting due process lawsuit documented and discussed on Wrightslaw, the parents might even convincingly allege to a due process hearing officer that a decline in standard scores represented regression. The results, if that interpretation of those scores was accepted as represented, could be catastrophic for a school district trying to show it had provided a student with more than trivial benefits. See "Letter to a Stranger: James Brody Case 1996" (Brody & Brody, 1996) on www.wrightslaw.com/advoc/stranger/brody.html as well as the 1997 State Hearing Officer Decision, *Brody v. Dare County Public Schools.*

For example, in their "Letter to a Stranger" (Brody & Brody, 1996), the parents argued that these data proved regression: G.E. showed 1.5 years of progress after 3 years of special education (2.9 G.E. to 4.4), but the percentile rank declined 12%.

The hearing officer ruled for the parents, providing them with tuition reimbursement. In *HISD v. Caius* (2000) (on CD), however, the circuit court ruled that the school properly used G.E.'s rather than percentiles to document progress. The school argued for the use of G.E.'s, and it won. (See Chapter 1 for a more thorough discussion of the case as well as the case itself on the CD.)

In short, percentiles and standard scores are best for demonstrating relative weaknesses and strengths as required by federal regulations. G.E.'s can be most effective when trying to document progress ("educational benefit" that is more than merely trivial). However, on many individual achievement tests, one year's growth in grade-equivalent scores may be less than 3 raw score points, so chance variation may have more impact than actual growth, stagnation, or regression. As one association has written:

> Resolved, that the International Reading Association strongly advocates that those who administer standardized reading tests abandon the practice of using grade equivalents to report performance of either individuals or groups of test-takers and be it further resolved, that the president or executive director of the Association write to

test publishers urging them to eliminate grade equivalents from their tests"(International Reading Association, p. 464; see also Smith, 2009).

Rasch-Wright (Item Response Theory) scores, such as Ability Scores, Growth Scale Value scores, Growth Scores, or W scores, may be the most statistically defensible means of assessing growth (Elliott, 2007; Embretson & Hershberger, 1999; Embretson & Reise, 2000; Jaffe, 2009), but that is a technical, not a legal issue. The challenge is in presenting a child's growth to parents in a way that is both statistically defensible and also comprehensible to the target audience—in this case, parents or guardians.

AGE NORMS VERSUS GRADE NORMS

Since many achievement tests allow evaluators to compute results based on either age- or grade-based norms, while most cognitive assessment tests (the Woodcock-Johnson III [WJ III] being an exception) provide only age-based norms, evaluation team members often raise the issue of which normative standard is better (legally or psychometrically). (Do *not* confuse age- and grade-based standard-score *norms* with age-equivalent scores ["mental ages"] and grade-equivalent scores. They are two entirely separate animals.)

Grade-Based versus Age-Based Norms

In discussions on the National Association of School Psychologists list-serv, the general, though not unanimous, consensus was that the only time an eligibility group should use grade-based achievement test standard scores was when it was also using a grade-based intellectual standard score (e.g., from the WJ III Test of Cognitive Abilities). Most test manuals that provide tables for discrepancy calculations include a warning not to mix norms based on the child's grade placement with norms based on the child's age. (Note: Grade-based scores are standard scores normed by comparing a child to children in his or her grade; do not confuse them with grade equivalents, an easy error.)

Neither OSERS nor OSEP has taken a clear stand one way or the other. Even the Preface to the current regulations seems to reflect this ambivalence. The thing is, when you retain students, their standing will leap in comparison to their grade peers, but retention in and of itself rarely affects rate of learning. Just as two students age 6 and age 16 might have the same mental age of 6-0, that certainly does not mean the 16-year-old will learn in the same way as the 6-year-old—or have the same educational needs.

In the 2006 Preface, OSERS wrote:

> The performance of classmates and peers is not an appropriate standard if most children in a class or school are not meeting State-approved standards. Furthermore, using grade-based normative data to make this determination is generally not appropriate for children who have not been permitted to progress to the next academic grade or are otherwise older than their peers. Such a practice may give the illusion of average rates of learning when the child's rate of learning has been below average, resulting in retention. A focus on expectations relative to abilities or classmates simply dilutes expectations for children with disabilities. (p. 46652)

Although seeming to support these precepts, in the very next paragraph, when referring to the use of end-of-grade test results on high-stakes testing, OSERS wrote: "The reference to 'State-approved grade-level standards' is intended to emphasize the alignment of the Act and the ESEA, as well as to cover children who have been retained in a grade, since age level expectations may not be appropriate for these children" (p. 46652).

In short, OSERS has provided two opposing rationales on the same page, leaving it up to the user to decide which makes the most sense.

Additionally (and ultimately unhelpfully), a couple of OSEP letters in the 1990s discussed the use of age versus grade norms; the first one said age norms only, but the second was much more permissive, leaving it up to the teams to decide what best reflected the child's performance and needs.

Whether the tests or other evaluation materials selected utilize age-referenced or grade-referenced norms is a matter that also falls within the purview of state and local educational authorities, with one possible exception: evaluations of student of having specific learning disabilities:

> [It] would appear that only the use of age-based norms rather than grade-level norms, would be appropriate in the selection of testing

or other evaluation materials for evaluations of students suspected of having specific learning disabilities. (OSEP, 1996, Hehir letter to Cole)

But then in 1997, OCR gave us these comments (excerpted here):

Part B does not specifically address the issue [of grade norms v. age norms.]. The reference in Part B regulations concerning specific learning disabilities appears to make only the use of chronological age norms, rather than grade level norms, appropriate to be used in evaluations of students suspected of having learning disabilities. . . .

The use of grade-level norms, consistent with the above considerations, in evaluating children for specific learning disabilities in appropriate cases is not prohibited by the regulations. (OSEP, 1997, Hehir letter to Matthew)

(We cannot resist noting that best practice, as opposed to laws and regulations, suggests reporting scores by *both* age norms *and* grade norms to give a complete picture of the situation and always to use the same norm basis to compare any two test scores. The full truth does not reside in either set of norms.)

RTI, Grade Norms, and Retained Children

If determining eligibility using CBM and an RTI model, and since CBM measures are grade norms, which grade norms do you use for retained children: the grade they are in or the grade they should have been in?

The movement to an RTI-based methodology (where CBM is typically normed locally and intelligence measures are not used to calculate discrepancy) permits districts to use methodologies that do not require the administration of a cognitive assessment,

CAUTION

OSEP's dicta on age-based and grade-based norms appear to be self-contradictory. However, it is clear that one cannot make a statistically valid comparison between two scores based on different normative bases.

but the team still is going to have to decide what to do about those children who were retained: Test them using probes and norms at the child's grade level, or use probes and norms for the grade appropriate for the child's age? We recommend the latter. Retention is not an intervention. If there is one thing most experts agree on, it is that a child who truly has a learning disability has a lifetime affliction. Waiting for him or her to fail again before providing appropriate interventions is therefore not a defensible position.

EXCLUSIONS

Consideration for Specific Learning Disability Identification

Some special education teams seem to think that children who have vision or hearing problems, who are culturally disadvantaged, or who have mental retardation or emotional disturbance cannot even be considered for specific learning disability identification. This is not true. As we discussed in Chapter 2, it is important to bear in mind that the so-called exclusions in the federal definition of specific learning disability. § 300.308(c)(10) and § 300.309(a)(3) rule out *learning problems* that are caused primarily by visual, hearing, or motor disabilities; mental retardation; emotional disturbance; cultural factors; environmental or economic disadvantage; or limited English proficiency. They do not rule out *children* who have those disabilities or disadvantages. See also Rapid Reference 4.4.

Rapid Reference 4.4

"Exclusions"
§ 300.309 Determining the existence of a specific learning disability (a)(3)

The group determines that its findings under paragraphs (a)(1) and (2) of this section are not primarily the result of—(i) A visual, hearing, or motor disability; (ii) Mental retardation; (iii) Emotional disturbance; (iv) Cultural factors; (v) Environmental or economic disadvantage; or (vi) Limited English proficiency.

SLD ELIGIBILITY CATEGORIES

Use of Single Subtest, Composite, and Broad Scores in Determining a Deficit

The underlying concepts in determining what tests may be used for determining eligibility are reliability and validity. Not only are these required ethically (see the *Standards for Educational and Psychological Testing* [AERA, APA, & NCME, 1999]) but legally under both the Final 2006 Regulations for the IDEA and Section 504 regulations.

In our opinion, scores reflecting reliabilities of less than .90 should not be used for individual decision making or in making eligibility determinations. Many of the individual (sub)tests on, for example the WJ III, in our opinion should not be used in making eligibility decisions because the subtest reliabilities do not justify that level of confidence. However, some single (sub)test scores on various assessments, such as the Wechsler Individual Achievement Test, could be appropriately used when their reliabilities exceed .90. See Sattler (2008) for more information.

Individual users are responsible for verifying the technical quality of every assessment tool they use. In general, technical manuals may be relied on, although the conscientious examiner will also read *Buros Mental Measurements Yearbook* reviews (e.g., Geisinger, Spies, Carlson, & Plake, 2007; www.unl.edu/buros/) and professional journals and current textbooks for independent opinions.

Additionally, users cannot simply assume composite scores are sufficiently reliable without knowing the basis for the subtest scores. For example, the WJ III scoring program will generate a composite score even if one of the subtests was based on a zero raw score, and many tests with printed norms tables allow examiners to look up total scores even when a component subtest has a zero raw score (or ignore the issue altogether). Consumer demand has driven publishers to permit the use of composite scores even when one of the subtests is zero. However, there is no reason to believe a composite so derived would be any more reliable or valid than the single subtest score from which the composite was generated.

Broad scores—for example, a composite score that is derived from combining three areas in reading (decoding, comprehension, fluency)—are also sometimes presented for consideration.

Sometime in the late 1980s or early 1990s, North Carolina tried to combine the SLD achievement areas of reading and math (four at that time) into two broad areas that could be measured by the WJ III broad scores. The Learning Disabilities Association of North Carolina complained to OSEP. OSEP (May 10, 1994) replied in part:

> None of the seven areas listed in 34 CFR 300.541(a)(2)(i)–(vii), the Part B regulation which establishes the criteria for determining the existence of a specific learning disability (SLD), can be categorically excluded from a multidisciplinary team's evaluation to determine whether a child has a SLD. To the contrary, each of these areas must be taken into consideration, and a state policy which requires otherwise may be suspect.

For more information on using your state's discrepancy alternative, see Dumont, Willis, and McBride (2001). The bottom line is that legally, ethically, and morally, knowing what we know about our instruments' limitations, we should not determine any child's eligibility based solely on the child achieving a certain numerical discrepancy, nor should we exclude any child because he or she has failed to achieve such a discrepancy. We need to consider the child within the context of *all* our assessment data.

REEVALUATIONS WHEN CHANGING METHODOLOGIES

Another question that came up often between the issuance of the draft regulations in 2004 and Final Regulations in 2006 was what would happen to all those children placed using discrepancy who did not qualify using a new methodology. OSERS recommended (and we agree) exercising great caution in dismissing students just because the procedure(s) had changed. At the very least, it seems to us, after three years of special educational services, an IEP team would have to conclude that, in addition to no longer meeting whatever arbitrary cutoff was established, the student would no longer need the support services he or she was receiving in order to continue progress before exiting him or her. OSERS's own words seem to in agreement with our suggestion.

> States that change their eligibility criteria for SLD may want to carefully consider the reevaluation of children found eligible for special education services using prior procedures. States should consider the

effect of exiting a child from special education who has received special education and related services for many years and how the removal of such supports will affect the child's educational progress, particularly for a child who is in the final year(s) of high school. Obviously, the group should consider whether the child's instruction and overall special education program have been appropriate as part of this process. If the special education instruction has been appropriate and the child has not been able to exit special education, this would be strong evidence that the child's eligibility needs to be maintained. (Preface, 2006 Final Regs., p. 46648)

A Special Case: Private or Home School Referrals when SLD Is Suspected

Private or home school referrals can seem particularly challenging when a school system is using RTI to identify children using a multitiered assistance team process. Generally, irrespective of methodology, OSERS said in the Preface to the 2006 Regulations regarding § 300.9 that "it may be necessary to obtain information from parents and teachers about the curricula used and the child's progress with various teaching strategies."

With respect to conducting an evaluation within the context of an RTI methodology, OSERS says in part:

[M]any private schools collect assessment data that would permit a determination of how well a child responds to appropriate instruction. The group making the eligibility determination for a private school child for whom data on the child's response to appropriate instruction are not available may need to rely on other information to make their determination, or identify what additional data are needed to determine whether the child is a child with a disability. However, under Sec. 300.306(b), a public agency may not identify any public or private school child as a child with a disability if the determinant factor is lack of appropriate instruction in reading or math." (Preface, 2006 Final Regulations, p. 46656)

Another option, if permitted by the state, would be to evaluate home- and private-schooled children using a discrepancy methodology.

SPECIAL EFFECTS

> For unto every one that hath shall be given, and he shall have abundance: but from him that hath not shall be taken away even that which he hath.
>
> —Matthew 25:29

> For he that hath, to him shall be given: and he that hath not, from him shall be taken even that which he hath.
>
> —Mark 4:25

Matthew Effects

"Matthew effects" is a term applied to the area of reading by Keith Stanovich (1986). It derives its name from the original biblical source, Matthew 25:29, above. It is popularly rephrased as "The rich get richer, and the poor get poorer."

Stanovich (1986) discusses many important aspects and apparent causes of the situation, but the fundamental point is that a student who starts off behind peers in reading (perhaps because of oral vocabulary or language deficits, perhaps for other reasons), is not likely to catch up because peers are developing reading skills at a rate at least as fast, and probably faster, from a higher starting point. Further, their reading experience helps them continue to develop oral language skills and reading comprehension abilities denied to the child who started off behind. "Waiting to see" how the slow-starting beginning reader develops is a recipe for reading failure. Stanovich strongly advocates intervening as early as possible.

The concept has been extended to other issues, such as declining IQ scores. See, for example, Peter Wright's successful argument in *Brody v. Dare County Public Schools* (1997).

Mark Penalty

Following Stanovich's (1986) example, Willis and Dumont (n.d.) have proposed the concept of the "Mark penalty" from the scripture cited above. The Mark penalty is incurred when a student's disability (e.g., visual impairment, hearing loss, or learning disability basic process disorder) is allowed to depress not only scores on tests of academic achievement but also estimates of the student's intelligence so that the examiner or team concludes that there is no significant difference between the student's academic achievement and the level of achievement that would be predicted from the student's score on the intelligence test. The same disability is depressing both the student's actual achievement and the estimate of the student's true intellectual ability. The IDEA 2006 Final Regulations address this issue (albeit not with regard to processing disorders).

> Assessments are selected and administered so as best to ensure that if an assessment is administered to a child with impaired sensory, manual, or speaking skills, the assessment results accurately reflect the child's aptitude or achievement level or whatever other factors the test purports to measure, rather than reflecting the child's impaired sensory, manual, or speaking skills (unless those skills are the factors that the test purports to measure). (§ 300.304(c)(3))

For example, most people would accept that a Full Scale IQ based on verbal and visual tests would not be a valid assessment of the intelligence of a child who is blind. Willis and Dumont (n.d.) contend that the same consideration might also apply to a child with severe visual perceptual weaknesses.

OSERS says that states are allowed to permit a severe discrepancy procedure (we cannot be required to use the method—but we are allowed to if our state permits it) but OSERS, in the Preface to the 2006 Final Regulations, also notes that "no single procedure" can be used to determine eligibility for a child:

> As required in § 300.304(b), consistent with section 614(b)(2) of the Act, an evaluation must include a variety of assessment tools and strategies and cannot rely on any single procedure as the sole criterion for determining eligibility for special education and related services. (p. 46648)

TEST YOURSELF

1. **When determining eligibility using a severe discrepancy model, the IDEA provides guidelines about how many test score points actually constitutes a severe discrepancy.**

   True or False

2. **Regardless of what procedure a school uses to determine special education eligibility, national norms from standardized tests must be used.**

   True or False

3. **If you use an RTI methodology in determining a specific learning disability, you need not show an intra-individual difference between ability and achievement.**

   True or False

4. **Because the definition of a specific learning disability always has described it as being caused by a psychological processing disorder, schools are required by IDEA to document a processing disorder when determining a child eligible for special education services.**

   True or False

5. **The two most important underlying concepts in determining what tests may be used for determining special education eligibility are:**

   (a) Age of the test norms

   (b) Reliability

   (c) Size of the standardization sampling

   (d) Validity

Answers: 1. False; 2. False; 3. True; 4. False; 5. b and d

Five

IDEA AND CLASSIFICATION/ ELIGIBILITY

Get your facts first, then you can distort them as you please.

—Mark Twain

DETERMINING ELIGIBILITY

Assessment professionals are often invited to participate on eligibility teams to provide expert assistance in making an entitlement decision.

Before testing, an individualized education program (IEP) team (the 2006 Final Regulations call it an "IEP team," even though the child might never receive an IEP, because all the required members of an IEP team are mandated participants) is convened to determine whether the child needs to be tested and what evaluations are needed. After testing, an eligibility group is convened, which must include qualified professionals and the parent. A local education agency (LEA) representative is not a required member at that meeting. There are a few more required members if a specific learning disability (SLD) is under consideration. The Office of Special Education and Rehabilitative Services (OSERS) has said (1999 Final Regs., Appendix A, p. 12473) that IEP team decisions are not made by a democratic vote. There is no similar dictum with respect to eligibility group decisions, so in

> ## CAUTION
>
> ### § 300.321(c) Determination of knowledge and special expertise
>
> The determination of the knowledge or special expertise of any individual described in paragraph (a)(6) of this section must be made by the party (parents or public agency) who invited the individual to be a member of the IEP Team.

some schools eligibility meeting decisions (and all SLD eligibility meeting decisions in at least one state) may be made by vote. Also, if the general rule in your LEA is that those decisions are made by vote (even IEP team decisions), that rule cannot be changed just for one case. The IEP team, with different membership requirements and a different task, is reconvened only if the eligibility group says the child is entitled to special education The IEP team meeting may be held separately from the eligibility meeting, but it does not have to be.

The eligibility group meeting has a different task than an IEP team, which is reconvened only if the eligibility group says the child is entitled to special education. If both meetings are held together, Jackie Teague, retired Education Consultant, New Hampshire Department of Education, recommended to one of the authors (personal communication, April 4, 1981) having everyone stand up, walk once around the table, and sit down again to emphasize the change in the purpose of the meeting.

DON'T FORGET

Each meeting (or each segment of a meeting with more than one purpose) must include all of the required members. Required members can be excused by mutual agreement of parents and the LEA but only when the member's expertise is not required (§ 300.321(e)).

SERVICES AND LABELS

Entitlement for services to children with disabilities seems to befuddle some people. Just as an example, at least one education administrator decided one time that children who are qualified under the developmental delay (DD) category could receive special education instruction for academics only if one of their qualifying areas is "cognitive." His justification was that "academics" is not a qualifying area in DD, so only children with "cognitive" delays should receive services for pre-academic or academic skills.

In order to qualify for entitlement under the DD label, a student must under the federal regulations be experiencing developmental delays in one or more of these areas: physical development, cognitive development, communication, development, social or emotional development, or adaptive development (§ 300.8, p. 46756). The regulation goes on to say, as it does for every disability, "who by reason thereof needs special educational and related services."

However, the services in an IEP are determined by the child's needs, not by the category or area of classification (Preface, 2006 Final Regulations, p. 46588). Also, an evaluation is not "comprehensive" just because it addresses those elements required for entitlement; it must also be sufficiently comprehensive to address all of the child's "special education and related services needs, whether or not commonly linked to the disability" (§ 300.304, p. 46785). See Rapid Reference 5.1 for a quick reference summary of this evaluation requirement.

Speech or Language Impaired Services in a Learning Disability Resource Room

It is also a common misunderstanding that in order for a child identified as speech or language impaired to receive services in an LD resource room, he or she must qualify as SLD. This just is not true. If a student is identified with a speech language impairment (SLI) as the primary disability, then the speech language pathologist must be the primary service provider, but the student may also receive special educational services from the SLD teacher in a resource setting if are they needed for the student to receive a free appropriate public education (FAPE).

> The Act does not require children to be identified with a particular disability category for purposes of the delivery of special education and related services. In other words, while the Act requires that the Department collect aggregate data on children's disabilities, it does not require that particular children be labeled with particular disabilities for purposes of service delivery, since a child's entitlement under the Act is to FAPE and not to a particular disability label. (Preface, 2006 Final Regulations, p. 46737)

The 2006 federal regulations reiterate language from the Code of Federal Regulations (CFR) from 1999 as part of the prefatory language:

> In all cases, placement decisions must be individually determined on the basis of each child's abilities and needs and each child's IEP,

and not solely on factors such as category of disability, severity of disability, availability of special education and related services, configuration of the service delivery system, availability of space, or administrative convenience. (Preface, 2006 Final Regulations, p. 46588)

Section 300.320(a)(2)(i), consistent with section 614(d)(1)(A)(i)(II) of the Act, requires that annual IEP goals be measurable and designed to meet the child's needs that result from the child's disability to enable the child to be involved in and make progress in the general education curriculum, and to meet each of the child's other educational needs that result from the child's disability. (Preface, 2006 Final Regulations, p. 46664)

So in spite of the requirement that an IEP be designed to address needs that "result from the child's disability" (§ 300.320), except in very rare cases, the general dictum that "a child's needs determine his or her IEP, not his or her label" appears sound advice. Regardless, even if one were inclined to seek a nexus in this specific instance, the links between a child's oral and receptive language skills and both reading and writing achievement are well established in the literature (Exceptional Children Division, 2006).

Severe Discrepancy and Service Delivery

Another area of common misunderstanding happens in schools using a discrepancy methodology for entitlement. In those schools, the question often raised is whether a child who only has a severe discrepancy in reading could be served in any or all of the other seven areas despite there being

---

≋ Rapid Reference 5.1

Evaluation Procedures

In evaluating each child with a disability under §§ 300.304 through 300.306, the evaluation is sufficiently comprehensive to identify all of the child's special education and related services needs, whether or not commonly linked to the disability category in which the child has been classified. (§ 300.304)

no severe discrepancy for those areas. The answer to that question is a qualified yes. The child's right to services in the other seven areas would be dependent on his or her present levels of performance establishing a need for remediation in those areas. It is *not* based on the area(s) for which eligibility was established for classification as SLD. In response to a query submitted by one of the authors (G. M. M.), the Office of Special Education Programs (OSEP) opined:

> Specifically, you [G. M. M.] pose the following question: When applying a state's ability achievement discrepancy methodology, can a student who qualifies for specific learning disabilities (LD) placement with a fifteen point discrepancy in either mathematics, reading or language be served for all three areas if the evaluations also document a need for specially designed instruction in those areas?
>
> Part B of IDEA and the Department's final regulations do not impose any limitation on the services to be provided to a child identified as having a specific learning disability based on the areas of severe discrepancy between intellectual ability and achievement that the LEA identifies in making that determination. (OSEP, 2008, on CD)

The underlying principles cited by OSEP were similar to those we cited earlier:

> Although the severe discrepancy is the mechanism the LEA has elected to use in making its determination of whether the child has a specific learning disability (34 CFR § 300.307(a)(1)), that determination is one part of a multifactored evaluation that must he conducted under Part B in accordance with the requirements of 34 CFR §§ 300.304 through 300.311. Under 34 CFR § 300.304(b)(1), the public agency must use a variety of assessment tools and strategies to gather relevant functional, developmental, and academic information about the child, including information provided by the parent, that may assist in determining whether the child is a child with a disability under 34 CFR § 300.8; and the content of the child's individualized education program (IEP), including information related to

enabling the child to be involved in and progress in the general curriculum (or for a preschool child, to participate in appropriate activities). Further, *no single measure or assessment may be used as the sole criterion* for determining whether a child is a child with a disability and *for determining an appropriate educational program for the child.* (34 CFR § 300.304(b)(2)) (emphasis in original)

OSEP (2008) went on to say: "The Department's longstanding policy is that special education and related services are based on the identified needs of the child and not on the disability category in which the child is classified."

That said, a long-standing legislative history indicates that it is not the label but the child's needs arising out of his or her disability that determine the IEP. Needs determine the IEP. The IEP determines placement.

DON'T FORGET

A child's services and accommodations are dictated by the child's needs, not on the identified disability category or subcategory or other considerations (34 CFR § 300.304(b)(2); § 300.39(b)(3); OSEP, 2008).

Since needs determine the IEP and the IEP determines placement, if a child has been labeled as having a developmental delay, or any other qualifying label, he or she has a right to a free appropriate public education that addresses all of the child's special education and related service needs.

Need to Label

In the Preface to 2006 Final Regulations, OSERS said:

The Act does not require children to be identified with a particular disability category for purposes of the delivery of special education and related services. In other words, while the Act requires that the department collect aggregate data on children's disabilities, it does not require that particular children be labeled with particular disabilities for purposes of service delivery, since a child's entitlement under the Act is to FAPE and not to a particular disability label. (p. 46737)

States may, however, impose regulations requiring specification of disability categories. Check your state regulations.

Overruling a Decision Made by an IEP Team

There may be times when an administrator feels that the decision made by an IEP team is wrong and therefore feels the need to overrule the team decision. In our

> **DON'T FORGET**
> ....
> Disability categories do not determine services. The child's needs arising out of his or her disability determine the IEP. *Needs, not labels, determine the IEP.*

opinion, if this were to happen, it would be prima facie evidence, in any adversarial proceeding, that the provision of due process had been denied with a consequent loss of a free appropriate public education (FAPE). One can never be sure what a hearing officer or judge is going to do, but cases have hinged and fallen on lesser transgressions than that based on the court's perception that the basic right of the parent to full participation was trampled on. The administrator could, of course, reconvene the IEP team with him- or herself as LEA representative and within the context of that meeting impose her or his will, which would not be on the face of it be unlawful but would be risky if everyone else in the room were recommending services.

Additional Documentation Establishing Eligibility

Any time a school holds an eligibility meeting, regardless of the expected outcome, parents certainly have the right to bring in additional documentation that could establish eligibility. The additional documentation must be considered if it meets agency criteria (§ 300.502, p. 46791). If the documentation is extensive or not immediately persuasive (one way or the other), the meeting may be adjourned and rescheduled to give team members more time to review the new information. An IEP team meeting may be rescheduled at a later date if appropriate, but not more than 30 days after the eligibility determination.

Drafting the IEP

Although the LEA usually combines the eligibility group and IEP team meetings, the federal regulations do not require that the meetings be held on the same day. Alternatively, the eligibility group can make an entitlement

CAUTION

We cannot say this often enough: Practitioners must be familiar with their state regulations. States cannot deprive a child or parents of rights granted by federal law (any more than they could forbid women from voting), but states can and do grant additional rights to children and parents and can and do impose additional requirements on schools.

decision and then reconvene to develop an appropriate IEP. *Your state regulations may differ* (imposing additional timelines for the delivery of services) from the IDEA 2006 Final Regulations (§ 300.323(c), p. 46789), which require that the IEP meeting be held within 30 days of the determination of eligibility and that IEP services be made available "as soon as possible" after development of the IEP. OSERS declined to alter the 30-day time limit, which has been in place since 1977 (Preface, IDEA 2006 Final Regulations, p. 46680).

EVALUATION REPORTS

Evaluation Report versus Psychological Evaluation

There is a difference between the evaluation report and the psychological evaluation. The evaluation report is a summary of all screenings and evaluations used in making an eligibility determination. It is important to distinguish between the team's "evaluation report" and the separate "reports of the evaluations" by the individual evaluators. Parents must be given a copy of the evaluation report (§ 300.306, p. 46786). Schools are obliged to let parents inspect the various and sundry evaluations that have been completed, but they are not (at least under federal law) obliged to provide copies of those evaluations. However, schools often do provide parents with copies, particularly to share with other professionals, such as a family doctor. It is more prudent, however, for the schools to obtain written consent to release the reports directly to the professional; parents sometimes have removed whole pages they deemed offensive before sharing with their healthcare provider. While the required content of the team's evaluation report will vary from state to state, typically it will include a listing of all screenings and evaluations administered (even those not necessarily required for an eligibility

⦦ *Rapid Reference 5.2*

The evaluation report should be completed before the eligibility meeting. Education agencies must permit parents to inspect *any* education records they request before an IEP meeting.

determination) along with a summary of the results of each screening and evaluation.

The evaluation report should be completed before the eligibility meeting. In some states it *must* be. The 2006 Final Regulations do not specify a time frame for providing parents with a copy of the evaluation report, although state regulations may. However, parents have a right to participate meaningfully in meetings about their child, which includes the right to inspect all relevant evaluations prior to the meeting. The 2006 Final Regulations do require (§ 300.321(a), p. 46788), that, if the parents ask to see any education records, "each participating agency must permit parents to inspect and review any education records relating to their children that are collected, maintained, or used by the agency under this part. The agency must comply with a request without unnecessary delay and *before any meeting regarding an IEP*" (emphasis added). See Rapid Reference 5.2.

Nonstandardized Procedure

Ethically, if an evaluation was conducted using nonstandardized administration procedures (e.g., if the directions for a nonverbal test were translated into American Sign Language for a deaf child), that information should be included in the report of that evaluation. Best practice would dictate that that information also be included in the team evaluation report. There is nothing in the current federal language requiring that, but the burden on the evaluator is still more than a "should" though less than a "must." OSERS, in the Preface to the 2006 Final Regulations, (p. 46643) wrote: "It is standard test administration practice to include in the evaluation report the extent to which an assessment varied from standard conditions, including the language or other mode of communication that was used in assessing a child. It is, therefore, unnecessary to include this requirement in the regulations." We cannot think of any good reason for withholding such information and can think of many good reasons for including and explaining it. Obviously, if the team determines that the variance from standard conditions invalidated the test (e.g., the reading comprehension portion of a reading test was read aloud to the child), that would adversely affect the degree of credibility given to the results. As OSERS wrote in the discussion section of the 1999 Final Regulations:

> An assessment conducted under non standard conditions is not in and of itself a "substandard" assessment . . . if an assessment is not conducted under standard conditions, information about the extent to which the assessment varied from standard conditions, such as the qualifications of the person administering the test or the method of test administration, needs to be included in the evaluation report. . . . This information is needed so that the team of qualified professionals can evaluate the effects of these variances on the validity and reliability of the information reported and to determine whether additional assessments are needed. (p. 12634)

The 1999 Final Regulations (§ 300.532) required evaluators to provide that information, but that language was removed from the 2006 Final Regulations for the IDEA.

Excusing Members from Team Meetings

> If you don't have the right people at a team meeting, you don't have a team meeting; you have a little social gathering, a party.
>
> —Jackie Teague, personal communication, 2010

We would also recommend having refreshments, but then we always do. Although the IDEA 2004 and many states allow for members to be excused if both the school and parent agree in writing, we would not recommend doing that in this context even if permitted by state regulations. The only legal reason for excusing someone is because "the member's area of the curriculum or related services is not being modified or discussed in the meeting" (§ 300.321, p. 46788), not because he or she forgot to show up.

ELIGIBILITY CRITERIA

Adherence to Criteria Established by States

Eligibility teams must adhere to the criteria established by their state in determining whether a child is eligible for services, but state criteria, even for SLD, must not rely on a single testing tool or strategy or a single procedure for establishing eligibility. Each child must receive a comprehensive evaluation before entitlement consideration, and, for SLD decisions, schools must not rely solely on a discrepancy formula or a child's response to intervention in determining his or her entitlement. With respect to SLD, the 2006 Final Regulations require LEAs to adhere to the criteria established by their state (if any; some states may prefer to pass the buck to LEAs). Section 300.306 contains a special rule for SLD eligibility that reads: "*Consistency with State criteria. A public agency must use the State criteria adopted pursuant to paragraph (a) of this section in determining whether a child has a specific learning disability.*"

That means if your state uses a 15-point nonregression discrepancy rule, the team may not elect, when using a discrepancy formula, to apply an 18-point rule from another state that uses regression. With respect to both discrepancy and RTI methodologies, as noted in the previous chapter, eligibility decisions always must be based on comprehensive evaluations.

SPECIFIC LEARNING DISABILITY

Primary Classification

There are times when a child qualifies for several disabilities at the same time. For example, a child might meet eligibility criteria as having a specific learning disability in oral expression or listening comprehension and at the same time also qualify as speech/language impaired. Must the eligibility group determine which classification is primary?

The IDEA 2006 Final Regulations do not require eligibility groups to designate primary, secondary, or tertiary disabilities, but states may mandate such hierarchies (or their computer forms impose them). Section 300.641 requires states to report only one disability (e.g., developmental delay, deaf-blind, multiple disabilities, or one particular disability) to the Department of Education. In any case, the decision really does not impact the child's eligibility for services since it is the child's needs, not the label, that determine the IEP.

High IQ Exclusion

High IQ is not an exclusion from SLD classification. OSEP has said:

> There is no categorical exclusion for children with high IQs in Part B; therefore, if a student with a high I.Q. is not achieving at his expected performance standard for reasons other than those specified in 34 CFR 300.541(b), (the criteria for determining the existence of a specific learning disability (SLD)), and otherwise meets the criteria for that disability in accordance with that provision, the child can properly be identified within the meaning of that disability. Each child who is evaluated for a suspected learning disability must be measured against his own expected performance, and not against some arbitrary general standard. (OSEP letter to Lillie/Felton, 1994; on CD)

Academically Gifted/Learning Disabled Children

When Congress changed the definition of a disability, authorizing the use of a response to intervention methodology in identifying SLD, it also changed who will be identified and who will not be identified. Because an RTI methodology does not take into account the level of children's IQ but only the level of their academics, and since, in the problem-solving model, the standard of comparison is an age-appropriate peer, not an intra-individual comparison, there was some question whether there would any longer be academically gifted/learning disabled children. OSERS attempted to ameliorate the impact of this change by adding an 8th area of eligibility, reading fluency, to the seven areas traditionally assessed in IQ/achievement models since publication of the SLD Regulations for P.L. 94-142 in 1978. Explaining why reading fluency was added, the Preface to the 2006 Final Regulations states: "No assessment, in isolation, is sufficient to indicate that a child has an SLD. Including reading fluency in the list of areas to be considered when determining whether a child has an SLD makes it more likely that a child who is gifted and has an SLD would be identified" (2006 Final Regulations, p. 46652).

SERVICES

Emotional Disturbance

Is the classification label for an emotional disturbance seriously emotionally disturbed (SED), emotionally disturbed (ED), or emotionally disturbed/behaviorally disturbed (EB/BD)? Two terms, "serious emotional disturbance" (§ 300.8 (a)) and "emotional disturbance" (§ 300.8 (c)(4)), have been used in the IDEA and regulations promulgated under IDEA. The term "emotional disturbance/behavioral disturbance" does not appear anywhere in the IDEA. References to "serious emotional disturbance" in case law or decisions should be read to have the same meaning as "emotional disturbance." P.L. 105-17, the IDEA Amendments of 1997, changed "serious emotional disturbance" to "emotional disturbance." Despite that change, the phrase "serious emotional disturbance" still appears once in the 2006 Final Regulations. The change has no substantive or legal significance. The change was intended strictly to eliminate any negative connotation of the term "serious."

Diagnosing Emotional Disturbances

There is nothing in the IDEA regulations that would require the school to obtain a psychiatrist's diagnosis to classify a child as having emotional disturbance. IEP teams may not diagnose; but neither may psychiatrists, medical doctors, or school psychologists determine entitlement under the IDEA (although they may not understand that fact). States impose their own rules for specific assessments required and qualifications examiners must possess for various disabilities. (And remember that the LEA must pay for any assessments required for identification of a disability under IDEA or Section 504.)

Using *DSM-IV-TR*

Unless it is required by your state, a child does not need to be given a diagnosis based on the *Diagnostic and Statistical Manual of Mental Disorders, Fourth Edition, Text Revision* (*DSM-IV-TR*; American Psychiatric Association, 2000) in order to qualify as a child with an emotional disturbance. There is no specific diagnosis that by itself qualifies a student as eligible for ED consideration (although schizophrenia is mentioned specifically as part of the federal definition). Nor is any specific diagnosis (including oppositional defiant disorder [ODD] or conduct disorder [CD]) in and of itself disqualifying. Regardless of any specific *DSM-IV-TR* or other diagnosis, a student is eligible if and only if he or she meets all of the qualifiers of ED set forth in IDEA, including the need for special education. A *DSM-IV-TR* diagnosis alone does not adequately describe the student's behaviors to determine whether the student has ED.

Qualifiers for Emotional Disturbance

To qualify for special education and related services under the category of ED, the student must meet all six of these key elements:

1. The student must have a condition (for which the *DSM-IV-TR might* be useful).
2. The student must have one or more of the five ED characteristics (one is sufficient).
3. The ED characteristics must have been present over a long period of time (not defined).
4. The ED characteristic(s) must be present to a marked degree (also not defined).
5. The student's education performance must be adversely affected.
6. As a result, the student must require special education to achieve FAPE. (300.8 Child with a disability, p. 46756 of the 2006 Final Regulations).

Definition of "Condition"

As we have come to see with many other terms, the word "condition" is not defined in the federal regulation. A dictionary definition of a condition is "a particular mode of being of a person or thing; existing state; situation with respect to circumstance" (Webster's, 1996). Since IDEA provided no clarification as to this word's meaning, we infer that the intent was for end users to apply the usual and customary definition(s).

Clinical versus Educational Definition

The *clinical* definition of an emotional disturbance is different from the IDEA *special education* definition of ED. "Thus, a child may suffer from an emotional disturbance clinically, but not suffer from such educationally so as to be eligible for special education" (*Fauquier County Pub. Sch.*, 1993).

"To a Marked Degree"

There is no legal definition. Some authorities define "a marked degree" as having two components: pervasiveness and intensity. "Pervasiveness" refers to the continuity of the behaviors; "intensity" to demonstration of behaviors in an overt, acute, and observable manner. This definition may provide guidance but it does not carry the force of law (Exceptional Children Division, n.d.)

"Over a Long Period of Time"

The IDEA does not define this phrase either (no surprise). Individual states' and professional criteria and standards may set forth a minimum length of time before a particular disorder is considered to exist, such as 6 months for a diagnosis of schizophrenia (*DSM-IV-TR*, 2000, p. 312). Temporary or transient periods of instability caused by such problems as a death in the family, separation or divorce, or a new school probably would not qualify as "a long period of time" (e.g., *In re Pflugerville Indep. Sch. Dist.*, 1994).

"Adversely Affects Educational Performance"

As with any disability, this determination is based on the unique facts and circumstances of the particular case. "Educational performance" does *not* apply only to grades in classes and "academic" concerns but also to peer interaction, participation in class activities, and classroom conduct as well as standardized testing, homework, quizzes, and following directions (*New York City Sch. Dist. Bd of Educ.*, 1992). An assessment of the disability's adverse effect on educational performance can incorporate *all aspects* of the child's functioning at school, including *behavioral difficulties* at school, *impaired or inappropriate social relations*, and *impaired work skills*. Schools are required to address the effects of a child's disability in all areas of functioning, including academic, social/emotional, cognitive, communication, vocational, and independent living skills (e.g., *Oakland Unified Sch. Dist.*, 1985; *West Chester Area Sch. Dist.*, 1992). (Also see our discussion of this standard in Chapter 2.)

The five characteristics of ED as cited in the Congressional Definition and Section 300.8 of the 2006 Final Regulations are as follows:

"An Inability to Learn that Cannot Be Explained by Intellectual, Sensory, or Health Factors"

To meet this criterion, a student need not be totally incapable of learning (a condition rare in living organisms) but, rather, the student's emotional condition must significantly interfere with the ability to benefit from instruction (e.g., New York City Sch. Dist. Bd. of Educ., 1992).

"An Inability to Build or Maintain Satisfactory Interpersonal Relationships with Peers and Teachers"

Students can exhibit this characteristic in a variety of ways, such as a student who has no friends at home, in school, or in the community; who is extremely fearful of teachers and peers; who avoids communicating with teachers and peers; who does not socialize, play, initiate, or engage with others; or who shows a marked avoidance of others or is severely withdrawn. Hearing officers and courts have interpreted this phrase in a variety of seemingly contradictory ways; see, for example, *Babb v. Knox County School System* (1992), *Dallas Sch. Dist. v. Richard C.* (1996), *Emery Unified Sch. Dist.* (1995), and *Merrillville Community Schools* (2002).

"Inappropriate Types of Behavior or Feelings under Normal Circumstances"

This characteristic requires two things: an inappropriate behavior or feeling and normal circumstances. Inappropriate types of behaviors or feelings could include a lack of appropriate fear reactions; unexplained rage reactions; flat, blunted, distorted affect; manic behavior; inappropriate affect (laughing at a funeral, etc.); bizarre ideas or statements; hallucinations; delusional thinking. Several court cases have described the behaviors of students who were found to meet this particular characteristic. See, for example, *Lapides v. Coto* (1988) and *M.R. v. Lincolnwood Bd of Educ.* (1994). Behavior or feelings displayed in normal circumstances might, of course, have originated in abnormal circumstances.

> ## CAUTION
>
> While decisions at the hearing officer and state hearing review officer level may give some guidance, they do not have precedential value in a court of law. Wherever possible, legal arguments should be based on case law and should reference previous Supreme Court, circuit court, or district court findings, in that order of preference.

"A General Pervasive Mood of Unhappiness or Depression"

This specific term is also not defined in IDEA, so a dictionary definition can be useful. "Pervasive" is defined as "spreading widely or present throughout something" (Microsoft Corporation, 2009). This definition suggests that pervasiveness, when it comes to IDEA, carries the meaning of across domains (home, school, community). In a case where a student exhibited a mood of unhappiness or depression at home but not at school, it was held not to be pervasive (*Berkeley Unified Sch. Dist.*, 1986). A pervasive mood of unhappiness or depression may be manifested in different ways, such as irritability, sadness, lack or loss of interest in activities, sleep disorders, disruptions of eating, unwarranted self-blame, poor self-concept, destructiveness, or suicidal thoughts.

"A Tendency to Develop Physical Symptoms or Fears Associated with Personal or School Problems"

Physical symptoms have included headaches, nausea, asthma, ulcers (not caused by, but possibly aggravated by, stress), and colitis; tiredness and stomachaches; as well as nausea, severe headaches, body aches, light sensitivity, and other vision problems. Fears might include, for example, phobias, social anxiety, or obsessive-compulsive behaviors. This listing is not intended to be exhaustive or definitive.

Almost as an afterthought, Congress added the following language to the federal definition, language that has been repeated in the federal regulations ever since: "Emotional disturbance includes schizophrenia. The term does not apply to children who are socially maladjusted, unless it is determined that they have an emotional disturbance under paragraph (c) (4)(i) of this section." (Section 300.8, 2006 Final Regulations)

"Socially Maladjusted"

"Socially maladjusted" is not defined in federal law either, nor does the *DSM-IV-TR* recognize it as a mental disorder. Social maladjustment, whatever it is, is not exclusionary. (See Rapid Reference 5.3.) What the regulations have said for more than 30 years is that "[t]he term [serious emotional disturbance] does not apply to children who are socially maladjusted, *unless* it is determined that they have an emotional disturbance" (Ibid, 2006)(emphasis added). Despite the opinions of many authors and speakers, it is possible to be socially maladjusted *and* to have a serious emotional disability. One does not preclude the other. See, for example, *Springer v. Fairfax County School Board*, 1998) (on CD). One state has addressed this issue by adding social maladjustment as an additional educationally handicapping condition (State of New Jersey Administrative Code, 2006 [NJAC 6A: 14-3.5(c)11]), but under federal law, students who were only socially maladjusted, would not qualify.

OSERS and OSEP have avoided taking a position, despite the long-standing controversy. We found only three OSEP letters on emotional disabilities, all at least six years before the 2006 Final Regulations were promulgated. None addressed social maladjustment. Neither the 1999 nor the 2006 Final Regulations offered any additional guidance. Therefore, practitioners must look to the courts for authoritative advice. One always hopes to learn vicariously from the experiences of others in court rather than firsthand.

Social Maladjustment and Court Decisions

We found a few court decisions that may be of interest to special educators. All are in the references and some are on the CD. Obviously, the entire court decisions provide more detail.

Since the regulations specifically state that the label emotionally disturbed "does not apply to children who are socially maladjusted, *unless* it is determined that they have an emotional disturbance," the decision in *A.E. v. Independent Sch. Dist.* (1991) seems very relevant: "That a child is socially maladjusted is not by itself conclusive evidence that he or she is seriously emotionally disturbed." A U.S. District Court in California accepted an expert witness's definition of "socially maladjusted" as being "a persistent pattern of violating societal norms with lots of truancy, substance and sex abuse, i.e., a perpetual struggle with authority, easily frustrated, impulsive, and manipulative" (*Doe v. Sequoia Union High School District*, 1987). See also *Corpus Christi Independent Sch. Dist.* (1992). Students who externalize blame and are oppositional and argumentative were found to meet the definition of social maladjustment in a Connecticut case (*Doe v. Bd of Educ. of the State of Connecticut*, 1990). In *Henry County Bd of Educ.* (1995), the courts described a socially maladjusted child as one who demonstrated "chronic misbehavior."

Springer v. Fairfax County School Board (1998) (on CD) is informative for the court's decision about juvenile delinquency, drug use, and serious emotional disturbance. Parents sought reimbursement from their school board for tuition paid to a private school in which they had enrolled their son (Edward) after he failed the 11th grade. The school board determined that Edward was not suffering from a "serious emotional disturbance," as his parents had claimed, and that Edward was therefore ineligible for special education services under the IDEA.

Regarding use of the "characteristics" of emotional disturbance in the IDEA definition, the court rejected the claim of inability "to build or maintain satisfactory interpersonal relationships with peers and teachers" because of "ample evidence" of friendships and social relationships. Based in part on reports of psychologists chosen by the parents, the court noted "that the record simply does not support [the] contention [of] a general pervasive mood of unhappiness or depression." The court concluded: "The Springers still have failed to establish the critical causal connection between this condition and the educational difficulties Edward

CAUTION

Change the facts, change the outcome. Beware of precedents with different facts.

experienced, the final step in proving a serious emotional disturbance."
The facts (and the court's interpretation of the facts) matter.

The court then noted: "Prior to his eleventh grade year, E had made steady educational progress, advancing from grade to grade on schedule." It went on say,

> It seems incontrovertible that Edward was socially maladjusted. Although neither the federal nor the Virginia regulations define the term, Edward's behavior fits the definition offered by experts and accepted by the LHO and the SRO. The LHO rightly understood the term to refer to "continued misbehavior outside acceptable norms." See also In re Sequoia Union High Sch. Dist., 1987-88 EHLR Dec. 559:133, 135 (N.D. Cal. 1987) ("socially maladjusted [is] a persistent pattern of violating societal norms with lots of truancy, substance … abuse, i.e., a perpetual struggle with authority, easily frustrated, impulsive, and manipulative").

It did not end the inquiry there. It went on to consider the five characteristics listed in the federal regulations that we discussed above and found that Edward could not be found to meet any one of them, a consideration we will come back to later in this chapter.

The court cited *A.E. v. Independent Sch. Educ.* (1991) and *In re Morgan Hill Unified Sch. Dist.* (1992) and commented that "the fact '[t]hat a child is socially maladjusted is not by itself conclusive evidence that he or she is seriously emotionally disturbed' (*A.E. v. Independent Sch. Educ.*, 936 F.2d at 476). Indeed, the regulatory framework under IDEA pointedly carves out 'socially maladjusted' behavior from the definition of serious emotional disturbance" (*Springer v. Fairfax County School Board,* 1998).

The court declined to equate a diagnosis of dysthymia with "pervasive … depression." Referencing *In re Pflugerville Indep. Sch. Dist.* (1994), the court noted that when student had made passing grades prior to drug involvement, "it is inferentially permissible to attribute any lowering of his grades to his unwise choice to spend less mental energies on his academics and to spend more mental energies on [drug activities]" (on CD).

It then affirmed the district court's finding that Edward was not disabled "because the applicable IDEA regulations do not equate mere juvenile delinquency with a 'serious emotional disturbance.'"

≡ Rapid Reference 5.3

Social maladjustment is *not* exclusionary based on a plain-English reading of the definition of SED in the federal regulations. A child *can* be socially maladjusted *and* emotionally disturbed under IDEA, just as a child can have red hair and be emotionally disturbed.

A diagnosis of a conduct disorder or oppositional defiant disorder does not automatically mean a child is or is not SED; in fact, no *DSM* diagnosis will automatically get you into, *or* keep you out of, special education. The federal definition of ED rules.

Externalizing versus Internalizing Disorders

There is also no distinction in the federal regulations between children with externalizing and internalizing disorders with respect to eligibility. The terms appear in only one comment and response in the Preface to the 2006 IDEA Regulations, not at all in the actual regulations. In its comment, OSERS said: "We do not believe it is necessary to make the recommended change because § 300.324(a)(2)(i) is written broadly enough to include children with internalizing and externalizing behaviors" (p. 46683).

Intent, Remorse, or Understanding

Determining the intent, remorse, or understanding of a student's actions is not a burden imposed by the federal regulation when determining the eligibility for ED. Each case should be evaluated on a case-by-case basis. For example, Johnny pulls wings off butterflies and feels intensely guilty. Sammy pulls the legs off insects and laughs. Hopefully, we would not put Johnny in special education just because he feels guilty and deny services to Sammy because he is a junior psychopath. Uncovering the intent can be a useful with respect to providing appropriate interventions or factors in deciding about a disciplinary change in placement. One author (R. P. D.) evaluated a student for ED eligibility because it had been reported that the boy had "bitten the heads off the frogs" in a biology class. Clearly the behavior was a bit disturbing to some, but was it a sign of disturbance? During the student interview, when asked, "Why did you do that?" he responded with a huge grin, "Because the girls love it." This student was probably in need of social skills training, but the stated reason for the behavior was not rooted in emotional disturbance.

Look again at the analysis used by the Fourth Circuit in *Springer v. Fairfax County* (1998), which is summarized next.

The judges asked these questions in reaching their decision.

1. Was Springer socially maladjusted? Answer: Yes. Like many adolescents, he made a lot of bad decisions, fell in with bad company, and ended up in a lot of trouble. The Fourth Circuit concluded that a conduct disorder constituted social maladjustment and that social maladjustment did not mean a child was ED. The court did not stop there, however.

2. The court went on to say: "As the district court recognized, finding that Edward was socially maladjusted does not end the inquiry. The regulations contemplate that a student may be socially maladjusted and suffer an independent serious emotional disturbance that would qualify him for special education services under IDEA."

3. It then proceeded to go through the IDEA definition of ED to address the points raised by the parents.

4. It referred to the testimony of one expert, who said that the student was "in complete control of his actions."

5. But then it asked if he had problems with interpersonal relationships. Answer: No. Everybody liked him, he had lots of friends. In short, he was quite capable of forming relationships with peers and teachers.

6. It asked if he suffered from a pervasive mood of depression. Answer: No. Edward was a little depressed ("dysthymia") about getting caught and tossed out of school, but that was not a cause of his misbehavior. The court concluded it was just the result of his bad choices.

7. With respect to his being afflicted with an inability to learn, the court observed, "Prior to his eleventh grade year, Edward had made steady educational progress, advancing from grade to grade on schedule."

Apparently, no one had suggested physical symptoms or fears associated with personal or school problems, so the court did not address that issue specifically.

The court concluded: "The precipitous drop in Edward's grades at this time appears to be directly attributable to his truancy, drug and alcohol use, and delinquent behavior rather than to any emotional disturbance." However, change even one no to a yes, and the outcome of that trial might have been different.

Evaluations for ED usually focus on determining whether a child has one of the characteristics listed in the federal regulations and whether there is evidence the child has exhibited them over "a long period of time and to a marked degree that adversely affects [the] child's educational performance." If the answers to those questions are all affirmative, then whether the child is also socially maladjusted is not relevant to the entitlement decision (although it could be very relevant in developing an appropriate behavior intervention plan [BIP] or IEP).

Slenkovich (1983), an attorney, made a name for herself by asserting that SED was to be used only for children with really severe emotional disabilities, such as childhood schizophrenia. Nowhere in the federal regulations, including the discussion sections, or in any OSEP letter has there ever been any support for such a restrictive interpretation. In the comments on the Final Regulations for the IDEA 2004, a number of people thought the social maladjustment clause should be removed. OSERS observed (unhelpfully) that there has since 1977 never been any consensus on what constituted ED, noted that social maladjustment was still in the congressional definition, and declined to do anything to change the regulations or to do anything else to clarify the situation. It indicated additionally that there has never been any instrument developed which can reliably differentiate between SM and SED.

According to one source:

This definition, with the exception of the exclusionary clause for social maladjustment, began with the work of Eli Bower in the 1950's. Initially, in July of 1972, it appeared essentially in its present form as an implementing regulation of Public Law 91-230. With the passage of Public Law 94-142 in 1975, serious emotional disturbance was established as a special education category. The undefined exclusion of socially maladjusted students and ambiguous language have presented a problem for school personnel since 1975. These ambiguities have led to alternative interpretations and disparate treatment of students and youth across jurisdictions (Cline, 1990). In a position paper on the definition, the Council for Students with Behavioral Disorders posits that students with emotional disturbances are underserved primarily due to poorly defined and restrictive federal eligibility criteria (1987). (Exceptional Children Division, Public Schools of North Carolina, n.d.).

Determining the intent of Congress from a historical context has proven futile. Practitioners can't reliably differentiate between SM [social maladjustment] and SED [Serious Emotional Disturbance] using any known instrument that has been scientifically validated. No one is quite sure what Congress intended. If it intended anything, it was probably to exclude children who engaged in delinquent behavior that they could control and for which they received social support—if they were not also emotionally disturbed. But in the final analysis, none of that matters. "Under the federal and state definitions, if the child meets one or more of the five identifying characteristics and the four considerations, he or she is eligible for special education services regardless of the presence or lack of social maladjustment." (Exceptional Children Division, n.d.)

DON'T FORGET

One argument for an RTI approach to referrals is that children who are only "at risk" or whose problems do not require special education services nonetheless receive additional services through regular education from the outset of the process and may continue to receive those services.

At Risk for ED

Children "at risk" for having a serious emotional disability cannot be classified in order to receive preventive services. Only children with disabilities may be classified. Children who are just likely to become disabled are not eligible. However, the behaviors and feelings that make the child appear to be at risk might already qualify him for the identification. Also, there is nothing that prevents a student support team (SST) from providing Tier III interventions as a regular education service.

LACK OF APPROPRIATE INSTRUCTION

Determination of a Lack of an Appropriate Education

The burden on the eligibility group is not to determine whether the student has had adequate instruction but whether a lack of appropriate instruction is the determinant cause of any deficits in reading or math. Words are important, and the difference between determining whether the student had adequate instruction or that a lack of appropriate instruction was determinant is a substantive, not just a semantic, difference.

> § 300.306(b), consistent with section 614(b)(5) of the Act, states that a child must not be determined to be a child with a disability if the determinant factor for that determination is lack of appropriate instruction in reading or math, or limited English proficiency. (Preface, 2006 Final Regulations, p. 46643)

The question would be more appropriately phrased as: "What data and factors do the eligibility group need to consider in determining whether a lack of an appropriate education was *the* determinant factor in causing a child's reading and/or math problems?" If the child is actually enrolled, his or her response to appropriate educational interventions might be one factor to be considered, but as previously noted, OSERS goes on to say that for every child evaluated:

> A public agency must use a variety of data gathering tools and strategies even if an RTI process is used. The results of an RTI process may be one component of the information reviewed as part of the evaluation procedures required under §§ 300.304 and 300.305. As required in § 300.304(b), consistent with section 614(b)(2) of the Act, an evaluation must include a variety of assessment tools and strategies and cannot rely on any single procedure as the sole criterion for determining eligibility for special education and related services. Although not in the current regulations. (Preface, 2006 Final Regulations, p. 46648)

The Office for Civil Rights (OCR) in the U.S. Department of Education has issued a similar advisory regarding the need for a comprehensive evaluation. Section 504 requirements are equally applicable to children identified under the IDEA, although it is generally held that if an LEA meets all the requirements under the IDEA, it will also have met the Section 504 mandate. The advisory was based on § 34 CFR 104 of the 504 Regulations, which also carries the force of law, specifically § 104.35, which also requires documenting and carefully considering "information from a variety of sources and a "placement decision . . . made by a group of persons . . . in conformity with § 104.34" (34 CFR § 104.35) of the 504 Regulations (on CD).

For example, if the parents are claiming a variety of medical problems that are potentially disabling, written consent should be requested asking the child's medical providers to release the relevant medical records.

IDEA requires parental participation in an eligibility determination, so the final decision should be made only at an eligibility group meeting. There is no explicit requirement that parents participate in a Section 504 group meeting, but generally speaking, it is prudent to include them—if only to ensure that group members can say afterward that the group conducted a comprehensive evaluation and considered all the relevant data, including information from the home. Home-schooled children have been found on average to exceed national norms when compared to children in regular schools. However, even if the eligibility group found that a child had not received an adequate (or appropriate) education, there are an infinite number of scenarios wherein it might

DON'T FORGET

If a school insists that a medical evaluation is required to determine eligibility, because it suspects the child might have such a disability, and such an evaluation is not available, then the school would be liable under either 504 or the IDEA to provide such an evaluation at no cost to the parents. The school may ask, but may not require, that the parents use their insurance. If you want to suggest that the family pursue a medical evaluation for their own information, not for identification of a disability under IDEA, be very clear in your explanation of that suggestion and document that they were given their rights.

conclude that the lack of appropriate instruction was secondary to the disability, that is, not determinant. One question to ask is: "Why was the child home-schooled?" If it was because of chronic health problems, the eligibility group might conclude that the health problems, not any lack of instruction, were determinant. As another example, if the eligibility group found that the parents withdrew the child from public school because the child was failing and teachers had suggested the child might have a disability or were recommending retention for the second time, the group might find that the math and/or reading problems predated the home schooling and that, therefore, any lack of appropriate instruction was not determinant. In our view, however, given the extensive positive research on home schooling, the presumption should be that home school instruction was appropriate absent evidence to the contrary.

ADVERSE EFFECT

Passing from Grade to Grade

A child's performance in the classroom is only one factor to be considered. Both the 1999 Final Regulations and the 2006 Final Regulations are quite specific in saying that schools must provide children with disabilities who need special education in order to receive FAPE with those services even if the child has been passing from grade to grade.

Section 300.306 states explicitly that a child does not have to fail or be retained in a course or grade in order to receive services. In the Preface to the 2006 Final Regulations, OSERS further clarified its intent by writing:

§ 300.101(c) (p. 46762) provides that a child is eligible to receive special education and related services even though the child is advancing from grade to grade. Further, it is implicit from paragraph (c) of this section that a child should not have to fail a course or be retained in a grade in order to be considered for special education and related services. A public agency must provide a child with a disability special education and related services to enable him or her to progress in the general curriculum, thus making clear that a child is not ineligible to receive special education and related services just because the child is, with the support of those individually designed services, progressing in the general curriculum from grade-to-grade or failing a course or grade. The group determining the eligibility of a child for special education and related services must make an individual determination as to whether, notwithstanding the child's progress in a course or grade, he or she needs or continues to need special education and related services. (p. 46580)

We found only one letter from OSEP (Letter to Clarke, 2007; on CD) that addressed the issue post IDEA 2004. In that letter OSEP said in part:

It remains the Department's position that the term "educational performance" as used in the IDEA and its implementing regulations is not limited to academic performance.

Whether a speech and language impairment adversely affects a child's educational performance must be determined on a case-by-case basis, depending on the unique needs of a particular child and not based only on discrepancies in age or grade performance in academic subject areas. Section 614(b)(2)(A) of IDEA and the final regulations at 34 CFR § 300.304(b) (p. 46785) state that in conducting an evaluation, the public agency must use a variety of assessment tools and strategies to gather relevant functional, developmental, and academic information. Therefore, IDEA and the regulations clearly establish that the determination about whether a child is a child with a disability is not limited to information about the child's academic performance.

The broad interpretation of "educational performance" as encompassing something more than academic performance did not differ significantly from guidance issued in 1980 with respect to children with speech and language impairments (OSERS, Martin to Dublinske, 1980).

If children do not need specially designed instruction in order to meet their needs, then they would not be eligible for identification as SLD, nor would they be eligible for related services paid for out of special education funds. This requirement is explicit in the federal regulations, was affirmed in an OSEP letter from Davila to Hartman in 1989 and reaffirmed in the OSEP (1995) letter to Lillie/Felton: "[I]f . . . a child has one of the disabilities identified in paragraph (a)(1) of this section, but only needs a related service and not special education, the child is not a child with a disability under this part" (2006 Final Regulations, 34 CFR 300.8, p. 46756).

TEAM MEETING

Psychologist and Eligibility Teams

In general, all the federal regulations require is that the decision regarding eligibility must be made by a group of qualified professionals and the parents. Special rules when SLD is being considered (§ 300.308) include, in addition to the child's regular teacher (or, if there is none, the closest possible approximation), "(b) At least one person qualified to conduct individual diagnostic examinations of children, such as a school psychologist, speech-language pathologist, or remedial reading teacher."

The federal regulations leave it up to the states and local LEAs to make those decisions. Some state regulations require school psychologists to be part of those teams, but most states do not, leaving it up to the individual schools to decide who is needed. It is up to each school, absent state regulations to the contrary, to decide whether it is "appropriate" to invite a school psychologist to an eligibility group meeting. In the Preface to the 2006 Final Regulations, OSERS said, however, that the person conducting the evaluation may not be the person best qualified to interpret the instructional implications for the team; so the federal regulations do not require the presence of a school psychologist (p. 48670).

MEDICAL AND PSYCHOLOGICAL "DIAGNOSES"

Other Health Impaired and Medical Diagnosis

Under federal law, a medical diagnosis is not required for the identification of a child as having an attention deficit disorder, potentially qualifying him or her for classification as other health impaired (OHI). Many states require a medical evaluation before classifying any child as having

OHI, but a careful reading of the regulations in those states will almost always reveal that there is no explicit requirement for a medical diagnosis, just a medical exam. Not that we recommend that a school psychologist, even a school psychologist with appropriate training in diagnosing attention deficit disorders, do so unilaterally. Some sources assert more than 50 different conditions that might mimic ADHD. Few people have the time or qualifications to rule them all out. One of us (J. O. W.) made a medical referral that resulted in a diagnosis of a vaginal yeast infection as the actual cause of hyperactivity and inattention in a young girl. He was reluctant to attempt that diagnosis himself. An appropriately trained school psychologist might diagnose ADHD, pending a rule-out of various and sundry medical/physical problems. A medical doctor could rule them out without making a diagnosis; in many states, that would not invalidate the psychological diagnosis, but some states do require a medical diagnosis regardless. However, even in states requiring a medical diagnosis of ADHD before classification as OHI, the diagnosis of an appropriately trained school psychologist could still be sufficient in and of itself for use in a 504 proceeding. Once all the required screenings and evaluations have been obtained, it is up to the eligibility group to weigh them and reach a conclusion regarding the child's eligibility based on all the evidence provided.

Diagnosis versus Classification

Qualified professionals diagnose a disability. As we also noted in Chapter 1, eligibility groups determine whether a child with a disability should be classified under one of the IDEA categories as listed in state regulations (which do differ). Qualified professionals do not individually have the authority to classify children. Eligibility groups have no authority to diagnose a child for any purpose (including Section 504 eligibility), only to classify or label a child with a disability under the IDEA.

Recommendations and the Obligation to Pay

If a psychologist recommends a related service, such as counseling, for a student, parents may believe that, therefore, the schools are automatically

≣ Rapid Reference 5.4

§ 300.34 Related services

(a) *General.* Related services means transportation and such developmental, corrective, and other supportive services *as are required to assist a child with a disability to benefit from special education.* (p. 46760, emphasis added)

obliged to pay for that service. (See Rapid Reference 5.4 for the IDEA definition of related services.) The school is required to pay for a related service under the IDEA only if (1) a child is classified by the eligibility group as entitled to special educational services and (2) the IEP team concludes that the related service is needed for that child to benefit from his or her special education. It is a myth that schools must provide whatever is recommended by an evaluator. Under Section 504, a school would be required to pay only if the group concluded the service was needed in order to address the disabled child's needs as well as the needs of nondisabled students were addressed. Two evaluators might make mutually exclusive recommendations.

In North Carolina, the Exceptional Children Division's policy guideline is that evaluation reports should emphasize findings and interpretations based on multiple sources of data.

Recommendations based on the professional's clinical and diagnostic impressions of the child are an important part of the report and provide relevant information for teams to use in making decisions regarding educational placement and programming. On the basis of his/her assessment of the child, an evaluator should render a professional opinion as to the nature of the child's difficulty and specific intervention strategies, rather than a global statement regarding special education eligibility and program placement. (Harris, 2001; on CD)

✎ TEST YOURSELF ✎

1. The determination of the "knowledge or special expertise" of any individual invited to be a member of an IEP team is determined by the public agency (school).
   True or False

2. According to the IDEA, the evaluation report is not the same as the psychological evaluation.
   True or False

3. If a child is identified as having emotional disturbance, he or she can certainly receive counseling services because of the disturbance but may not receive speech and language services.
   True or False

4. A child who has a severe discrepancy only in reading could be served in any or all of the other seven areas despite there being no severe discrepancy for those areas.
   True or False

5. With regard to emotional disturbances, the IDEA regulations require that IEP teams obtain a psychiatrist's diagnosis in order to classify a child.
   True or False

6. Having a *DSM-IV-TR* diagnosis automatically qualifies a student as having a "condition" of emotional disturbance and therefore eligible for classification as ED.
   True or False

7. Before any child can be provided with special education services under the IDEA, that child must first be labeled as having one of the 13 disabilities listed in § 300.8.
   True or False

Answers: 1. False; 2. True; 3. False; 4. True; 5. False; 6. False; 7. False

Six

IDEA AND BEHAVIOR

> Do not train a child to learn by force or harshness; but direct
> them to it by what amuses their minds, so that you may be
> better able to discover with accuracy the peculiar bent of the
> genius of each.
>
> —Plato

Not all children are angels, and many, in fact, break school rules. If a student is a student eligible for services covered by the Individuals with Disabilities Education Act (IDEA) or Section 504, disciplining such behaviors becomes more complicated. The process for discipline can at times be very different for one student versus another, especially if one is identified as having a particular disability. When dealing with discipline issues, school personnel must be mindful not only of the IDEA protections but also of protections provided under Section 504 and the Americans with Disabilities Act (ADA).

Manifestation hearings to determine whether there was a nexus between the behavior and the disability are discussed at length later in this chapter. Evaluators can become key members of a manifestation determination tion hearing team because of their expertise in helping determine whether the behavior in question was caused by or directly and substantially linked to the student's disability. Since every evaluator is a potential expert witness in this type of proceeding, we believe it is important to be aware of the general rules of law as they now apply.

CAUTION

So-called zero tolerance policies can get schools into terrible legal difficulty when they are rigidly applied to students with disabilities. It is worthwhile to discuss such policies with regular education administrators before there is a crisis.

Disciplining Children who Are Protected by the IDEA

The most authoritative sources of information are the federal regulations, your state regulations, and the Office of Special Education Programs' (OSEP's) handy handouts on discipline. We have included federal regulations and some of OSEP's handouts on discipline on the accompanying CD. We have also included on the CD links (current, we hoped) to all 50 states' regulations. (It was not feasible to provide updated regulations/codes/procedures or policies for all 50 states because states revise their regulations so frequently and at such unpredictable times).

It is not that we cannot provide you with some helpful hints in this chapter (we are going to try), but if push comes to shove, and a student's parents are challenging the changes a school is proposing, having the law or an authoritative interpretation of the law to give the school board attorney (who may have even less expertise in special education law [spedlaw] than those he or she is representing) would be a lot more helpful than quoting from this book.

Children with disabilities under Section 504 and the IDEA generally can be disciplined to the same extent as children without disabilities as long as they are not disciplined more severely than children without disabilities for similar infractions.

IDEA or 504 Procedural Safeguards

When disciplining students with disabilities, several principles must be considered. The first applies to discipline that might result in a change of placement (see Rapid Reference 6.1). If disciplinary consequences,

≡ Rapid Reference 6.1

A suspension of more than 10 consecutive days is considered a change of placement under IDEA.

Shorter, nonconsecutive suspensions adding up to a total of more than 10 days in the same school year may be considered a change of placement if they result in a pattern of removals.

whatever they are, do not result in a disciplinary change of placement, the child may be disciplined with the same procedures used for all students, and there would be no need to conduct a manifestation hearing. The second principle, as mentioned earlier, deals with "fairness." As long as the disciplinary consequences being applied to a

> **CAUTION**
>
> In order not to count toward the more-than-10-day suspension issue, a child's in-school suspension must not impair services designed to allow the child to meet IEP goals and progress in the regular curriculum.

student with a disability were the same as would have been applied to a child without a disability, Section 504 protections against discrimination would not come into play. The third principle deals with length of time. If the disciplinary action taken by the school will result in a suspension of more than 10 consecutive days or if the suspension, in conjunction with other disciplinary changes, results in more than 10 days of cumulative placement resulting in pattern of removal, then IDEA and 504 procedural safeguards are triggered.

In-School Suspensions

Under federal regulations, in-school suspensions do not count toward the more-than-10-day suspension issue as long as the child continues to receive services enabling him or her to meet the goals of his or her individualized education plan (IEP) and to progress in the general education curriculum (Preface, 2006 Final Regulations, p. 46715).

Suspension Length

Schools can suspend a child with a disability up to 10 days without triggering rights related to a disciplinary change of placement.

Consecutive or Cumulative Days

As we said before, if the suspension is for more than 10 consecutive days, it is automatically a disciplinary change of placement, and due process rights, beginning with the right to a manifestation hearing, apply. A series of cumulative suspensions would be considered a change of placement triggering due process rights under the IDEA (or Section 504) only if the school concluded "that a change in placement has occurred." The school must review all prior suspensions and determine if the student "has been subjected to a series of removals that total more than 10 school days in a school year, the behaviors are substantially similar in nature, and such additional factors as the length of each removal, the total amount of time the child has been removed, and the proximity of the removals to one another support the premise that the series of removals constitute a pattern." It is the finding that the series of removals constituted a pattern, *not* the impact of those suspensions on the child's learning, that triggers due process rights related to disciplinary changes in placement (Preface to the 2006 Final Regs., p. 46729).

Disciplining for Different Conduct Issues

When considering the 10-cumulative-day suspension limit, there may be times when it matters if the discipline is for different conduct issues (e.g., the first suspension was for fighting and the second was for skipping school). If school personnel conclude the behaviors were substantially similar in nature (both indicative of negativistic and defiant behavior, or both indicative of high levels of personal stress), then one requirement in establishing a pattern adding up to a disciplinary change of placement would have been met. If school personnel decide that they were substantially dissimilar, then that requirement for establishing a pattern would not have been met. Without putting too fine a point on it, it is our opinion that, if school personnel believe that the behaviors reported *might* be a manifestation of the child's disability, they should (to be on the safe side) consider them "substantially similar."

DON'T FORGET

When there have been or will be more than 10 cumulative days of suspension, the school must consider whether they resulted or will result in a change of placement.

Suspension Limit and Change of Placement

The Supreme Court determined in *Honig v. Doe* (1988) (on CD) that 10 consecutive days' of suspension was a change of placement and that 10 cumulative days' of suspension *might* be a change of placement for a student with a disability. The decision applied equally to children with disabilities under the IDEA and Section 504. The 2006 final regulations regarding school suspensions and the rights of children with disabilities to a manifestation hearing merely reflect the Office of Special Education and Rehabilitative Services' (OSERS's) reinterpretation of that decision and are, therefore, reliable as guidance under Section 504 as well.

MANIFESTATION DETERMINATION

If a student's behavior is going to result, or has resulted, in a disciplinary change of placement for more than 10 consecutive days, the school must initiate a manifestation determination (MD) hearing. It must also do so if it concludes that similarities between the reasons for suspensions resulting in more than 10 cumulative days are sufficiently similar so as to constitute a pattern. It is the pattern, not the effect of those suspensions that triggers that right under the IDEA.

A manifestation hearing under the IDEA is an IEP team meeting held after a disciplinary change of placement (e.g., suspension of more than 10 days) to determine if the child's behavior, for which he or she is being disciplined, was, in fact, directly a result of his or her disability. All the appropriate members of an IEP team must be invited. It is, however, not just a meeting; the process, if conducted properly, also meets the Section 504 requirement that a child be reevaluated before any change of placement. (Under 504, there is no mandated membership list for the panel conducting the manifestation hearing.)

Satisfying IDEA and 504 Safeguards

The 2006 Final Regulations simplified the manifestation determination process considerably from what was in the 1999 Regulations, which many schools have found so complex that they were unable to follow them without a crib sheet listing all the steps. The revised procedures under the IDEA require these four steps (and would meet all Section 504 requirements as well):

1. The team must review all relevant information in the student's file, including the child's IEP, any teacher observations, and any relevant information provided by the parents.

2. Based on that review, the team must determine
    (i) If the conduct in question was caused by, or had a direct and substantial relationship to, the child's disability; or
    (ii) If the conduct in question was the direct result of the local education agency's (LEA's) failure to implement the IEP.

3. If *neither* of these conditions is found to be present, the student is subject to the same disciplinary action that any student without a disability would receive for the same violation. If *either* of these conditions is met, the team must find that the behavior was a manifestation of the child's disability. If it is determined that the conduct was a result of the IEP not being implemented properly, the school must take steps to correct those deficiencies immediately. "Stay put" (the right of a child with a disability to remain in his current placement pending the outcome of the hearing—see Chapter 2) applies unless the school and parents agree to an alternative placement or the student has committed an offense triggering the school administration's authority to unilaterally place the student in an interim alternative placement for 45 days.

4. If the manifestation hearing results in a finding that the behavior was a manifestation of the child's disability, the team must also conduct a functional behavioral assessment (FBA), if one has not already been completed, or review a behavior intervention plan (BIP), if one has already been developed, revising it if appropriate (§ 300.530, 2006 Final Regulations). It is also important to remind readers once again to consult with state codes or regulations; some states (e.g., North Carolina) retain the language from the 1999 regulations requiring FBAs to be completed anytime a school recommends a disciplinary change of placement for an IDEA-eligible child, whether the behavior was found to be a manifestation or not. (See also Rapid Reference 6.2).

≡ *Rapid Reference 6.2*

If the conduct in question was caused by, or had a direct and substantial relationship to, the child's disability or was the direct result of the LEA's failure to implement the IEP, the LEA must review any existing BIP or conduct a FBA. States may impose additional requirements.

Parental Permission

Parental consent is not needed for a manifestation determination hearing, but written consent is required before conducting a Functional Behavioral Assessment.

Behaviors that Do Not Apply

If the proposed suspension is for using (not just possessing) drugs, then under Section 504, the school would not have to have a manifestation hearing at all. (*This exception would not apply, however, if the student had also been entitled under IDEA.*) However, if a school system alleges that it is suspending a 504 student for drug use, it may only do so if under similar conditions it would have suspended a child without a disability. (For example, if the alleged drug use occurred off campus, then the school could invoke the drug use exemption only if it disciplined non-504 children for using drugs off campus.)

DON'T FORGET

Parental consent is not needed for a manifestation determination hearing, but it is required before conducting an FBA.

Differences between 504 and IDEA Procedures

Under § 300.504 of the 2006 Final Regulations (p. 46798) or Section 504, if the team determines that a student's behavior is a manifestation of that child's disability, he or she may not be suspended and services must be continued ("stay put" applying under both statutes).

If the behavior is not a manifestation of a disability under Section 504, then the child may be disciplined just as a child without a disability would be, but the student would not have to have services continued. Schools (or any educational institution receiving federal funds) cannot discriminate by imposing a tougher penalty, but that is the only limitation.

Under the IDEA, however, regardless of whether a child is removed for behavior that is *or* is not a manifestation of his or her disability, that student is still entitled to services. The relevant portion of the law in § 300.530, p. 46798 is excerpted next.

(d) Services. (1) A child with a disability who is removed from the child's current placement pursuant to paragraphs (c), or (g) of this section must—

(i) Continue to receive educational services, as provided in § 300.101(a), so as to enable the child to continue to participate in the general education curriculum, although in another setting, and to progress toward meeting the goals set out in the child's IEP; and

(ii) Receive, as appropriate, a functional behavioral assessment, and behavioral intervention services and modifications that are designed to address the behavior violation so that it does not recur.

REMOVAL FROM SCHOOL

School's Unilateral Authority

Additional authority is given to school personnel with respect to the school's or a hearing officer's unilateral authority to place a child with a disability entitled under the IDEA in an interim alternative placement for up to 45 days if a (1) child carries a weapon or possesses a weapon; (2) possesses or uses illegal drugs or tries to buy a controlled substance; or (3) has inflicted serious bodily injury upon another person at school, on school premises, or at a school function supervised by the LEA. Although school administrators have that authority, *they must convene an IEP team meeting in order to exercise that right.* In instances where the school's concerns about safety are even more severe, it does also have the option of seeking a *Honig* injunction from a court for longer periods (§ 300.530, 2006 Final Regulations). These days, schools rarely invoke that option.

Honig Injunction

A *Honig* injunction refers to a court injunction obtained by a school system from a court forbidding (enjoining) a student from attending school. See Rapid Reference 6.3. There is a presumption in favor of the child's current educational placement that school officials can rebut, the Supreme Court noted, "only by showing that maintaining the current placement is substantially likely to result in injury to the student or to others." It is named after the 1988 Supreme Court decision, *Honig v. Doe* (1988; on CD).

The term is not heard very often, because the IDEA now gives school authorities or a hearing officer the authority to order a child removed to an interim alternative educational setting for up to 45 days (an IEP team determining the services needed, but not necessarily the setting) if the child has violated drug policies, possessed a weapon on school grounds, or caused serious harm to another child. However, *Honig* still can be invoked if the school system is seeking a longer exclusion, and it would still apply if a school were seeking to exclude a 504 student. Although the IDEA 1997 and IDEA 2004 gave schools additional options to use when dealing with students who were dangerous to others, brought drugs on campus, or had weapons on campus, nothing in the statute precludes a school system from seeking relief in the courts or requires the schools to exhaust the procedures in the IDEA 2004 (and its implementing regulations) before going to the courts. It is just a lot easier to use the additional authority granted by the IDEA than to have to present evidence to convince a judge the student should be in an alternative educational setting because he or she posed an imminent threat.

CONFUSING QUIRKS AND TWISTS

Victim Rights

Schools have an affirmative obligation to protect the safety of all their students. School officials need to protect their students against any kind of harassment or assault. As indicated in OSERS's Q and A on discipline (OSERS, 2009; on CD), some federal courts have equated rape to serious bodily injury, but, in any case, the IDEA is not the only concern that school administrators should have if allegations are being made that a student, with a disability or otherwise, is being harassed.

≣ *Rapid Reference 6.3*

A *Honig* injunction is a court injunction obtained by a school system forbidding a student from attending school because maintaining the current placement is substantially likely to result in injury to the student or to others.

Section 1983 of the Civil Rights Act has ofttimes been invoked by the parents of special education children as providing grounds for lawsuits against school officials for malfeasance. Those lawsuits were routinely rejected by the courts, both state and federal, in spedlaw cases as in regular education cases, the courts saying that since the various education laws imposed their own system of compensation, a Section 1983 complaint, including complaints alleging sexual discrimination that were covered under Title IX of the Education Act, was precluded. However, in January 2009, the Supreme Court ruled in *Fitzgerald v. Barnstable* that parents could sue school officials personally under Section 1983 for civil rights violations, irrespective of Title IX. The case itself involved a kindergarten child who had allegedly been sexually harassed on a school bus by a peer. The legal issue addressed by the Supreme Court was whether such lawsuits could be brought only under Title IX, which just allows for institutional lawsuits; or whether it could also be brought under Section 1983 of the Civil Rights Act, which allows for lawsuits to be filed against individuals. The court said the Civil Rights Act was still applicable. The world suddenly got a little more dangerous for school administrators, whether the victim does or does not have a disability. In situations where the victimizer has a disability (and victims, sadly, can become victimizers themselves), schools sometimes have responded by hiring one-to-one assistants to protect the child from him- or herself as well as other students.

CAUTION

Schools have an affirmative obligation to protect the safety of *all* their students.

Parental Disagreement with MD

It is entirely possible that an IEP team meets and determines that the behavior of a student is not a manifestation of the child's disability, but the parent disagrees and argues that it is. In this case, "stay put" goes into effect, except in those situations where drugs, weapons, or serious bodily injury was involved and the district invoked its right to a unilateral 45-day placement. In any dispute, the rules regarding "stay put" apply unless overturned by a judge or hearing officer or when both parties agree to an alternative placement.

Determining Behaviors Are Not Related to a Disability

It is of course possible to determine that a child's behavior is not related to his or her disability. The standard for determination is a legal, not a philosophical or theological, one. Within a legal context, "free will" is generally assumed except in cases where the accused is so deranged that he or she does not understand the difference between right or wrong. In manifestation hearings, if the team concludes that the conduct in question was caused by, or had a direct and substantial relationship to, the child's disability, then it would be considered a manifestation. If, however, the team concludes that there was no relationship, it may still consider factors such as intentionality, remorse, and the ability to understand consequences in determining whether a change of placement is warranted on a case by case basis (Final Regulations, 2006, p. 46714).

Also note that even if a MD team finds that the behavior is a manifestation of the disability, disciplinary actions that would not result in removal or a change of placement still may be used to the extent and duration that they would for a student without a disability. Disciplinary actions other than suspension or expulsion or a long-term change of placement—say, to homebound—would therefore be allowed. See Rapid Reference 6.4 for this rule regarding disciplining students with disabilites.

Triggering Procedural Safeguards when a Child Has Not Been Identified

Under the IDEA 2004, safeguards are not triggered unless a concern has been expressed by the parent in writing to supervisory personnel or a teacher prior to the incident. An oral statement of concern would not be sufficient. If, however, the facts were that a parent had made the request in writing, there was documentation that the request had been reviewed, and that someone had decided that the child was not special education eligible without affording the student all his or her due process rights, these facts probably would be fatal to any argument that the school might want to make in a judicial or quasi-judicial forum. Schools in that instance would be protected against parent claims only if they have referred the child, evaluated the child (with informed written parental consent), and found the child ineligible for services, all the while handing out due process handbooks when the child was referred and then again when found ineligible for identification.

Limits to FAPE

Since the school must provide a free appropriate public education (FAPE) to students with a disability who have been suspended, there may be times when schools argue that their services should have some limits as to how much must be given. For example, must the child receive a "full day" of education?

The limits are defined only by what is necessary to insure that the child has an opportunity to progress in meeting both the goals of his or her IEP and to progress in the general curriculum. If the school system asserts that it can do so with homebound instruction for 1 hour 3 days a week, it can do so unless that assertion is challenged by the parent in due process or is overturned by a hearing officer. In that case, the school system probably would lose the argument, especially if any of the child's goals included improved behavior with respect to peers. It is pretty hard to teach or provide an opportunity to practice good behavior with peers when a student's only regular social contacts are parents.

FBAs and IEPs

The FBA is an evaluation. The results of an evaluation when the team has concluded that the behavior was a manifestation of a child's disability help

≡ Rapid Reference 6.4

Students with disabilities can be disciplined under customary school rules as long as the discipline is no harsher than discipline for students without disabilities and any days suspended do not result in a change of placement.

to determine current levels of performance, which may be incorporated into an IEP in the form of a behavior intervention plan (BIP).

Parental Consent for a FBA

As noted previously, the LEA does need written parental consent to do a FBA if the purpose is to help determine eligibility *or* prefatory to making changes in a BIP in the child's IEP. In addition to the previous reference, for a more thorough discussion of OSEP's reasoning, see the Posney letter to Christiansen (February 9, 2007; on CD) in which OSEP's rationale that an FBA is an evaluation requiring informed written parental consent is discussed in great detail.

Although this point is not addressed specifically in this part of the regulations, if a parent disagrees with any evaluation conducted under the IDEA, he or she would have the right to request an independent educational evaluation (IEE) under § 300.502 of the 2006 Final Regulations at district expense. The school district could either provide the requested IEE or initiate due process hearing procedures to try to show that the school's evaluation was adequate.

Disabled IDEA Student Using Drugs

Special education is an entitlement that a qualified child has; it is not a carrot to be given and taken away in some reward/punishment procedure. School administrators can, however, unilaterally send a child with a disability identified under the IDEA to an alternative educational placement for up to 45 days, but only if the possession, sale, or use of the drugs (1) was done knowingly by the student and (2) happened on campus or at a school-sponsored event.

Infractions "Off School Grounds"

Generally, in our opinion, the school does not have any authority to discipline the child for the behaviors that occur off the school

CAUTION

Schools cannot deny special education as a punishment or offer it as an incentive.

grounds, but this issue continues to be litigated with students without disabilities with respect to cyberbullying. The only absolute exception would be if the infraction occurred at a school function off campus (including infractions at school bus stops).

Schools' Codes of Conduct

Neither Section 504 nor the IDEA dictates schools' codes of conduct. Disciplinary decisions are left to the school administrators on a case-by-case basis within the context of their respective school districts' board of education policies. Rules about suspensions apply regardless, of course, and codes of conduct cannot override the rights afforded to disabled children by federal and state laws.

45-School-Day Placement versus Long-Term Suspension/Expulsion

School districts are not required to use 45-school-day interim alternative placement for drugs, weapons, or serious bodily injury but may go right to a long-term suspension/expulsion if conduct is unrelated to the student's disability. However, school systems do not have the unilateral right to suspend students with disabilities long term under either Section 504 or the IDEA. The only way they could suspend a student with a disability long term would be, as indicated earlier, through a *Honig* injunction. The burden of proof, as noted, would be on the school system to show that continuing the child in regular education would pose unacceptable risks for the other children and/or staff.

> The "stay-put" provision prohibits state or local school authorities from unilaterally excluding disabled children from the classroom for dangerous or disruptive conduct growing out of their disabilities during the pendency of review proceedings. Section 1415(e)(3) is unequivocal in its mandate that "the child *shall* remain in the then current educational placement" (emphasis added), and demonstrates a congressional intent to strip schools of the *unilateral* authority they had traditionally employed to exclude disabled students, particularly emotionally disturbed students, from school. This Court will

not rewrite the statute to infer a "dangerousness" exception on the basis of obviousness or congressional inadvertence. . . . However, Congress did not leave school administrators powerless to deal with such students, since implementing regulations allow the use of normal, nonplacement-changing procedures, including temporary suspensions for up to 10 school days for students posing an immediate threat to others' safety, while the Act allows for interim placements where parents and school officials are able to agree, and authorizes officials to file a § 1415(e)(2) suit for "appropriate" injunctive relief where such an agreement cannot be reached. In such a suit, § 1415(e)(3) effectively creates a presumption in favor of the child's current educational placement which school officials can rebut only by showing that maintaining the current placement is substantially likely to result in injury to the student or to others. (*Honig v. Doe*, 1998; on CD)

Bus Suspensions

According to OSERS, for all children protected under IDEA, bus transportation suspensions trigger manifestation determination rights only if transportation has been written into the IEP as a related service. The 2006 Final Regulations do not address bus suspensions per se, but they do reaffirm the right of children to receive transportation as a related service.

According to OSERS, "if the IEP Team determines that a child with a disability requires transportation as a related service in order to receive FAPE, or requires supports to participate in integrated transportation with nondisabled children, the child must receive the necessary transportation or supports at no cost to the parents" (Preface to the 2006 Final Regulations). Yet OSERS reiterated the principle found in the 1999 regulations that if it was not written into the child's IEP, then parents of children with a disability had the same obligations to get their children to school as the parents of children suspended in general education (p. 46715).

Once again, however, we reiterate our all-too-frequent caveat urging readers to double-check their own state regulations. California, for example, apparently requires special education students to receive alternative transportation for any bus suspension (Community Alliance for Special Education & Protection and Advocacy, 2005). Wisconsin's attorney general has also opined that bus suspensions "would count" as suspensions toward the 10 days. Options for providing alternative transportation could include either contracting with a taxi cab service or formally contracting with the child's parents (assuming they were willing) to transport their child in return for payments reimbursing them for mileage.

> He who spareth the rod hateth his son: but he that loveth him correcteth him betimes.
>
> —Proverbs 13:24

> Withhold not correction from a child: for if thou strike him with the rod, he shall not die. Thou shalt beat him with the rod, and deliver his soul from hell.
>
> —Proverbs 23:13–14

POSITIVE BEHAVIORAL INTERVENTIONS AND SUPPORTS

With the revision to IDEA 2004 and the introduction of response to intervention (RTI) as a method for determining eligibility for specific learning disabilities, many schools are adopting the use of response to behavioral interventions as part of a comprehensive evaluation to determine eligibility as having an emotional disability. It is not the purpose of this book to provide a road map for LEAs attempting to develop such a system. However, we probably would be negligent if we did not at least mention that the debate between those who support corporal punishment (as seemingly recommended by the Bible) and the use of aversive punishments versus those who favor an approach modeled after Plato's recommendation cited at the beginning of this chapter has, for all intents and purposes, been settled by Congress. When referencing behavior and the tools for behavioral change, the Final Regulations specifically refer to positive behavioral interventions and support (or positive behavioral intervention strategies [PBIS]) no fewer than 22 times in the Preface and another 6 times in the Regulations themselves. Additionally, OSEP has established a separate Web site dedicated exclusively to the use of PBIS at www.pbis.org as well as a comprehensive set of evaluation tools (on that same Web site) at www.pbis.org/evaluation/evaluation_tools.aspx. We believe any school system using interventions based on federally recommended assessments would be in an excellent position to show it was implementing a state-of-the-art intervention program. A system documenting unimproved behavior "after three separate paddlings" would in our opinion not be in defensible position. Corporal punishment or other negative behavioral intervention (including aversives) would also fail to meet federal standards in addressing disproportional suspension or expulsion rates (§ 300.170, p. 46774 of the 2006 Final Regs.); or as behavioral interventions in a IEP if the team found that the child's behavior was impeding the learning of himself or others (§ 300.324 Development, review, and/revision of IEP, p. 46790).

✐ TEST YOURSELF ✐

1. **According to the IDEA, in-school suspensions are considered the same as out-of-school suspensions.**
   True or False
2. **According to the IDEA, when determining the amount of suspension a child has had, the school should count only the number of consecutive days the child has been suspended.**
   True or False
3. **Parental consent is not needed for a manifestation determination hearing.**
   True or False
4. **A *Honig* injunction refers to a court injunction obtained by a school system from a court forbidding a student from attending school.**
   True or False
5. **If a child with an IEP commits a crime at school, the school is not allowed to report that child to the police.**
   True or False

Answers: 1. False; 2. False; 3. True; 4. True; 5. False

Seven

IDEA, SECTION 504, AND ADA

> Congress acknowledged that society's accumulated myths and
> fears about disability and disease are as handicapping as are
> the physical limitations that flow from actual impairment.
>
> —Supreme Court Justice William J. Brennan, Jr.,
> *School Board of Nassau County v. Arline*

Although the application of Section 504 is generally thought of as being a regular education responsibility, related service providers may be asked to evaluate children referred under Section 504 or even to take responsibility for chairing 504 committees in their respective buildings. Regardless, special education service providers are often regarded as the go-to persons when questions regarding special education law (spedlaw) arise. Hence this chapter's comparatively brief review of Section 504 and listing of more authoritative references.

OVERVIEW OF SECTION 504

Most people involved in public education, and almost certainly all of those involved with special education in public school probably have heard about Section 504, but it seems that almost every school district addresses Section 504 in a different manner. It is, in fact, all too common to hear parents report that they have been told by someone representing a school district that "We don't do that in this district." However, compliance with Section 504, which is a federal statute, is *not* optional.

Section 504 is a federal law designed to protect the rights of individuals with disabilities in programs and activities that receive federal financial assistance from the U.S. Department of Education (ED). Section 504, and specifically, 34 Code of Federal Regulations (CFR) § 104, provides: "No otherwise qualified individual with a disability in the United States . . . shall, solely by reason of her or his disability, be excluded from the participation in, be denied the benefits of, or be subjected to discrimination under any program or activity receiving Federal financial assistance."

Section 504 regulations, similar to those of the Individuals with Disabilities Education Act (IDEA), require school districts to provide a free appropriate public education (FAPE) to each qualified student with a disability who is in the school district's jurisdiction, regardless of the nature or severity of the disability. Under Section 504, FAPE consists of the provision of regular or special education and related aids and services designed to meet the student's individual educational needs as adequately as the needs of students without disabilities are met.

School systems are directly responsible for applying 504 regulations. Since the states do not have the same responsibilities for oversight as they do under the IDEA, there is unfortunately an almost infinite opportunity for misconceptions to arise as local boards struggle to develop relevant policies.

As an introduction, we address some of those misconceptions along with what the law actually requires for schools. (Many rules are different at the postsecondary level.)

MISCONCEPTIONS ABOUT 504

Misconception: Under the IDEA, students receive special consideration for disciplinary infractions. Under Section 504, they do not.

Reality: Under both IDEA and Section 504, if a student is being suspended for more than 10 consecutive days, or if a series of short-term suspensions amounts to a change of placement resulting in a loss of FAPE, the school must conduct a "manifestation hearing." If the behavior was a manifestation of the child's disability, the student may not be suspended. Unlike the IDEA, under Section 504, if the behavior was not a manifestation, then a student identified as disabled may be suspended without services to the same degree a student without a disability would be suspended. There is one exception under Section 504. If a 504 student is suspended long-term for using drugs (not just for possession), the student has no right to a manifestation determination hearing.

Misconception: Under the IDEA, the school is responsible for providing a comprehensive evaluation at district expense if the school suspects a student has a disability. Under Section 504, the parent is responsible.

Reality: Under both the IDEA and Section 504, the school is responsible for providing a comprehensive evaluation at district expense if it suspects the child has a disability. Under both laws, the school has the option of using evaluations provided at parent expense but is not required to rely on them solely although they must consider them if they meet agency criteria.

Misconception: IDEA evaluations are free, but parents must pay for 504 evaluations.

Reality: This is true only at the postsecondary (college or university) level. All public elementary and secondary schools are responsible for providing a free comprehensive evaluation for children suspected of a disability under both laws.

Misconception: There are more guarantees for student success under the IDEA than under Section 504.

Reality: Neither law guarantees student success. Under the IDEA, the school is responsible for providing an individualized education program (IEP) that is reasonably calculated to benefit the child. Under Section 504, the burden is to provide services that "level the playing field." Those differences are largely semantic, as Section 504 includes the same guarantees for services (including the right to residential placement at public school expense) that the IDEA provides, if those services are needed for the child to receive FAPE (Final Regulations, Section 504, § 104.33; on CD).

Misconception: Under the IDEA, a child may receive special education services; under Section 504, he or she may receive only accommodations.

Reality: The full continuum of services under the IDEA is also available under Section 504; Section 504 is a large umbrella covering all children with disabilities, including those students protected by the IDEA. Some courts have held, however, that if a 504 child were entitled to special educational services, the school system would have entitled him or her to that under the IDEA.

Misconception: Related services are available under the IDEA but not under Section 504.

Reality: Related services are available under the IDEA only if needed for the child to benefit from his or her IEP. However, those same related services also would be available under Section 504 if needed to meet the student's educational needs as adequately as nondisabled children's needs are met.

Misconception: Only the disabilities listed in the Final Regulations for IDEA 2004 are eligible for consideration under Section 504.

Reality: Section 504 does not limit the eligible disabilities. There must be an identifiable disability, but it does not have to be one named in IDEA. In fact, to be eligible for the civil rights protections (not services) under Section 504, an individual does not even have to have a disability. Section 504 prohibits discrimination based on a perceived handicap, such as AIDS, even when the handicap is not substantially limiting to the person him- or herself. Although many people do have substantial limitations arising out of their illness (such as AIDS), "discrimination based solely on the fear of contagion is discrimination based on handicap when the impairment has that effect on others" (Office of Civil Rights, 1991).

Misconception: ADA/Section 504 apply only to public schools, not to private schools.

Reality: Both private and public schools that are recipients of federal funding must provide their students with the rights afforded under those laws.

Misconception: Under the IDEA, a child may be served only if he or she has a covered disability. Under Section 504, a child is automatically eligible if he or she has exited from (has a history of a disability) a special education program.

Reality: A child may have a disability but not need special education and be eligible for 504 services; but a child does not become eligible for services simply because he or she was in special education. He or she still must have a current disability. (See Rapid Reference 7.1 for a quick reference list of common myths about Section 504.)

SECTION 504 AND ADA

Children with disabilities identified under Section 504 have substantially the same rights to a FAPE as children identified under the IDEA. The major difference is that Section 504 is an unfunded federal mandate; IDEA is a partially funded federal mandate. While some people describe

≡ Rapid Reference 7.1

Persistent myths about Section 504 include those listed. All are untrue.

* Section 504 is optional for schools. *Not even close.*
* Under the IDEA, students receive special consideration for disciplinary infractions. Under Section 504, they do not. *False.*
* Under the IDEA, the school is responsible for providing a comprehensive evaluation at district expense if the school suspects a student has a disability. Under Section 504, the parent is responsible. *Wrong.*
* There are more guarantees for student success under the IDEA than under Section 504. *Untrue.*
* Under the IDEA, a child may receive special education services; under Section 504, he or she may receive only accommodations. *Myth.*
* IDEA evaluations are free, but parents must pay for 504 evaluations for preschool and school children. *Not true.*
* Related services are available under the IDEA but not under Section 504. *Contrary to fact.*
* Only the disabilities listed in the Final Regulations for IDEA 2004 are eligible for consideration under Section 504. *A canard.*

Section 504 as a civil rights law and the IDEA as an educational rights law, the difference when it comes to services available are at most trivial. One significant difference is that, in order to be identified under the IDEA, a child must demonstrate a need for special education. Under Section 504, a child needs only to require (at the minimum) accommodations to level the playing field (as adequately as the needs of children without disabilities are met) in order to qualify. This does not just mean providing academic accommodations. Back in the 1980s, one author's (G. M. M.) school district constructed a new middle school without providing handicapped access to the stage. When queried about this in an Office for Civil Rights (OCR) complaint, the school system said that when the student with paraplegia in chorus needed to be on the stage, two adult teachers were assigned to carry her up the stairs. OCR responded that the school's accommodation was inherently more unreliable, inherently more dangerous, and therefore inherently inadequate to meet the child's needs as adequately as a child without a disability. The school was given the choice of installing a ramp or a lift for her wheelchair. Terminology differs as well. Under Section 504, the disability must substantially limit a child in a major life function (in schools, that is often, but definitely not always, translated as meaning "learning"). Under the IDEA, the disability must adversely affect educational performance. (See Section 504 and specifically § 104.33 on the CD.)

SECTION 504 AS A CONSOLATION PRIZE

If a child referred for special educational services under the IDEA is determined to need only non–special education services, should we automatically consider that student for 504 placement? The answer is "It depends." "Need" does not, in and of itself, determine eligibility for services under Section 504. It must be a need arising out of a substantial limitation resulting from a disability. If a child does not qualify under IDEA because he or he does not need special education services, then the child still might qualify for 504 accommodations.

If, however, the reason the child does not qualify under the IDEA is that he or she does not have any identifiable disability (and not just those listed in the IDEA), then the child could not qualify under 504.

Section 504 was not intended to be a consolation prize and should not be routinely used as such. Even with the expanded eligibility requirements under the Americans with Disabilities Act Amendments Act (ADAAA) (see the next main section), the basic process remains the same: first, identification of a disability, establishing a child's rights to the civil rights protection under both the Americans with Disabilities Act (ADA) and 504; and then, if a substantial limitation is identified after mitigating factors are considered, development of a 504 plan to ensure the student's needs are met as adequately as those of students without disabilities.

CAUTION

Only students with identifiable disabilities can be served under Section 504. This law is *not* a consolation prize for low-achieving students without identifiable disabilities. Serving those students is an obligation of regular education, and there is no statutory or regulatory restriction or exclusionary factor limiting a school's right to continue providing school support team (SST) interventions at any level or tier to any student.

Eligibility Team for 504?

The same people who serve on an IEP team, assuming they are knowledgeable about the child, could also serve on a 504 committee. However, there are no mandated members as under the IDEA; not even the parent is a required participant. The only mandate is that the local education agency (LEA) must "ensure that the placement decision is made by a group of persons, including persons knowledgeable about the child, the meaning of the evaluation data, and the placement options." For reasons we discuss elsewhere, we recommend parental participation regardless (504 Regulations, § 104.35 (c)). Group members can become knowledgeable by reviewing the materials accumulated in the course of evaluating the student. Section 504 regulations do not define "a group," but the common definition of "a group" is given as "two or more people." While the criteria for entitlement under Section 504 are much broader than under the IDEA, a diagnosis of a disability by a qualified professional still would be a sine qua non. As noted previously, eligibility groups cannot diagnose.

SECTION 504 AND THE AMERICANS WITH DISABILITIES AMENDMENTS ACT

Expand Definition of a Disability by the Americans with Disabilities Act Amendments Act of 2008

The Americans with Disabilities Act Amendments Act of 2008 removed a factor (consideration of mitigating circumstances) that had been used to deny civil rights to people who had managed to compensate for their disabilities through medical or physical aids; it expanded the list of potentially qualifying disabilities; and it broadened the list of life functions that

DON'T FORGET

If the U.S. Supreme Court declares a law or a lower court decision unconstitutional, the only recourses are to wait for the court to someday reverse itself or to begin the laborious process of trying to amend the Constitution. However, if the court makes a ruling on the basis of federal law other than the Constitution, Congress has the option, as it did with *Sutton v. United Air Lines* (1999) and the ADAAA, of amending or passing a law to address the issue raised by the court.

might be substantially limited. In doing so, Congress basically overturned a Supreme Court decision (*Sutton v. United Air Lines*, 1999; on CD). In that decision, the Supreme Court ruled that if a disability did not result in a substantial limitation in a basic life function because of mitigating circumstances, then the protections of Section 504 and the ADA did not apply. In 2008, Congress said they did, except for people whose eyesight was corrected by eyeglasses. The *Sutton* Supreme Court decision is included on the CD, but remember: It no longer is representative of current law.

Those Who Are Regarded as Having a Disability or Have Had a History of a Disability

There is still a considerable amount of misinformation being disseminated about just who might be eligible for entitlement as having a disability under Section 504. (See Rapid Reference 7.2 for a quick reference summary of eligibility requirements.) A question one might hear is something to the effect that "Section 504 says that people covered under that Act include those who are regarded as having a disability or have had a history of a disability or are suspected of having a disability. So if we regard a child as having a disability even though he hasn't qualified under the IDEA, what is wrong with our qualifying him for, and providing him with, accommodations under Section 504?"

This is not rocket science. OCR letters on the topic date back at least to 1992. An individual can receive services to eliminate discrimination only if he or she has a substantial limitation resulting from a disability. If someone does not have a disability, he or she could not have a substantial limitation resulting from it; so, no substantial limitation resulting from a disability would mean no entitlement. *The second and third legs of the definition (a history of and regarded as disabled) provide only civil rights protections against discrimination.* It is those civil rights that the ADAAA of 2008 restored to people who would have had a substantial limitation except for mitigating factors.

The definition of students protected from discrimination under 504 does include those with a "record" of a disability or "regarded as" having a disability (34 CFR § 104.3(j)(1)).

These provisions have led to much confusion among school districts. The main misconception seems to be that if a child is currently not

≣ Rapid Reference 7.2

- To be eligible for services or accommodations under Section 504, a student must have a current and identifiable disability that substantially limits a major life activity.
- The ADAAA has expanded the lists of disabilities and of major life activities.
- If the student needs accommodations for those limitations, the school must provide them.
- If the student does not need accommodations, the student is still protected by Section 504 from disability-based discrimination.

identified as disabled, but that child has a record of a disability, or is regarded as having a disability, the school would be obligated automatically to evaluate and place the child under 504 by a Section 504 committee. Repeat: This is a misconception! Only children who currently suffer from, or are suspected of suffering from, an impairment substantially limiting learning or another major life activity (or who are suspected of having one) are eligible for referral, evaluation, and educational services under 504. "Logically, since the student qualifying under prong two or three is not, in fact, mentally or physically handicapped, there can be no need for special education and related aids and services" (OCR Senior Staff Memo, 1992). Protection from discrimination and provision of services are separate issues.

School Board Policy on Section 504

First, and foremost, there must be a school board policy on Section 504. There is no required format for a district policy; some are brief, some are extensive.

The main thing to look at in reviewing and/or revising a school system's current policies is to be sure the school has deleted any reference to mitigating factors (except for correction of vision) from its statement of rights, its forms, and its directions for completing local 504 plan forms (whatever the district may call them).

If you have questions about it, take a look at OCR's Web site or the accompanying CD (which includes copies of many of their materials on the ADA/504). Their materials, including the FAQ on 504 (on CD), have been updated. Only the regulations themselves, however, carry the force of law; all the rest (even what OCR has written) is just interpretation. If you are asked to help a committee write a 504 policy, we recommend that, rather than reinventing the wheel, you Google school board policies for Section 504, checking, of course, to insure that they were revised after the ADAAA was passed, and presenting representative results to the local school board for consideration. The problem in coming up with a generic policy suitable for all users is that Section 504 allows each district to develop its own due process procedures. Some districts may elect to use the same procedures outlined for students identified under the IDEA, but others may not.

Section 504 and Transition Plans

Children identified under Section 504 do not have rights to a transition plan. However, remember that, if the team or a court finds that the accommodations, modifications, and related aids or services a child is receiving rise to the level of special education, the district could entitle the child under the IDEA and develop an IEP, which does include a mandate for transition plans at least by age 16 (14 in some states). For that matter, if a parent wants a transition plan for a child and is threatening litigation, we see nothing in the 504 regulations that would prohibit a district from providing one as part of a 504 plan. Going to court just for the principle of it would never be our first recommendation. The IDEA defines "*specially designed instruction* as adapting the content, methodology, or delivery of instruction to address the unique needs of the child and to ensure access to the

CAUTION
....

A student who qualifies for modifications and accommodations under Section 504 actually may be qualified for an IEP under the IDEA. It might be better for the team, including parents, to make this decision than to wait for a hearing officer or court to do so. Also, Section 504 is a completely unfunded mandate, but IDEA is partially funded.

general curriculum so that the child can meet the educational standards within the jurisdiction of the public agency that apply to all children" (§ 300.39(b)(3)). The "or" is significant. It is therefore not beyond the realm of possibility that a court might find that the level of accommodations provided under a 504 plan rose to the level of special education, finding that 504 child eligible for IDEA services anyway. (All court proceedings involve a roll of the dice.)

DIAGNOSES

Medical Diagnosis and Section 504

A child diagnosed with attention deficit hyperactivity disorder (ADHD) by a physician, but who does not need special education, does not automatically qualify for services under Section 504. By now, it should be obvious that nothing is ever automatic. A medical doctor's diagnosis is neither a requirement under Section 504 (as long as there is a diagnosis by some qualified professional) nor is it sufficient to meet the requirements under Section 504 that every child with a disability receive a comprehensive evaluation.

A physician's medical diagnosis may be considered among other sources in evaluating a student with, or believed to have, an impairment that substantially limits a major life activity. Other sources to be considered along with the medical diagnosis include aptitude and achievement tests, teacher observations, physical condition, social and cultural background, and adaptive behavior. The Section 504 regulations require school districts to draw on a variety of sources in interpreting evaluation data (§ 104.35) and making placement decisions.

A medical diagnosis of an illness also does not automatically mean a student can receive services under Section 504. The illness or disability must cause a substantial limitation of the student's ability to learn or another

DON'T FORGET

- Nothing is automatic in sped-law.
- School committees and groups of professionals determine whether a diagnosed disability is a disability under Section 504 or the IDEA.
- Hearing officers and courts may, of course, disagree with school teams and groups.

major life activity. For example, a student who has a physical or mental impairment would not be considered a student in need of services under Section 504 if the impairment does not in any way limit the student's ability to learn or other major life activity, or results in only some minor limitation in that regard. (See OCR's FAQs on Section 504 included on the CD.)

504 PLANS

Personal Liability Lawsuits

We have seen anecdotal reports on the Internet of teachers refusing to sign 504 plans because they believe it will increase their personal liability. If a teacher signs a 504 plan, this does not increase the teacher's exposure to personal liability lawsuits. There is actually nothing in the 504 regulations that requires a 504 plan be written or that the parent be invited to the 504 team eligibility team meeting. Nevertheless, 504 plans represent an enforceable agreement to provide specified services. The LEA is obliged only to inform teachers of the services it has agreed to provide. If a teacher fails to provide services promised by the school system, he or she would be subject to disciplinary action, including early termination, regardless of whether he or she signed a 504 plan. With the exception of an early case involving a teacher named Withers (*Doe v. Withers*, 1992) who failed to implement a child's IEP accommodations (resulting in the child's failure and subsequent loss of sports eligibility), the courts have not held teachers individually liable for either IDEA or Section 504 violations resulting in a loss of FAPE. Compensatory services or reimbursement of costs incurred by a parent in securing FAPE for a child generally have been deemed sufficient compensation under both laws. However, those decisions will not necessarily save a teacher or school administrator from the consequences of an intentional tort. See Chapter 8, on damages, for more extensive discussion of that alarming/encouraging (depending on whether you are a school employee or parent) trend.

Regardless, whether a teacher signs or does not sign a 504 plan is not a material fact with respect to increasing his or her personal liability. The courts will instead look at whether the teacher knew of his or her obligations (e.g., was informed of them) and whether he or she chose to intentionally ignore them.

See www.wrightslaw.com, specifically www.wrightslaw.com/law/caselaw/case_Doe_Withers_Juryorder.html, for the jury decision.

Responsibility for Convening 504 Meetings and Writing 504 Plans

Unlike the IDEA, Section 504 bypasses state education agencies (SEAs) and puts the responsibility for implementing and enforcing the requirements of Section 504 directly on the LEAs Therefore, the issue of "who is responsible" is one that is addressed at the local level based on local board and administrative policies. In one school, an assistant principal may be assigned that responsibility; in another, a school counselor. However, Section 504 does require that each school district appoint a 504 contact person. He or she would be responsible for authoritatively determining responsibility for convening meetings and writing plans under Section 504 (§ 104.7, 504 Regulations) both for staff and students.

Section 104.7 Designation of Responsible Employee and Adoption of Grievance Procedures

The responsibility for affording children with disabilities their rights under Section 504 is placed by Congress directly upon the public schools. The fact that state departments of public instruction have no specific responsibility for oversight may explain at least in part why some school systems

DON'T FORGET

Wrightslaw provides links to many special education cases in the Wrightslaw Law Library at www.wrightslaw.com/law.htm.

Not all cases are automatically strong precedents, especially if the jurisdiction of the court does not include your location, the facts are unusual and specific, the decision is different from most other decisions on similar issues, or the case has been appealed since the most recent available citation.

CAUTION

Your district *must* have a 504 contact person. Be sure to stay in contact with that person and share information. You could buy a copy of this book for your 504 contact person.

were late in recognizing their responsibilities under Section 504, including the following:

(a) Designation of responsible employee. A recipient that employs fifteen or more persons shall designate at least one person to coordinate its efforts to comply with this part. (b) Adoption of grievance procedures. A recipient that employs fifteen or more persons shall adopt grievance procedures that incorporate appropriate due process.

MAJOR LIFE FUNCTIONS

Defining "Major Life Functions"

The ADAAA says "major life activities include, but are not limited to, caring for oneself, performing manual tasks, seeing, hearing, eating, sleeping, walking, standing, lifting, bending, speaking, breathing, learning, reading, concentrating, thinking, communicating, and working." Again, the key phrase is "not limited to." The ability to take tests, for example, without accommodations or modifications is not listed but is generally regarded as "a major life function." See Rapid Reference 7.3 for a quick reference list of major life activities as defined by the ADAAA.

The ADAAA (the definitions therein also applying to Section 504) also added major bodily functions: "a major life activity also includes the operation of a major bodily function, including but not limited to, functions of the immune system, normal cell growth, digestive, bowel, bladder, neurological, brain, respiratory, circulatory, endocrine, and reproductive functions." Learning is the major life function that schools most frequently address, but substantial limitations in other major life activities may also require accommodations. For example, a child might be severely asthmatic with no learning problems but need to carry medication in order to attend school. Section 504 would require the accommodation even if a local board policy prohibited self-medication. The list, even though it is expanded, is not intended to be exhaustive. For example, if a child with sweaty palms could not take tests using computer-compatible answer sheets because his sweat smeared his answers, rendering the page unscorable, then the committee could consider him for testing accommodations if the child was diagnosed by a qualified professional with palmar hyperhidrosis—which is not specifically listed in the statute.

≡ Rapid Reference 7.3

Major life activities now include, but are not limited to:
- Caring for oneself
- Performing manual tasks
- Seeing
- Hearing
- Eating
- Sleeping
- Walking
- Standing
- Lifting
- Bending
- Speaking
- Breathing
- Learning
- Reading
- Concentrating
- Thinking
- Communicating
- Working
- Functions of the immune system
- Neurological and brain functions
- Normal cell growth, digestive, bowel, and bladder functions
- Respiratory, circulatory, endocrine, and reproductive functions

RIGHTS, ACCOMMODATIONS, AND SERVICES

Reasonable Accommodation and Cost

Section 504 includes the term "reasonable accommodations." School districts may struggle with deciding what is reasonable and what is not, and, more important, schools may question whether a needed accommodation could ever be unreasonable based on the cost. OCR's answer to the second question (is cost a relevant factor?) when applied to public education, would be that if a service (up to and including residential placement) is needed for the student to receive FAPE, there is no limitation on the school system's financial obligations. The short answer according to OCR, therefore, would be "Never."

Section 504 and the IDEA 2004 and Least Restrictive Environment

An education in the least restrictive environment (LRE) within which the child can be provided an appropriate education is a right, not an option. The mandate under Section 504 is very specific and applies to all students with disabilities, including those who have been entitled under the IDEA.

Some parents have argued that LRE actually means the environment (such as a private school) that least restricts the child's ability to reach his or her highest potential. The IDEA Final Regulations actually explain LRE clearly and differently.

§ 300.114 LRE requirements. (a) (2) Each public agency must ensure that—(i) To the maximum extent appropriate, children with disabilities, including children in public or private institutions or other care facilities, are educated with children who are nondisabled; and (ii) Special classes, separate schooling, or other removal of children with disabilities from the regular educational environment occurs only if the nature or severity of the disability is such that education in regular classes with the use of supplementary aids and services cannot be achieved satisfactorily. . . .

§ 300.115 Continuum of alternative placements. (a) Each public agency must ensure that a continuum of alternative placements is available to meet the needs of children with disabilities for special education and related services. (b) The continuum required in paragraph (a) of this section must—(1) Include the alternative placements listed in the definition of special education under § 300.38 (instruction in regular classes, special classes, special schools, home instruction, and instruction in hospitals and institutions); and (2) Make provision for supplementary services (such as resource room or itinerant instruction) to be provided in conjunction with regular class placement. (IDEA 2006 Final Regulations, pp. 46764–46765)

Rejecting IDEA and Services under Section 504

Can a parent demand that his or her child be provided the same services under Section 504 (an unfunded mandate) after rejecting IDEA special educational services offered by the school system?

No. If, in exercising their rights found in the amendments to the IDEA in 2008, parents reject the special educational services offered by the school system, they in essence are, at the same time, rejecting those services under Section 504. OCR has found that when a child qualifies under the IDEA, the district satisfies the provisions of 504 for that child by developing and implementing an IEP under IDEA. Therefore, when parents reject that IEP developed under IDEA, they "would essentially be rejecting what would be offered under Section 504. The parent could not compel the district to develop an IEP under Section 504 as that effectively happened when the school followed IDEA requirements" (OCR, *Letter to McKethan*, 1996). Similar findings were expressed in a Texas Section 504 hearing (*Errol B. v. Houston ISD*, 1995) and by a federal district court. "The Court believes that the only students likely to be entitled to special education under Section 504 are the same students also entitled to special education under the IDEA" (*Lyons v. Smith*, 1993).

Evaluations under Section 504 to Determine if Accommodations Are Needed to Provide FAPE

Section 504 independently requires schools to conduct child find for unserved children with disabilities. A school system would not be obligated to evaluate a child just because a parent suspected the child had a disability under Section 504 or the IDEA; that burden is imposed only if the school shares in that suspicion or a due process hearing officer orders the evaluation. However, if a school evaluated a child under the IDEA, it would meet all of its obligations under Section 504 (OCR Clarification Letter from Lim, 1993; on CD).

Section 504 Plans and Manifestation Hearings

Sometimes children with disabilities are removed from special education services by parents exercising rights given to them by the 2008 Amendments to the IDEA. While, as discussed earlier, there is no obligation on the school's part to offer the child a 504 plan as an alternative to an appropriate IEP offering the same services, sometimes it may do so.

If that child incurs a disciplinary change of placement as a result of suspension, by law only 504 rules would apply. Parents' rejection of an IEP and special educational services means that they cannot invoke IDEA rights, including the right to have a team consider whether the behavior was the result of the school's failure to provide services in the child's IEP, or those rights pertaining to students whom a court might otherwise have deemed protected, because the parents then allege that the school system was knowledgeable about the child having a disability. However, it is our opinion that if the team decided the behavior was a result of the 504 plan not being followed, that finding would be relevant and stay put would apply.

Response to Intervention, Interventions, and Student Support Teams (SST)

Many school systems provide students who are having academic difficulty with interventions in a response to intervention (RTI) framework. If a parent withdraws from special education a child with behaviors that adversely impact his or her own learning or the learning of others, the school does have the option of providing the child with services through its SST, because the SST and its interventions are considered to be part of the regular education program, not special education.

IMMIGRATION ISSUES

Immigration issues related to the IDEA and Section 504 can be confusing. Consider this scenario: A child with limited English proficiency has physical limitations that ordinarily would require the school system to provide modifications, related aids and services under 504. However, the school has reason to suspect the child and the family are illegal immigrants. Does the school still have to serve that child under Section 504? Why can't schools simply report the child and family to the immigration department?

The answer to the first question is "Yes. The schools have to serve the child." The OCR also enforces Title VI of the Civil Rights Act, which prohibits discrimination based on sex, religion, or national origin. With respect to the second part of this question regarding reporting the family to immigration authorities, the answer is still "Probably not," following the Supreme Court decision in *Plyler v. Doe* (1982). The court in that decision declared unconstitutional a Texas law that withheld educational funding for children who were not legally admitted into the United States. In short, the court held that depriving innocent children of an education would result in incalculable harm to them and that it was not in the national interest to do so. The lawyers representing illegal migrants, not the court, have interpreted that as meaning that if schools reported illegal children to immigration, such reporting would have a chilling effect; and that if children do not have the social security numbers they need in order to access public education, then the schools would have to make up substitutes for social security numbers for school identification purposes. One author's (G. M. M.) school system has long been guided by those principles. However, those are inferences drawn from *Plyler*, not part of the *Plyler* decision itself (on CD). It seems likely as the current debate over illegal immigration unfolds, those long-standing and commonly held principles will once again be tested both in Congress and in the courts.

As political pressure to halt illegal immigration grows, the rights of illegal children to a free public education are slowly being eroded. For example, a number of states have passed laws restricting illegal immigrants from getting driver's licenses (Vock, 2007). Police in at least one state have set up checkpoints near schools where driver's licenses are checked and individuals dropping their children off at school without legal driver's licenses face having their cars impounded (McKinnon & Burge, 2008). State laws protecting children of illegal immigrants from being questioned for their social security numbers (e.g., in New York) are being offset by other states (e.g., Arizona) that are aggressively seeking out illegal immigrants for deportation. With all the other pressures being brought to bear on illegal immigrants, anything the schools might or might not do to chill or discourage parents lacking documentation of legal residence from exercising the rights of illegal immigrant children to an education could become irrelevant. Your superintendent or school board should consult with its attorney on this issue and should keep staff informed of any changes in policy.

Also remember that if the parents do not understand English, they have the right to have the prior notices and proceedings translated

CAUTION

Laws regarding undocumented immigrants are complex and are changing very rapidly in different ways in different jurisdictions. It is essential to stay up to date and to seek and follow qualified, expert legal guidance.

into their native language (Preface, 2006 Final Regulations, p. 46689; § 300.503, p. 46792; see Chapter 2, Rapid Reference 2.2). Sometimes, of course, as we noted earlier, the only way to know is to ask the parents. Parental preference should be respected.

CONSENT

504 Plans and Written Consent

A school is not required by law or federal regulation to get written consents for 504 plans. (Just because the government allows you to shoot yourself in the foot, it does not mean you should.) The phrases "written consent" and "504 plan" are found nowhere in the Final Regulations for Section 504.

As noted, since there is no requirement for a written 504 plan, there is no requirement that the parent even be there when the 504 committee draws one up. OCR does throw just a little cold water on that feeling of freedom you might be experiencing, because in its FAQ (on CD) in 2009, it does say that consent is required (in response to Question 41) before conducting an initial evaluation. However, even there, OCR does not specify that the consent be in writing. Presumably, then, oral consent would meet the standard.

In our experience, however, the question has largely been moot, because federal funding is available to evaluate children under the IDEA, and it is not available to evaluate children under 504 only. So (assuming a district does not want to establish a separate, and separately funded, evaluation process for children suspected of being eligible under 504 only), the IDEA rules (which require prior written informed consent) would apply to any child referred through the child find process. In the event that a district wants to bypass all the strictures of IDEA, paying for an evaluation outside of the special education framework, we still strongly recommend getting written consent to test and (if IDEA rights were not given) that 504 due process rights be provided in writing and that provision recorded. We also recommend that the 504 plan always be in writing. Plus we always recommend that parents be invited to those 504 meetings, whether required by law or not. A separate written consent would not be required for 504 plan implementation, but we recommend asking parents to sign the plan (or whatever other name the school system has given to it). Mostly, however, we recommend evaluating all children under IDEA rules. Concluding before a comprehensive evaluation has been completed that a child might be disabled but not in need of special education could be construed as predetermining the outcome of the evaluation—a potential violation of the child's civil and educational rights. Hawaii has had problems with that. See *Pasatiempo v. Aizawa*, Ninth Circuit, 1996 (on CD), an IDEA case. As we interpret the results in that case, the court concluded that when the parents or a teacher indicated that they suspected the child had a disability, if the state evaluated the child, it had to do so under IDEA rules, and it had to give the parents their rights under the IDEA. Hawaii, it said, also had the option of not evaluating the child at all; but even in that instance, if the child had been referred, it must give parents their IDEA rights (what Hawaii referred to as "Chapter 36"). The same principles also apply if a parent asked for a child to be tested, and instead the district assigned the child to a prereferral process involving (God forbid) the use of screening tests, such as the Kaufman Brief or Slosson Intelligence Test to "screen out" children who "probably would not qualify." Determining that a child was not entitled to services based on screening tests (we are not talking about the documentation required in assessing student progress in a multitiered RTI problem-solving process) without completing a comprehensive evaluation or giving the parents their rights potentially would be a violation of their rights.

The reason we recommend written consents for testing and written 504 plans, of course, is based on the old adage, "If it isn't in writing, it didn't happen." If you do not have it in writing, it is just your word against theirs.

The reason we recommend parental invitation to and involvement in the development of 504 plans in part is because exclusion breeds distrust. Distrust inhibits communication. And when communication between school and parent fails, requests for due process hearings, OCR complaints, and litigation are more likely to flourish. Also, and not just as a by-the-way, including the parent

DON'T FORGET
....
If it isn't in writing, it didn't happen.

DON'T FORGET

Parental involvement, even when not legally required, improves the breadth, depth, and quality of information available to the team or group; improves communication; and may reduce the chance of litigation.

will enable the school to more accurately address specific needs arising out of the disability, which will in turn maximize instructional impact, and—last but by no means least in our brave new world of accountability—positively impact children's scores on high-stakes testing. We all need to work together to bring those test scores up.

⬛ TEST YOURSELF ⬛

1. **If the school suspects a student has a disability under Section 504, the parent is responsible for providing a comprehensive evaluation.**

   True or False

2. **Under Section 504, a child may receive not only accommodations but also special education services.**

   True or False

3. **Under Section 504, a medical diagnosis would be considered enough of an evaluation for the purpose of determining eligibility.**

   True or False

4. **Under Section 504, reading is not considered to be a "major life function."**

   True or False

5. **Section 504 and the IDEA 2004 provide children with disabilities with the same rights to an education in the least restrictive environment.**

   True or False

6. **Schools must provide services to qualified children with disabilities of illegal immigrants under both IDEA and Section 504.**

   True or False

Answers: 1. False; 2. True; 3. False; 4. False; 5. True; 6. True (for now)

Eight

IDEA AND DAMAGES

Avoid lawsuits beyond all things; they pervert your conscience, impair your health, and dissipate your property.

—Jean de la Bruyere

Compromise is the best and cheapest lawyer.

—Robert Louis Stevenson

In the arena of education, one often hears about the fear teachers, administrators, and evaluators have of being sued. Probably without knowing it, they are echoing the concerns raised during the 1600s by the French philosopher Jean de la Bruyere.

How prevalent is the fear of suit, and has this perceived fear resulted in any specific changes in how teachers and administrators do their jobs? A recent Harris Interactive Market Research (2004) survey conducted for the organization Common Good revealed these issues:

- Approximately two-thirds of teachers and principals worry, to varying degrees, that a decision they make will be legally challenged.
- One-quarter of teachers and one-fifth of principals have avoided making a decision they believe is right because of fear of legal challenge.
- Almost 80% of teachers and principals say the current legal climate has changed the way they work. More than 60% of principals surveyed said they had been threatened with a legal challenge.
- Sizable proportions of teachers and principals have experience with or knowledge of lawsuits or legal challenges by students or parents.

- Nearly two-thirds of principals have been threatened with legal challenges by parents, students, or teachers. Nearly half have been threatened with other harm or assaulted.
- More than 1 in 10 teachers have been threatened with legal challenges by students or parents, and almost 1 in 3 have been threatened with other harm or assaulted.

Although special education issues are most often resolved through mediation or due process procedures, there may be times when someone is actually accused of some personal malfeasance and is sued in court. Given that the provision of special education services is so intimately entangled with the day-to-day life of students and their parents, it is no wonder that heated conflicts often turn into protracted court debates.

What are the rights and protection afforded by the laws governing educational practice? This chapter addresses several of the more common aspects of the educational laws encountered by special education professionals.

Having reviewed the laws ourselves, we do believe that there is probably good reason for some people to say that special education law (spedlaw) gave parents every due process right known to man and then invented a few more.

Basic Rights Given to Parents through IDEA or Section 504

When most people think of "due process," they usually think of a due process hearing. Parents have many (many) other alternatives to resolve complaints. Not all are available in every state, but because they are federally based, most are. In no particular order, these alternatives are divided into alternatives for the Individuals with Disabilities Education Act (IDEA) and for Section 504.

Under the IDEA

1. Parents can obtain the support of an advocate to represent them at individualized education program (IEP) team meetings.
2. Parents can employ an attorney to represent them at IEP team meetings.

3. Parents can request the state to assist them in using a mediator to help in the development of what is called a "facilitated IEP." (This is not explicitly required by the Act, but available in many states. Both parties would have to agree.)

4. Parents can report alleged procedural violations directly to the state education agency (SEA) for resolution. Some SEAs have forms to assist parents. Information on all of these rights usually is found in the parent rights handbook provided by the state for use by the schools.

5. If the issue is a dispute over whether the school has or has not provided a free appropriate public education (FAPE), the parents can request (or agree to) mediation with an impartial mediator. It is not required, but it is free.

6. Parents can skip mediation, or if mediation is unsuccessful in producing an agreement, they can go directly to a due process hearing.

7. Parents can appeal a due process hearing officer's decision to a state hearing review officer (SHRO).

8. Parents have the option of appealing a SHRO decision to state or federal court (depending on which venue their lawyers thinks will afford them the greatest chance of success).

9. Parents can appeal a federal district court's decision to a circuit court.

10. Parents can appeal a circuit court's decision to the U.S. Supreme Court.

Under Section 504

This can get a little tricky. Since 504 covers all IDEA students, you might think that the parents of an IDEA child could use these options, and you would be right. However, before going to federal court over an issue involving special education, there has been a pattern of decisions requiring parents to exhaust their remedies under the IDEA before going to federal court (*Polera v. Newburgh*, 2nd Circuit, 2002).

1. Parents presumably have the right to representation as they would under IDEA, but there is no explicit requirement that parents even be invited to 504 committee meetings.

2. If parents are alleging a violation of their child's civil rights, they can appeal directly to the regional offices of the federal Office for Civil Rights (OCR). OCR provides parents with guidelines along with a form on its web pages to initiate the process and a method for parents to contact the OCR electronically. (Electronic complaints would have to be followed by a signed written complaint.)

3. When the issue involves a dispute over FAPE or least restrictive environment (LRE) but does not involve special education, parents must use the due process procedures that have been approved by their school system's school board before going to court. Sometimes these are the same as under the IDEA; sometimes they are not.

4. If parents disagree with the hearing officer's decision (or if the school has not, as required by law, established a structure for resolving 504 disputes), parents may then proceed directly to U.S. District Court.

DEFINITIONS OF "DAMAGES"

Before going any further, it might be helpful to describe the different types of awards that are generally given by the courts. Not every law makes every type of damage available to a plaintiff.

Compensatory services. Compensatory services in the form of compensatory education may be awarded when a hearing officer or court finds that a school system has failed to provide a child with a FAPE under the IDEA. Monetary compensation may be awarded under the IDEA for "in-kind" services—for example, private school tuition—as well for legal fees if the parents prevail in a due process hearing or court of law. (Attorney fees actually were not available until the IDEA 1997; 2006 Final Regulations, §§ 300.504, 300.517.) The school system may not use federal funds to defend itself against a due process lawsuit.

Compensatory damages. These are monetary awards to compensate someone for what was lost, nothing more. Compensatory damages are not available under the IDEA, the Americans with

Disabilities Act (ADA)/Section 504 (at least when educational torts are being cited), or the Family Educational Rights and Privacy Act (FERPA; at least not in federal courts). However, compensatory damages may be available for torts under Title VI, Section 1983, or Title IX.

Punitive damages. These are monetary awards in addition to the compensatory damages designed to punish someone for what he or she did. Punitive damages are not available under the IDEA or Section 504. The Supreme Court has ruled that both compensatory and punitive damages are available for intentional discrimination under Title IX (which prohibits discrimination on the basis of gender) but are not, available under Title VI (which prohibits discrimination based on national origin). See Rapid Reference 8.1.

Under the IDEA, a parent can sue for relief in the form of monetary reimbursement for expenses incurred in providing the child with a FAPE. Under Section 504, when parents are alleging deliberate indifference to their child's needs, additional compensatory monetary damages may be sought (*Mark H. v. Hamamoto*, 9th Cir., 2010; on CD). The Supreme Court has ruled that punitive damages are not available in civil suits under the ADA, Section 504, or Title VI (*Barnes v. Gorman*, 2002; on CD).

Tuition Reimbursement for Private School

If parents enroll a child with a disability in private school, and that child has never been in special education, there are certain specific circumstances under which the parents could get tuition reimbursement. If parents asked for a child to be evaluated and the school refused, and if the parents then had their child evaluated independently and the child was found to have

≡ *Rapid Reference 8.1*

Because punitive damages may not be awarded in private suits under Title VI, it follows that they may not be awarded in suits under Section 202 of the ADA and Section 504 of the Rehabilitation Act (*Barnes v. Gorman*, 2002).

a disability, and if they then placed their child in a private school that the court determined did provide the student with an appropriate education, the Supreme Court said "yes" to reimbursement (*Forest Grove v. T.A.*, 2009, on CD).

The *Forest Grove* case involved a student who had been evaluated by his school system and found ineligible for services. According to the Oregon Administrative Law Judge at the first hearing (*T.A. v. Forest Grove*, 2003), the school psychologist had erred in two respects. First, after completing an assessment consisting primarily of a review of previous testing, the psychologist told the parents that he thought their child might have an attention deficit disorder but did not recommend or complete an evaluation for ADHD that might have entitled the student as having an other health impairment. Second, he allegedly told the parents that even if their child was diagnosed with ADHD, he did not think that would entitle the student to services. In the normal course of events, if parents believed that their child had not received a comprehensive evaluation, they would have simply asked for an independent evaluation at district expense. However, the parents interpreted the psychologist's comments as precluding any possibility of their child receiving services and, subsequent to their child being diagnosed as having ADHD by an independent evaluator, placed him in private school because they didn't believe there was any point in taking the evaluation back to the school. As it turned out, the school psychologist was right, but (in our opinion) it was not his decision to make. After hearing all the evidence, the Administrative Law Judge made several important determinations. The judge ruled that the school had not provided the student with a comprehensive evaluation; the student was eligible as having an other health impairment under the IDEA; and the student was also eligible under Section 504. The judge ordered the school system to pay for the private school and recommended they develop an IEP for the student.

The school system, based on their interpretation of the 2006 Final Regulations, provided neither an IEP nor a Section 504 plan. They instead appealed the Administrative Law Judge's decision because they believed that the Final Regulations required that a student be identified and receive special educational services before parents could seek compensation for private school tuition. At that point, the case was no longer about a child's right to a comprehensive evaluation but about the student's right to a free appropriate education even if it was denied by the public school system. Nevertheless, while the main point of law decided in this case was that parents in situations such as these may seek and receive compensation when appropriate, this case viewed in its entirety also gives support to a principle we have suggested all evaluators adopt: that the buck never stop here.

As the Administrative Law Judge found, once ADHD was suspected, the school psychologist should have evaluated for it; or at the very least should have referred the matter back to the IEP team for review and possible action. He did not. Additionally, while the school system seems to have given credence to the school psychologist's assertion that an ADHD diagnosis would make no difference, that decision should not have been on his head. Once a referral has been made, only a properly convened IEP team or Section 504 committee has the authority under the federal disability statutes and regulations to make an eligibility decision.

Some reviewers (e.g., Dixon, Eusebio, Turton, Wright, & Hale, 2010) have interpreted this case as supporting the use of cognitive assessments, cognitive profiling, or as somehow suggesting that using RTI in the identification of specific learning disabilities (SLD) is a deficient methodology. The events leading up to this lawsuit actually occurred before 2004, and while there was much testimony at the hearing level about executive functioning and processing problems, those problems were cited in the decision only as evidence that had the school assessed for ADHD, it might have found the student eligible as other health impaired (OHI). It was the failure to assess for ADHD, not the lack of cognitive measures or assessments of executive function per se, that led to the hearing officer's censure of the school and school psychologist.

Being Sued for Compensatory Damages Related to Special Education

Obviously, anyone can be sued for compensatory damages related to special education about anything, in any place, at any time, but in the context of special education there is some good news. First and foremost, cases in which teachers or administrators have been held personally liable for compensatory or punitive damages are relatively rare. Also, virtually every circuit court that has addressed the issue has found that while compensatory *services* are available under the IDEA, compensatory or monetary *damages* (and punitive damages) are not, except to the extent, of course, necessary to reimburse parents for educational and legal expenses incurred in order to provide their child with FAPE when the school failed to do so (e.g., private school tuition reimbursement). However, that is no reason to feel complacent. The IDEA is only one law; lawyers have lots of them at their disposal. Plaintiffs may, under certain circumstances, still invoke Section 504, Section 1983 of the Civil Rights Act (34 USC 1983), and state statutes allowing for lawsuits seeking damages for emotional distress. One author (J. O. W.) was one of the evaluators in a case in which the parents eventually sued both regular and special education administrators individually for violating their child's rights. Even though evaluators were not included as defendants and, in any case, the suits ultimately were dismissed, the experience was not pleasant.

Doe v. Withers

Doe v. Withers was one case with unusual circumstances and has little precedential value today. As the Unnamed Law (Dickson, 1978, p. 180) states, "If it happens, it must be possible." However, in spedlaw, just because something happened in the past does not necessarily mean it is possible today. *Doe v. Withers* (1992) tells us that, in one instance, one teacher was successfully sued for blatantly refusing to provide an accommodation in an IEP, despite being told by administrators to provide it. This case, by itself, is probably not all that important; its relevance lies in its use as a precedent for other cases. Peter Wright (2009) also observed, "This case paved the way for subsequent special ed damage cases, including *W.B. v. Matula* [1995, on CD], a case from the U. S. Court of Appeals for the Third Circuit, and *Witte v. Clark County School District*, a 1999 case from the U.S. Court of Appeals for the Ninth Circuit" (on CD). In *Matula*, the Third Circuit had ruled Section 1983 damages could be obtained in a lawsuit over special education. However, the Third Circuit reversed itself on *Matula* in *A. W. v. Jersey City Public Schools* (2007). Reviewing dissents from two other circuits (including *Sellers v. Manassas* in the Fourth Circuit) and additional guidance from the U.S. Supreme Court, the Third Circuit concluded that Section 1983 relief was available only for constitutional violations of civil rights, not for violations of statutory rights as under the IDEA. (For their complete analysis, see *A. W. v. Jersey City* on the CD.) Witte (unlike *A. W.* or *W.B.* or *Doe*) was suing the system for damages based on alleged emotional and physical abuse, which the IDEA did not address. (See our additional discussion regarding Section 1983 claims in the *Goleta v. Ordway* case later in the chapter.)

Invoking Section 504 and the ADA to Sue for Damages

In a 2006 case in Brookline, NH (*Alexandra R. v. Brookline School District*, 2009; *Burke v. Brookline Sch. Dist.*, 2008; *Burke & Rolfhamre v. Brookline School District*, 2007), the parents sued for damages under Section 504. The court ruled that the parents were trying to evade the restrictions under the IDEA (limiting their right to compensatory services only); the parents appealed first to the First Circuit, which affirmed the lower court decision, and then to the Supreme Court, which refused in June 2008 to hear the case. It does seem clear for now that only if the alleged behavior were intentionally malicious or grossly deviant from established norms (or rising to the level of intentional indifference to the child's rights) would any of those laws come into play. Still, this appears to be an evolving area of litigation, and the dust has not settled. Many states have whistleblower laws, which also could be invoked in a retaliation lawsuit. One rule appears trustworthy: Adherence to the procedures set forth in the IDEA is the single best protection against lawsuits based on alleged retaliatory behavior or intentional discrimination (see Rapid Reference 8.2); special education administrators who shortcut those procedures, whatever their intent, put themselves and their districts at financial risk.

≡ *Rapid Reference 8.2*

Adherence to the procedures set forth in the IDEA is the single best protection against lawsuits based on alleged retaliatory behavior or intentional discrimination.

Being Sued for Emotional Damages Related to Special Education

In the cases we have seen, most of the actions invoking lawsuits for emotional damages related to special education have involved what we would consider clear violations of accepted norms, not just a statutory violation. In one such case, a child was fed his own regurgitated food as a punishment (see *Witte v. Clark* [1999], Ninth Circuit, in the Damages folder on the accompanying CD). In another case, a teacher denied a child the right to participate in the choir telling her that she believed that depressed children could not be relied on; attempts by the parent to resolve the situation only made it worse. The circuit court affirmed that the ADA prohibited discrimination based on disability and allowed the lawsuit to proceed (see *Baird v. Rose* [1999] on CD).

> # CAUTION
>
> ....
>
> Courts may not be able to award punitive damages, but schools cannot afford to be going to court over compensatory services just because someone did not do his or her job. Courts may not be able to hurt an individual school employee, but school administrators can put a school employee on welfare pretty quickly for violating a child's rights.

Section 1983 Claim

As mentioned, a Section 1983 claim refers to Section 1983 of the Civil Rights Act (42 USC § 1983), "Civil action for deprivation of rights." It allows injured parties to take legal action if they have been deprived of their constitutional rights by a person functioning under "color of any statute, ordinance, regulation, custom, or usage, of any State or Territory or the District of Columbia," such as a school official working in his or her official capacity.

Success with Section 1983 Claims

Aside from *Doe v. Withers* (1993), discussed earlier, parents have not had a great deal of success in pursuing Section 1983 claims under the IDEA or Section 504.

That has not, however, been the case with respect to cases brought under Title VI of the Civil Rights Act (which prohibits discrimination on the basis of race, color, and national origin in programs receiving federal funds) and Title IX of the Education Act (which prohibits sexual discrimination in any education program receiving financial assistance; see *Fitzgerald v. Barnstable School Committee*, 2009, in the Damages folder on CD; also see Chapter 6, "Confusing Quirks and Twists.")

Schools also need to be careful to distinguish between simple bullying and bullying rising to the level of discriminatory harassment prohibited by Title VI, Title IX, and/or Section 504 of the Vocational Rehabilitation Act. OCR has stepped up its monitoring and enforcement in this area (OCR Letter to Colleague from Russyln Ali, 2010). When school officials fail to address harassment based on race or religion, harassment based on sex, or harassment based on discrimination, they may find themselves accused of having violated children's rights. In Mr. Ali's own words,

> Harassment creates a hostile environment when the conduct is sufficiently severe, pervasive, or persistent so as to interfere with or limit a student's ability to participate in or benefit from the services, activities, or opportunities offered by a school. When such harassment is based on race, color, national origin, sex, or disability, it violates the civil rights laws that OCR enforces.

That is not to say parents have had no success in invoking Section 1983 for IDEA rights violations. One troubling case was *Goleta Union Elementary School District v. Ordway* (2002), an unpublished California District Court decision in which the plaintiff went after the special education director personally alleging she unilaterally changed a student's placement without verifying that the new placement would be appropriate. In this case the judge asserted that the only thing necessary for someone to assert a Section 1983 claim was a violation of the IDEA statute. It should still be cautionary to anyone who thinks shortcutting the IDEA regulations could possibly be a good idea. The complete text of the *Goleta* decision and an analysis from parents' perspective by Peter Wright (2003) can be accessed at www.wrightslaw.com/news/2003/ca.goleta.ordway.damages.htm on Peter and Pam Wright's special education legal Web site (www.wrightslaw.com).

However, the Supreme Court ruled subsequently in *Rancho Palos v. Abrams* (2005) that:

> Even after a plaintiff demonstrates that a federal statute creates an individually enforceable right in the class of beneficiaries to which he belongs, see *Gonzaga Univ. v. Doe*, 536 U. S. 273, 285, the defendant may rebut the presumption that the right is enforceable under §1983 by, *inter alia*, showing a contrary congressional intent from the statute's creation of a comprehensive remedial scheme that is inconsistent with individual enforcement under §1983.

However, the *Goleta* case apparently was never appealed and was settled with the payment of damages to the plaintiffs, which brings us to two other points: (1) Going to court is always a gamble, because even when the law appears to be on your side, the judge might not be; and (2) sometimes trying to prove you are right could end up being a whole lot more expensive than admitting you were wrong even when you were not.

CAUTION

Never, ever, skip steps or fail to follow all federal and state procedures when carrying out activities under IDEA, even if you believe you are just trying to help the parents and the child. Even if you have hit the ball out of the park, you need to touch all of the bases.

Make sure all provisions of the IEP or 504 plan are followed by all staff as written.

Do not intentionally inflict emotional distress on students and do not condone it by your silence if others do. Accusations of "deliberate indifference" can get you in trouble even (especially?) if you have not done anything.

It also may be reassuring that while in *Goleta*, the case was as personal as personal can get (the parent was after the administrator's own personal cows and chickens), in most instances, it is the school system, not specific employees, who are listed as defendants. Still, when lightning burns your house to the ground, it is of little comfort to know that millions of your neighbors escaped unscathed.

Special educators sometimes skip steps in the IDEA process with the best of intentions—for example, in an effort to expedite services for a child—but that is never prudent.

Freedom of Speech

When advocating for their children, school employees may at times express their concerns publicly and then find themselves retaliated against by a public school supervisor. As a result, they *may* have a case for seeking damages.

However, the odds for a litigant to prevail in such a case would depend on the individual facts and whether their "right to freedom of speech" actually applied to their case.

The Freedom of Speech amendment to the U.S. Constitution (the First Amendment) only protects citizens from persecution from their government for expressing an idea about a matter of public concern. It does *not* protect employees from their employers when addressing personal concerns, such as the terms or conditions of one's employment.

The Fourth Circuit in *Boring v. Buncombe County Bd of Educ.* (1998; on CD) found against a teacher who complained about her treatment after trying to put on a play her principal found objectionable. Deciding against the teacher, the court found her case "does not present a matter of public concern and is nothing more than an ordinary employment dispute. That being so, plaintiff has no First Amendment rights derived from her selection of the play Independence." A more recent case (*Fox v. Traverse City Area Pub. Sch. Bd. of Educ.*, 2010; on CD) involved a special education teacher who alleged she was fired for expressing concern about her class size; that litigation also resulted in a loss for the plaintiff with the court finding that the teacher's speech was about her conditions of employment, not a matter of public concern.

The "a matter of public concern" standard was and is key. If you speak out on a matter of public interest—for example, a matter concerning the welfare of students in your district—you may be protected. Pamela Settlegoode (*Settlegoode v. Portland School District*, 2004; on CD; you have to love that name in this context) settled for more than $1 million when her district administrators retaliated against her for speaking out on behalf of her children. The Ninth Circuit, in supporting her claims under Section 1983, adopted three standards based on *Pickering v. Board of Ed. of Township High School Dist.* (U.S. Supreme Court,

1968; full decision on CD) to be applied in making a determination of liability:

> When a government employee alleges that he has been punished in retaliation for exercising his First Amendment rights, we engage in a three-part inquiry: To prevail, an employee must prove (1) that the conduct at issue is constitutionally protected, and (2) that it was a substantial or motivating factor in the punishment. Even if the employee discharges that burden, (3) the government can escape liability by showing that it would have taken the same action even in the absence of the protected conduct. (*Settlegoode v. Portland School District,* 2004)

Also see *McGreevy v. Stroup,* Third Circuit, 2005 (on CD), in which the court allowed a damages lawsuit to proceed on behalf of a school nurse who alleged, among other things, that she was fired for defending the rights of children with disabilities. (She also alleged retaliatory action because she refused to allow the terms of her employment to be misrepresented.)

Obviously, in *Settlegoode,* the school administrators were arguing the point that they would have taken the same action even if the teacher had *not* engaged in the protected conduct, which is why that particular case, after a series of wins and losses for the plaintiff, went all the way to the Ninth Circuit, where she finally prevailed. Different courts weighed the school district's arguments differently.

In another case in the U.S. District Court for Connecticut (*Sturm v. Rocky Hill,* 2005; on CD), that court also ruled in favor of a special education teacher's right to sue for damages based on a claim of retaliation.

Not all special education teachers' complaints about the treatment of special education children have been upheld as constituting protected speech, however.

In *Lamb v. Booneville School District* (2010), a federal court upheld the firing of a special education teacher who had objected to the paddling of an autistic child. The case was decided on the same standards as cited earlier, but in the court's view, the record did not support the teacher's contention that she was speaking out on a matter of public concern (the defense of the child's rights). The court wrote:

> Finally, in Plaintiff's email to Kilgore, she explains that her problem was not necessarily that C.J. was paddled, but that C.J. should

have been brought to her when his behavior issues escalated in Murphy's classroom. In other words, as his primary teacher, Plaintiff felt it was her responsibility to deal with his behavioral issues as she saw fit." (*Lamb v. Booneville School Dist.*, 2010; complete decision on CD)

The federal court regarded that as an employment issue. In *Pickering v. Board of Ed.* (1968), the Supreme Court ruled that teachers had the right to speak out on matters of public concern (complete decision on CD). In applying the balancing test first advanced in *Pickering*, as noted, the Mississippi court determined that the speech in question was primarily work related (the amount of deference by administration to the teacher), not about a matter of public concern (the inappropriate application of corporal punishment to an autistic child).

The court's conclusion is debatable, but it is nevertheless both cautionary and illustrative of another basic principle in spedlaw: Nothing is ever as black and white as the litigants sometimes surmise, and while all cases depend on the facts, which facts a judge will find most important and weigh most heavily always involves a gamble on both sides.

A second, incidental lesson is that electronic mail can and probably will become part of the court record, sometimes with disastrous consequences for the author of the email, sometimes the recipient, and sometimes both. You might get away with emailing things you would not want your mother to see, but never email anything you would not want a judge to see. One of the authors (J. O. W.) received and quickly replied to an email inviting him to a team meeting. In his hurry to reply, he did not delete an exceptionally snarky comment about the parents that the sender had gratuitously included in the message. That oversight put the school at a tactical disadvantage.

CAUTION

Electronic mail (even with impressive disclaimers about confidentiality posted at the top and bottom) may become exhibits in a due process hearing or court case and may (except when protected by FERPA) even be subject to state sunshine laws. Within the context of litigation, remember that FERPA was written to protect the child, not to protect public educators from their own loose lips.

Not all cases are decided based on the First Amendment, of course, and in some instances, it is relevant to remember that the IDEA and Section 504 are (obviously) laws affording statutory, not constitutional, rights. Virtually every state has a whistleblower law protecting citizens against retaliation when they report violations of law. A school-based professional who believes he or she was retaliated against for exposing a violation of a child's civil rights under the law could under those circumstances also be able to sue in state court. State courts, like federal courts, however, would require that the teacher provide evidence that the retaliatory action was triggered by his or her advocacy and that the teacher convince them that he or she would not, in the case of a firing, have been dismissed regardless.

So there are protections but no guarantees that the teacher's perception that he or she was speaking out on a matter of public concern will be perceived in the same way by a judge. In the final analysis, however, if school-based professionals do not advocate for and speak out on behalf of the children with disabilities they serve, among them the frailest and most vulnerable students in our school system, who will?

DON'T FORGET

If a situation arises in which you need to speak up for a child, be very careful to do precisely that and *not* to say or write anything that even remotely suggests your concern is for anything except the child's rights and needs (e.g., your job conditions or professional perquisites). Do not do, write, or say anything unrelated to the child's needs that would allow your employer to argue that you would have been fired anyhow, regardless of the areas of public concern that were being addressed.

Advice for Evaluators

Defensive practice is the best way to avoid litigation. Evaluators typically work with children one to one in closed rooms for hours at a time; they therefore are potentially vulnerable to suspicions and accusations of misconduct. Evaluators (generally speaking) cannot control whether their districts fail to provide children with minimal services or fail to keep agreements arrived at during due process hearings. However, if they conduct themselves professionally and take some rudimentary proactive measures, they can reduce their chances of becoming targets.

- Be aware of the obligations imposed by § 104.35 of Section 504 and § 300.304 of the IDEA with respect to providing every child suspected of a disability with an evaluation that is sufficiently comprehensive to evaluate the child in all areas of suspected disability and to identify all areas of special education and related services needs.
- Be aware of ethical obligations imposed by one's professional associations and state statutes regarding assessment and, to the extent practical, abide by them. For school psychologists, the applicable standards would be Standard 9 of the "Ethical Principles of Psychologists and Code of Conduct" (American Psychological Association, 2010) and Principle II.3 of the "Principles for Professional Ethics" (National Association of School Psychologists, 2010).
- More practically, never ever test a child behind a door locked from the outside. Sometimes custodians unlock doors for an itinerant evaluator, leaving it open; sometimes those doors are still locked from the outside even if they can be opened from the inside. If you cannot unlock the door without a key, either get a key or defer testing.
- If a teacher or parent requests that someone of a different sex test the child, and especially if the student has had a history of abuse, honor the request.
- If a child has a history of violence against adult caregivers, and the teacher wants the one-to-one assistant to sit in to provide the assessor with protection, honor the request. Better to have a nonstandard testing situation than have to explain how it came to be that a child was injured or you were injured while the child was in your care.
- Ensure meaningful parental participation in the decision-making process. It increases trust, avoids miscommunication, and affords both parties an opportunity to address problems before the situation becomes adversarial. Besides, it is the parent's legal right.
- Follow the procedural requirements; usually this is not hard to do because the forms drive the process. Do not take shortcuts to

save time. Do not falsify data under the guise of "cleaning up" a folder so as to appear compliant (see Chapter 9). All of these last suggestions may seem self-evident, but failure to take these simple precautions has been at the root of many a lawsuit.

- At the risk of being overly repetitious, never let the buck stop with you (that is what committees and teams are for).

- While various and sundry laws generally protect school employees from frivolous lawsuits, the courts have been reluctant to protect people, including school employees, from their own intentional torts when the injurious behavior is sufficiently egregious or shows a reckless disregard for (or deliberate indifference regarding) the safety of others. Hence our advice to "always be nice to parents" also applies to children, because (1) not being nice can bring about unexpected consequences; (2) when the time comes not to be nice, that is why schools have board attorneys; and (3) we are all in the field to help children.

- Always remember that, in spedlaw, good deeds never go unpunished, especially if the "good deed" also involves abridging parents' due process rights. In the *Ordway* case cited earlier, for example, the action for which the mother later sued and received damages because due process was not followed allegedly *was at her own request.*

- When informed of bullying behavior, be aware that what may seem like simple bullying may, depending on circumstances, rise to the level of racial, religious, sexual, or disability-based harassment prohibited by federal law. Report all such behavior to the appropriate school administrator(s), keeping a record of that report.

- This continues to be a rapidly evolving area of spedlaw; so if you find yourself in a real adversarial situation, obtain the services of a real lawyer . . . do not rely on this chapter for current legal advice!

☙ TEST YOURSELF ☙

1. Punitive damages may not be awarded in private suits under Section 202 of the ADA and Section 504 of the Rehabilitation Act.

   True or False

2. The single best protection against lawsuits based on alleged retaliatory behavior or intentional discrimination is strict adherence to the procedures set forth in the IDEA.

   True or False

3. The Freedom of Speech amendment to the U.S. Constitution protects employees from their employers when addressing valid and important personal concerns such as the terms or conditions of one's employment.

   True or False

4. Electronic mails with confidentiality disclaimers are protected by FERPA and therefore will not become exhibits in a due process hearing or court case.

   True or False

5. Parents are not allowed to employ an attorney to represent them at IEP team meetings within the public school system.

   True or False

6. In a dispute over whether the school has or has not provided FAPE, parents do not need to request mediation before going directly to a due process hearing.

   True or False

Answers: 1. True; 2. True; 3. False; 4. False; 5. False; 6. True

Nine

FERPA AND THE PPRA: CONFIDENTIAL RECORDS

Whoever wishes to keep a secret must hide the fact
that he possesses one.

—Johann Wolfgang von Goethe

A nyone who has ever been the least bit involved with public school systems (and who hasn't?) probably has noticed a tendency for those systems to create and maintain a heck of a lot of paperwork. Every student seems to have a paper trail that can follow him or her for quite some time. To the regular paper pile, those students who are involved with special education will be eligible for, and very quickly amass, another whole set of papers. These will include notices for special education meeting, individualized education programs (IEPs), and copies of reports written about the student along with the actual test record forms used during the multiple evaluations done.

This accumulation of paper comes with a whole raft of added legal and ethical responsibilities, typically assumed by the school professionals dealing with the specific students. Parents, however, also have a vested interest in these paper piles, and they may want more out of the pile then you or the school would like them to have. Many education professionals are unaware of the legalities related to student records, and some are, unfortunately, totally unfamiliar with the safeguards provided by the Family Educational Rights and Privacy Act (FERPA) and the Protection of Pupil Rights Amendment (PPRA) regulations. This chapter addresses some of the more common questions and concerns that relate to many students and specifically special education students when it comes to their educational files.

In addition to Individuals with Disabilities Education Act (IDEA), FERPA, and PPRA requirements for educational records, and any additional rules imposed by their respective states, school psychologists also may be bound by ethical requirements of the American Psychological Association (2010) and/or the National Association of School Psychologists (2000, 2010).

Parental Review of Educational Records

Parents have the right to review of all their child's educational records, including test protocols, if they contain "personally identifiable information." If they do *not* contain personally identifiable information, then the parents do *not* have a right to inspect them. This long-standing position of the Office of Special Education Programs (OSEP) was last reiterated in an OSEP Letter from Guard to Schuster (August 7, 2007; on CD).

Test protocols often contain personal information on the child and can be requested, for example, by any knowledgeable attorney for review by the parents' experts when the test record form (protocol) is also the recording of the child's responses made by the examiner. The scoring of these responses often can play an important role when determining a child's eligibility (or lack thereof) for special education services. Because of that, the common errors all evaluators have made at one time or another (e.g., Alfonso, Johnson, Patinella, & Rader, 1998; Watkins, 2009) can be fertile ground for someone intent on discrediting the school's position (Willis, 2001). While the thought of being discredited makes any of us flinch, it is far better in the long run to catch our mistakes and correct them than it would be to let a child suffer for a lifetime because we or a colleague used the wrong table to score a high-stakes test.

Parents are entitled by federal regulations to inspect their child's educational record, including test protocols, but not to make or have copies made except under very special circumstances. (Note: In California, state law requires the local education agencies [LEAs] to provide parents with copies of the test protocols. Be sure to check your state rules.) In a due process case, however, that is largely moot. The parent's attorneys want our protocols to share with their professionals, and there is absolutely nothing in the law, in professional ethics, or in publishers' dicta on the subject that would inhibit or prohibit our sharing hard copies with professionals bound by the same professional ethics that apply to us, as long as the parent has given informed consent and as long as the protocols are sent

≡ Rapid Reference 9.1

Parents or eligible students have the right to inspect and review the student's education records maintained by the school. Schools are not required to provide copies of records unless, for reasons such as great distance, it is impossible for parents or eligible students to review the records. Attorneys can, however, subpoena copies of all records. Schools may charge a reasonable fee for copies.

directly to the professional (not picked up, say, by the mother's secretary). The 2006 Final Regulations provide a list of some special education records that must be provided to the parent; those are discussed later in this chapter. See Rapid Reference 9.1.

DESTRUCTION OF PROTOCOLS IN SCHOOL RECORDS

Destroying Test Protocols

Even when framed in the best possible light ("We burned the protocols to protect the validity of our test, not because we were afraid someone would find out we had screwed up"), destroying protocols looks bad. And it is bad. First, parents have the right under the IDEA to prior notification before destruction of any educational record used in the special education process. In recent times, no one has seriously disputed that test protocols are education records once they are used to form the basis of a report. So destroying a test protocol without prior notification to the parents would be unlawful (§ 300.624, p. 46804). It is also not "best practice." As far back as 1996, the American Psychological Association was saying that if a psychologist is retaining the test results, he or she should retain the test record. In any adversarial situation, if the school expects to win on points, it cannot afford to give them away. Almost always one should expect a hearing officer or judge to attach more credibility to a report that can be supported by test data than one that cannot because, for whatever reason, the school psychologist or other evaluators destroyed important evidence. (Destroying protocols because they had been requested rather than before they were requested would be a violation both of the IDEA and FERPA; FERPA Regulations, §91.10 (e).)

The Office of Civil Rights (OCR) also issued a letter in 1990 which found that a district's policy of destroying protocols violated Section 504 because the protocols were relevant to the district's recommendation that a child be placed in a program for children with behavioral disorders, a recommendation with which the parents disagreed (Office for Civil Rights, 1990).

How Long to Keep Test Protocols

Special education records may be destroyed when they are no longer needed for educational purposes, but parents must be given prior notice first, in case they are needed for other purposes (§ 300.573). Our response to how long these records should be kept is the same as it is regarding all special educational records: They should be kept *at least* a year after a child is no longer age eligible for services in the public school system or 5 years after a child is dismissed from the program in case of an audit; some jurisdictions (e.g., Texas) would say for 3 years. The federal regulations, however, are clear in saying that once a school system has notified a parent that the records are no longer needed, then at parental request those records must be destroyed. Obviously, it would not be prudent to tell parents that special education records were not needed when the school still might need them to meet federal and state requirements.

Educators often are caught between test publishers and federal regulators on the proper treatment of test protocols. LRP Publications (http://www.lrp.com/) has addressed those issues in at least two national special education law (spedlaw) workshops, one in 1994, the other in 2000.

OSEP has defined test protocols as being educational records since 1981 (Inquiry of Hill, 1981). FERPA regulations applying to educational records also applied to test protocols if they contained personally identifiable information, according to OSEP. The argument being tested, apparently, was whether, since the test protocols were in the sole possession of the psychologist, they needed to be shared. OSEP said that once the scores had been released (in this case "released" meant used for an educational decision), the parents had the right to review the underlying paperwork.

FERPA itself also prohibits a district from destroying education records while a parental request to review them is pending. Although, in most states, parents generally are not entitled to copies of the protocols (unless failure to provide them would effectively prevent the parent from exercising his or her right to inspect them), OSEP and OCR have both opined that under Section 504 and IDEA that parents may have a right to a copy of the test protocol if those records are needed for a due process hearing. Although some test publishers have recommended that districts require a court to subpoena them, if they have been requested by a parent's attorney, we do not recommend making him or her jump through hoops to get them. That decision should, however, be made by the administrator designated by board policy as being in charge of the school records. Remember, if the school loses, it is going to end up paying for the time the parent's attorney spent getting over all our hurdles. (OCR, In re Tri-County, Illinois, 1984; OSEP, Inquiry of Hafner, 1979). When tests or test records do not contain personally identifiable information, parents do not have the right of access, according to OSEP. Do not let this point lull you into thinking that what you should do is simply tear off the "front sheet" of a record form—the part that typically contains the child's name and identifiable information—and turn the record form into a de-identified record, not open to review. "Personally identifiable information," as we discuss elsewhere, includes much more than the child's name and date of birth. Also, you never know what legal chicanery will impress a judge, but it goes back to our spedlaw maxim: "If you think you have found a loophole, then you have more than likely have found a noose."

There are a number of other possible pitfalls. Once you tore off the face sheet, you would not know to what protocol it belonged, so in essence you would have destroyed a child's special education record without giving the parent prior notification. You would still be unable to produce the protocol, which would give the impression that you were trying to hide something.

Although this seems simple, the problem is compounded by publishers such as Pearson and Riverside, which seem to interpret FERPA regulations a little differently than we do. How would a conflict between a lawyer's demand and publishers' conditions for purchase and use of their tests play out? Based on OSEP's long-standing position and the few court cases we have seen on this issue, the parents would almost certainly win.

Definition of "Personally Identifiable Information"

"Personally identifiable" does not just mean the child's name and date of birth, which is why writers who write emails about Johnny H. instead of Johnny Hart think they have met the FERPA burden. They have not. Personally identifiable information that generally requires written consent prior to release includes:

(a) The student's name;

(b) The name of the student's parent or other family members;

(c) The address of the student or student's family;

(d) A personal identifier, such as the student's social security number, student number, or biometric record;

(e) Other indirect identifiers, such as the student's date of birth, place of birth, and mother's maiden name;

(f) Other information that, alone or in combination, is linked or linkable to a specific student that would allow a reasonable person in the school community, who does not have personal knowledge of the relevant circumstances, to identify the student with reasonable certainty; or

(g) Information requested by a person who the educational agency or institution reasonably believes knows the identity of the student to whom the education record relates. (FERPA, § 99.3)

That "definition," including part (f), carries the force of law.

Inspection of Test Record Form and Test Security

As we have said, a school does not have the right to refuse a parent's request to inspect a test record form (protocol) because the test publisher claims that revealing the content to a layperson would compromise test security. Because test record forms containing personally identifiable information are considered part of a child's school record, they, along with all the other materials maintained as part of that record, are open for inspection. However, there are differences among the states over a parent's right to physical copies of the protocols. There is a tension between parental rights to access and publishers' rights to test security. In California, for example, state regulations give parents the right to obtain physical copies of test protocols containing personally identifiable information (e.g., an intelligence test protocol). A California court ruled that the parent's right to obtain physical copies trumped publishers' rights. This does *not*, however, establish a precedent in other jurisdictions.

This case (*Newport-Mesa Unified v. State of Cal. Dept. of Ed.* 2005) was a lawsuit between a school district and the California Department of Education. The court found that special education test protocols are "school records" for the purposes of California Education Code Section 56504 and that a copy of the special education test protocols must be provided to parents upon their request. Although the court said that schools could ask parents to sign nondisclosure agreements, the California Department of Education later disagreed, saying that they could not. For most of us, this simply illustrates that a right given to a school in one paragraph or ruling can be quickly taken away by a different court ruling, federal or state regulation, or even with the same statute and regulation. Again, these rights do *not* apply outside of the state of California and are reported here primarily to illustrate (once again) the need for familiarity with your applicable state laws, which is beyond the scope of this book to provide for all 50 states although we do provide links to codes, procedures, or regulations for all 50 states on the accompanying CD.

CAUTION

Any test record form (protocol) might wind up as an exhibit in a hearing or court case. It is prudent to make sure all of your protocols are completed correctly, scored absolutely accurately, and free from personal notes you should never have written.

Copying the Actual Test Manual

Parents do not have a right to copy the actual test manual or see the test kit. FERPA only allows parents to inspect the protocols if they have any personally identifiable information on them. Under some circumstances, such as when a parent cannot come to the school to inspect the record because of a physical ailment or a parent who lives 2,000 miles away from the school in another state, the school would have to provide the parent with copies. IDEA 2004 does not expand FERPA rights in that respect.

In Attachment 1 following Appendix B of the Final 1999 Regulations for the IDEA, the Office of Special Education and Rehabilitative Services (OSERS) said: "For example, a test protocol or question booklet which is separate from the sheet on which a student records answers and which is not personally identifiable to the student would not be a part of his or her 'education records'" (p. 12641). If a child marks a bubble sheet, that is the education record.

We find no burden to voluntarily offer parents the right to inspect the record other than in the annual notification required under FERPA in § 99.7 (on CD).

Copying Special Educational Records for Parents

As discussed in Chapter 2, under FERPA, schools are not required to provide copies of educational records to parents unless there is no other practical way for them to review them (see Rapid Reference 9.2).

The right to review does not include the right to copies, with the exception of the prior notices required by IDEA (including copies of the evaluation report and a copy of the child's IEP at no cost to the parent; § 300.322, p. 46789). With respect to the other exception in FERPA, if, for example, a parent were on military duty in a combat zone, the special education administrator might elect to send copies rather than personally carry the records overseas for the parent for review. Andrea Canter (2001a, b; 2002; 2005) has reviewed test protocol issues in the National Association of School Psychologists' (NASP) *Communiqué*. Rosenfeld (2010) recently has provided an update of this information. States may create other exceptions. As noted previously, California gives parents the right to receive copies of test protocols containing personally identifiable information.

≡ Rapid Reference 9.2

Remember that, regarding educational records, the right to review and the right to copy often are treated very differently by the educational laws. The right to review an educational record is quite clear; the right to a copy arises only in special circumstances.

Attorneys may subpoena any educational records. Even records otherwise classifiable as "personal notes" may be subpoenaed and introduced into evidence if, after review by a judge, they are found to be relevant to reaching a just outcome. Confidentiality is never absolute.

Protections for Student Records

Rights related to the protection of school records are covered by FERPA, not IDEA. Protecting those rights is a responsibility of regular education. Although the rights under FERPA are extensive, there is no burden placed on special education to keep students' special education records confidential from any regular education teachers who, according to school policy, have a legitimate educational interest.

Schools often maintain separate folders for special education records because special education teachers are responsible for maintaining the files for audits. We do not want these files mixed up with other records, and we certainly do not want people mucking with them. But just because something is common practice does not mean it is a legal requirement.

Some schools may put a sheet in the child's cumulative record saying when a child was tested, the date, and where the reports may be found. All educational records must be accessible to parents.

The burden on regular education teachers is to provide all of the regular classroom accommodations listed in the IEP, whether the teachers were at the meeting when the IEP was created or not, so special education teachers often provide regular education teachers with copies of the IEP. That is permitted under FERPA without parental consent. Tacking the IEP up on the regular classroom teacher's bulletin board "as a reminder" (as happened in one of G. M. M.'s schools) is not permitted.

How Long to Keep the Educational Records

How long a school must keep the educational records of special education students varies, of course, with respect to the nature of the records. Schools are given broad latitude in determining what records to keep or destroy under FERPA (FPCO Letter from Rooker to Anonymous, July 18, 2002). However, special education records do require special treatment.

There is no provision in FERPA comparable to § 300.573 of the Part B, IDEA regulations, requiring a "public agency [to] inform parents when personally identifiable information collected, maintained, or used under this part is no longer needed to provide educational services to the child" before it destroys that information. (FPCO Letter from Rooker to Mathews, September 13, 2005; on CD)

Repeating what we wrote with respect to test protocols, we recommend keeping records for at least 1 year after a child ages out of the program, 5 years (Texas says 3) after exiting from a special education program. (Test protocols containing personally identifiable information have the aforementioned protections afforded by the IDEA and may not even under FERPA be destroyed if a parent has a pending request for an opportunity to review them.)

DON'T FORGET

Each state may impose confidentiality requirements above and beyond those mandated by federal law and regulation. These opinions always should be read within the context of your state regulations. (This warning is more than just perfunctory, since § 300.123 of the 2006 Final Regulations requires each state to have policies and procedures in effect to ensure public agencies in the state comply with the IDEA confidentiality regulations related to protecting the confidentiality of any "personally identifiable information collected, used or maintained under Part B" (p. 46765).)

Parental Request to Change the Educational Records of a Child

Parents certainly have the right to request that the record be amended (see Rapid Reference 9.3). Schools also have the right to say "No way." If the school does object to changing the record, the parent then has the right to appeal and/or have a parental statement entered into the record. For example, Johnny is in his grandmother's care, and she tells the psychologist, "Mom was heavily involved in drugs during her pregnancy." Mom regains custody and reads the report. She says, "I used drugs, sure, but not when I was carrying Johnny. I want that report amended." You can either change the report to reflect Mom's version *or*, if your school records officer (usually a principal and/or special education director) believes it is just fine, Mom can either request a formal hearing or write her own statement and have it attached—for example, "I never did what my mother said about taking drugs when I was pregnant, and she's just a lying lady of the night." If possible, we would just change the report. Otherwise, you would have to write a correction (or make copies of the parent's addendum) and attach it to all copies of the disputed document(s) in school files. We would definitely not recommend having two versions of the same report in the school files as that is not an approved option.

Access to Inactive Special Education Records

School staff (related service providers, etc.) can access inactive special education records when a student is referred to a general education intervention team if, according to board policy, the participants meet the administrative requirements as having a legitimate educational interest in the records. Special education records are education records under FERPA, and as such are subject to board policies requiring access to be limited to personnel having a legitimate educational interest. While it is administrative policy, not FERPA regulations or Family Policy Compliance Office (FPCO) dicta, that ultimately would provide the basis for answering the question, Who has a legitimate educational interest in each school system? FPCO has suggested: "A school official has a legitimate educational interest if the official needs to review an education record in order to fulfill his or her professional responsibilities." That is a pretty broad brush, but as we explain later, it does not provide unlimited access by every Tom, Dick or Harriette employed by the school system.

≡ Rapid Reference 9.3

A parent or eligible students have the right to request that a school correct records that he or she believes to be inaccurate or misleading. If the school decides not to amend the record, the parent or eligible student then has the right to a formal hearing. After the hearing, if the school still decides not to amend the record, the parent or eligible student has the right to place a statement with the record setting forth his or her view about the contested information.

Ownership of Test Records

Educational records are educational records whether active or inactive (unless, of course, they are destroyed inactive records) no matter where they are kept. "Ownership" is not a word to be found in the federal regulations in regard to educational records. Schools have responsibilities, and parents have rights. The records are not "owned" by either party.

To further confuse matters, we have been told that some consent forms contain a statement similar to this one: "Psychological records are considered to be part of the student's education record and as such are the property of the school district." There has been some debate as to the accuracy of this statement. One side says the school district owns them and the parents have right of access. Others say the parent is the owner and the school district maintains them. *Neither is correct.*

According to FERPA Regulations, which carry the force of law,

> An educational agency or institution may disclose personally identifiable information from an education record of a student without the consent required by § 99.30 if the disclosure meets one or more of the following conditions: (1)(i)(A) The disclosure is to other school officials, including teachers, within the agency or institution whom the agency or institution has determined to have legitimate educational interests.

Additionally, FERPA goes on to say:

> An educational agency or institution must use reasonable methods to ensure that school officials obtain access to only those education records in which they have legitimate educational interests. An educational agency or institution that does not use physical or technological access controls must insure that its administrative policy for controlling access to education records is effective and that it remains in compliance with the legitimate educational interest requirement in paragraph (a)(1)(i)(A) of this section. (FERPA, § 99.31(a)(1)(i)(B)(3)(ii)); complete regulations on CD)

FERPA allows disclosures of personally identifiable information from education records without consent to school officials, including teachers, within an educational agency or institution—an LEA or its constituent schools—if the agency or institution has determined that the school officials have legitimate educational interests in the information.

> An LEA or school that discloses information under this exception must specify in its annual notification of FERPA rights the criteria it uses to determine who constitutes a school official and what constitutes legitimate educational interest. (a) If the educational agency or institution has a policy of disclosing education records under § 99.31 (a) (1), a specification of criteria for determining who constitutes a school official and what constitutes a legitimate educational interest.

(See 34 CFR § 99.31 (a)(1) and 34 CFR § 99.7 of the FERPA regulations.)

There is no explicit requirement for a board policy under FERPA as there is under the PPRA. However, § 99.31 (a) (ii) does require at the minimum an administrative policy defining legitimate educational interest. Many LEAs meet that obligation through board policy. In 1996, FPCO wrote:

> The regulations removed § 99.6—the requirement for a student records policy—and revised the annual notification requirements under § 99.7. As a result, school districts must annually notify parents of their FERPA rights, but are no longer required to maintain a student records policy. (www.ed.gov/policy/gen/guid/fpco/ferpa/library/california.html)

However, in 2008 FPCO wrote:

> A district or institution that makes a disclosure solely on the basis that the individual is a school official violates FERPA if it does not also determine that the school official has a legitimate educational interest. (www.ed.gov/legislation/FedRegister/finrule/2008-4/120908a.html)

and referenced the FERPA regulation cited earlier:

> An educational agency or institution that does not use physical or technological access controls must insure that its administrative policy for controlling access to education records is effective.

Loosely translated, this means that there is no explicit requirement that education records be kept under lock and key as long as they are protected in some way. The FERPA regulations also require districts to annually notify parents if they allow contracted personnel, parent volunteers, or others with a legitimate educational interest to view education records without prior written consent. For example, the annual notification might include a state defining a "legitimate educational interest" as occurring whenever a school official, someone contracting with the school to perform a function that the school would otherwise have to perform itself, a parent volunteer, or anyone else to whom the school has outsourced a function it would normally perform itself needs to review the records in order to perform his or her duty.

Special Education Status and Class Standing, Honor Roll, and the Like

Regional OCR offices have issued differing interpretations about whether a school can take into account a student's special education status with regard to class standing, honor roll, and the like, but the most authoritative ruling seems to be the 1996 OCR Dunbar Letter to Runkel (see OCR letter on CD). The standards herein are, however, broad and therefore may be interpreted differently in different settings.

(1) Eligibility for honor roll and academic awards cannot be denied automatically on the basis of disability status under IDEA or Section 504. Below-grade level performance should not automatically exclude a student from consideration.

(2) Notations on permanent transcripts are only appropriate to designate modified curriculum (i.e., reduced mastery criteria/modified essential elements)—not instructional delivery modifications.

(3) School districts can establish eligibility criteria for class ranking (e.g., weighted classes) as long as IDEA or Section 504 students are not arbitrarily excluded. The system must be based on "objective rating criteria" and special education or modified courses should not be weighted more lightly automatically. (OCR, Dunbar Letter to Runkel, 1996)

One thing seems clear to us, at least, and that is if the course require-ments are the same, if the child is required to pass the same end-of-course test, and all that is being modified is the method of instruction, then it would be discriminatory to imply in the record that there was something "special" about a special class.

Parental Permission and Release of Student Records

Generally, schools must have written permission from the parent or eligi-ble student in order to release any information from a student's education record. However, there are several specific circumstances (excerpted from FERPA 2009 Regulations, § 99.31) under which a school may disclose those records, without consent, to these parties:

> School officials with legitimate educational interest;
> Other schools to which a student is transferring;
> Specified officials for audit or evaluation purposes;
> Appropriate parties in connection with financial aid to a student;
> Organizations conducting certain studies for or on behalf of the
> school;
> Accrediting organizations;
> To comply with a judicial order or lawfully issued subpoena;
> Appropriate officials in cases of health and safety emergencies; and
> State and local authorities, within a juvenile justice system,
> pursuant to specific State law.

See the FERPA regulations on the accompanying CD or the FPCO Web site for detailed information: www2.ed.gov/policy/gen/guid/fpco/index.html

Nothing in FERPA or special education regulations specifies where the information is to be kept. Practically, a school would not want to keep financial records (which are really what special education records are, espe-cially if you have a headcount audit) someplace where some unauthorized person could easily access them. Also, ethically, test protocols are secure instruments that should be shared only as required by law. We recommend that test protocols be stored in a place other than the child's cumulative folder (e.g., a central office or in school files maintained by the school psychologist, special educator, or speech pathologist who actually tested the student).

Release of Directory Information

FERPA does allow us to share directory information without getting parental consent. Suppose a developmental optometrist, believing he had a cure for dyslexia, asks a school to provide him with directory information for all the children with specific learning disability (SLD) in the district. Is there any reason why the school should not comply?

Directory information based on nondirectory information is not directory information. The nondirectory information in the last example is, of course, that each child on the list has a disability. The information is protected both by FERPA and the IDEA. There would of course be nothing to prevent a district under either statute from itself forwarding the optometrist's information to all the families of SLD children, but there would be no obligation on its part to do so.

Shredding Testing Materials (Summary)

Once a school has completed an evaluation of a child, it should not shred the testing materials. Shredding test protocols without prior notification to the parents would be a violation of the IDEA, is contrary to generally accepted professional and ethical guidelines, and creates the impression that the district has something to hide.

Scanned Signatures and Emailed Files

Local policies aside, the legal and ethical concern does not seem to revolve around the scanning of the signature as much as about how reports are sent. Electronic transmittal of confidential information carries with it many problems that are only beginning to be recognized and addressed in this digital age. The previous, 2000 NASP ethical standards, section E. 6, stated in part:

> To ensure confidentiality, student/client records are not transmitted electronically without a guarantee of privacy. In line with this

principle, a receiving FAX machine must be in a secure location and operated by employees cleared to work with confidential files, and e-mail messages must be encrypted or else stripped of all information that identifies the student/client. (NASP, 2000, p. 31)

The new, 2010 NASP ethical standards are a little less explicit.

Standard II.4.7. To the extent that school psychological records are under their control, school psychologists protect electronic files from unauthorized release or modification (e.g., by using passwords and encryption), and they take reasonable steps to ensure that school psychological records are not lost due to equipment failure.

Standard II.4.1. School psychologists discuss with parents and adult students their rights regarding creation, modification, storage, and disposal of psychological and educational records that result from the provision of services. Parents and adult students are notified of the electronic storage and transmission of personally identifiable school psychological records and the associated risks to privacy. (NASP, 2010, p. 8)

Even if a school psychologist does not belong to NASP, the standard would still apply if a school psychologist's job description called on professional adherence to NASP ethical codes.

However, this standard does not necessarily apply to the administrators for whom a school psychologist works. FERPA does not explicitly forbid sharing student records via email with written parental consent. There are certainly varying opinions, some saying it is okay, some saying it is not, but for us the bottom line is that the Internet is a dangerous place. It is remarkably easy to misdirect an email intended for one specific recipient to another or even an entire address book or listserv. There have been anecdotal reports on the NASP listserv of recipients actually altering psychological reports transmitted electronically. So if you do, with parental permission, use email to share protected information, be very careful. Emailing a report as an unencrypted document file without any password protection would be insane, since the report could be edited (e.g., by removing the word "not" from "not disabled") by anyone who obtained a copy.

It is also all too easy to err. For example, one author (G. M. M.) sent an email with an extensive list of concerns about a special education folder to a new teacher, misdirecting the critique to the teacher's mother, an experienced teacher with the same name (and a working email box). Technically it was a FERPA violation, albeit unintentional, because the recipient had no legitimate educational interest in the child. On more than one occasion, professionals thinking they were writing a friend have accidentally posted personal emails on national listservs with literally thousands of members.

Although FERPA supersedes any state sunshine laws, affording protection to students' education records regardless of any state mandate, it should always be remembered that in many states, any emails sent or received on a state-supported email system are subject to public scrutiny. Additionally, virtually all organizations retain the right to access and inspect employee emails at the discretion of their chief administrator.

Revising a Submitted Report

Similar to the answer regarding a parent's right to amend information in a child's educational record, the short answer here is "Yes, it is permissible to revise a report that has already been submitted" but, as discussed, all copies should be amended if possible and the record and report heading should show it was amended on a particular date. The actual text of a report may be amended, or an amendment may be added to the original report. Typically, requests to amend reports come about because of obvious errors—for example, referring to a boy as "she" or arithmetic mistakes (saying there was a significant discrepancy based on state criteria when there was not). Sometimes the requests involve more substantial issues, such as a request that the psychologist withdraw recommendations against retention. The kinds of issues generally can be avoided if the psychologist has met with the parent and previously shared recommendations, but ultimately they would need to be decided on a case-by-case basis by each professional according to the dictates of his or her conscience. The bottom line, however, is that amending reports is permitted by the law.

In many schools, authority over records is established by board policy. Building records are usually under the authority of the principal. Central office special education records are often under the authority of the special education director. When problems arise with special education records in either setting, however, the principals usually defer to the special education director (at least in part because there is not much point changing the educational record in one place while maintaining an unmodified version in another).

As with disputed facts, as discussed earlier, federal regulations also say that parents may ask that records be amended if they constitute a violation of the child's privacy rights. See §§ 99.20, 21, and 22 for further details, but we have not found a good definition or example of a "violation of a child's privacy rights" other than if the data are misleading or inaccurate. At least theoretically, personal information that is unrelated to the child's educational needs might be removed—for example, a comment regarding a student's brother's sexual orientation or the parents' political affiliations. If the school chooses not to honor a parent request to amend the record, the parent is entitled to a hearing. See § 99.20 of the FERPA regulations for a more thorough review of this issue (34 CFR Part 99; on CD).

At least one Web site maintains a form letter than can be used to file a FERPA complaint with FPCO: www.deltabravo.net/custody/ferpa-complaint.htm.

Backdating a Record under FERPA

Consider this scenario: "My district is striving for 100% compliance with a 60-day timeline. A teacher schedules the meeting before the expiration date, but the parent cannot come in until a week past the expiration date. At the meeting, the principal asks the parent if she would agree to backdate the meeting date 'to help us with the paperwork.' Are there any potential penalties for backdating a record under FERPA?"

FERPA does not directly address the issue of student record falsification, but state statutes and/or state board of education regulations could apply. There is a natural desire to please one's supervisor, and the pressure to conform may be palpable. However, there have been instances where exceptional children program directors have been fired for falsifying student records by altering and/or backdating records or where teachers were (based on state law) accused of criminal misconduct.

In one case, a special education director was fired for falsifying special education records and appealed his dismissal (*Weems v. North Franklin School District*, 2002). The court affirmed the trial court's decision to uphold his termination.

In another instance, in Texas, a newspaper reported that special education personnel had been accused of potentially criminal misconduct by falsifying their student Admission Review and Dismissal (ARD) team meetings by backdating some records in order to avoid a negative review by their supervisors. In this particular case, the governing board declined not to take action against the two accused employees after an independent evaluation was completed. The investigation, however, did not clear the teachers, and their superintendent recommended their contracts not be renewed for the coming school year (Brosig, 2010).

Falsifying student records by backdating could in some instances also be used by parents in alleging a denial of due process even if they had been asked to participate in the falsification and complied. The standards, however, would be relatively high; the parents would have to prove the records were falsified and then they would have to prove some harm came from it. Even if the backdating could be proven (e.g., the psychologist testified to it), the second standard is very hard to meet. Thus, being frank, open, and honest not only is worthy of the best Boy Scout behavior, it also is low risk. Engaging a parent in a conspiracy to lie would not do much for a school employee's reputation.

Also, from a practical standpoint, these kinds of issues come up every day in our practice. Johnny has a 73 IQ, and he "needs" a score no higher than 72 to qualify for special education. What is the harm in dropping it one point? Once a practitioner starts down the road of record falsification, losing his or her grip on the firm moral bedrock of unconditional honesty, he or she finds himself on a very slippery slope with no bottom in sight. Almost none of us would falsify entire reports. However, in 2006, a school psychologist in Brooklyn, NY, did just that (falsifying entire reports of children she had not tested), and not only lost her job, but the case was referred to the district attorney for prosecution (Condon, 2006; Rogers, 2006). However, falsifying dates is not exactly like driving 72 mph in a 65 mph zone either. Small lie, big lie, it is all the same—you are still a liar in the parents' eyes.

If you are still unsure and need to document the risks of falsifying a special education record for a supervisor, we advise that you contact your state director of special education and ask three questions:

1. Is backdating special education records a common and accepted practice in your state?
2. If it is not, what penalties might a district expect to incur if found guilty of having condoned the practice?
3. Are there any state statutes or state board of education policies that could make a school employee liable to dismissal, loss of license, and/or charges of criminal misconduct by falsifying a special education record by backdating it?

Changing a Student's Grades

Only when there was a "ministerial error" (e.g., the teacher recorded the wrong grade) would FERPA require a teacher to change a student's grades. Disagreements based on the child's or parent's perception that he or she deserved a better grade are not covered under FERPA.

Students Grading Other Students' Papers

A teacher allowing students in a class to swap and grade each other's papers is one of those seemingly simple situations that went all the way to the United States Supreme Court (*Owasso Independent School Dist. v. Falvo*, 2002; on CD) in order to get a very expensive answer. The court reasoned that grades are not a part of the child's educational record until they are actually recorded (e.g., in a teacher's grade book). Also see the revised definition of an educational record in § 99.3 of the FERPA Regulations (2010 revision; on CD).

FERPA Requirements for Contract Work

The 2008 Amendments for FERPA (on CD) discuss the propriety of sharing educational records with contractors doing work the school would otherwise have done for itself and who are under the direct control of the school system. They are silent with respect to subcontractors, but we think it is fair to assume that the use of secretaries by attorneys and other contracted personnel is a common practice. (We know of one case in which the specific issue contested was whether the due process rights of a child with an educational disability were violated when a school district makes an unofficial stenographic transcript or electronic recording of a special education hearing. Appropriately, in our estimation, the court found "the issue wholly devoid of merit" [*Caroline T. v. Hudson School District*, 1990].) Regardless, it is the contractor who is responsible for preserving confidentiality, and § 99.31 says that if our "Office determines that a third party outside the educational agency or institution to whom information is disclosed under this paragraph (a)(6) violates paragraph (a)(6)(ii)(B) of this section, the educational agency or institution may not allow that third party access to personally identifiable information from education records for at least five years." Those same consequences could also be imposed if a contractor's employee, even one's spouse if employed to render secretarial services, violated the trust placed in them and a complaint was lodged with FPCO.

Additionally, after the 2008 revisions to FERPA, schools are permitted to share information from children's educational records only if they indicated in their annual notice that they may share information with specific contractors, consultants, volunteers, and the like.

Suits for Revealing Confidential Records

Under federal law, if a teacher or school administrator is accused of revealing confidential records to other persons without parental consent, he or she cannot be sued by the parent for damages. The Supreme Court ruled that the federal statute's only remedy was through FPCO, which has the power with the approval of the Secretary of Education to withhold a district's federal funding if the rules are not followed. (See *Gonzaga Univ. v. Doe* [U.S. Supreme Court, 2002] on the CD. Also see § 99.67 of the FERPA regulations for the steps FPCO must follow before taking action to terminate federal funding because of a system's policy or practice of violating the nondisclosure rules.) Violating children's

CAUTION

There may be state laws beyond the scope of this book allowing parents to seek damages for nondisclosure violations in state courts.

rights under FERPA could subject a school employee to disciplinary action from the school system. States, however, may impose stiffer penalties.

Guardian ad Litem Rights and Access to Confidential Records

A guardian ad litem (GAL) may have access to a student's confidential records without written consent from the parents, assuming the GAL has produced a court order and provided the school with a copy appointing him or her as the child's guardian with the right to review education records. Although a GAL is someone appointed by the court to represent a child's interests while that child is under the supervision of the court, he or she may not make educational decisions for the child *unless* the court order specifies he or she has that power (a rare occurrence) or that person has been lawfully appointed by the school system as the child's surrogate parent.

Participation of Other Agencies in Transition Planning

School systems do not have to ensure the participation of other agencies in IEP team meetings when they are to be involved in the child's transition planning. The school system should make an effort to obtain their participation, but the IDEA has never given them the authority necessary to compel other agencies to attend (Preface, 2006 Final Regulations, p. 46672).

Parent Consent, Confidentiality, and Outside Agencies

A parent can refuse consent to participate in an IEP team meeting, based on the confidentiality rights afforded by FERPA and the IDEA, for outside agencies providing transition services. However, a parent does not have the right to deny participation permission to any other mandated member of the team (Preface, 2006 Final Regulations, p. 46673).

Medical Emergency and Parental Consent

The old FERPA regulations provided no criteria whatsoever for what would constitute a medical emergency under which confidential information could be released without written parental consent, only saying that this provision was to be "strictly construed." Now, after the December 2008 revisions to

FERPA, the school system is to consider the totality of the information available to it, and only if there is an articulable and significant threat to the health or safety of the student or other students may that information be released. The school must, as a condition of exercising this exception, record those reasons in the record as well as the person to whom the information was disclosed (an additional burden not imposed prior to 2008) (§ 99.96). There is still no clear, bright line that would distinguish between significant and non-significant, but the regulations do say that FPCO will not substitute its judgment for that of school personnel as long as they had a rational reason for doing what they did. ("Articulable" was a curious addition, because it really does not seem to add any additional clarity; the dictionary definition of "articulable" merely means it is something someone could put into words. Perhaps implying rational reasons should be written by an English teacher?) There is no specific timeline for recording the reason(s). But those reasons must remain a part of the child's record as long as the record itself is maintained.

Other Federal Agencies and Confidentiality Issues

In addition to meeting those responsibilities required by FERPA, the 2006 Final Regulations (congruent with the Act) address confidentiality in §§ 300.123, 300.610, and 300.612 (which require as part of the prior notification a description of the policies pertaining to the protection of privacy of special education records). As indicated in Chapter 1, those regulations mean that OSERS also has enforcement authority along with FPCO, but complaints about procedural violations under the IDEA would be filed first with the state in accordance with the state policies promulgated in response to 34 Code of Federal Regulations (CFR) 300.123 requiring states to develop their own policies. That decision could then be appealed to OSEP if appropriate by either side; however, complaints alleging a FERPA violation could be filed directly with FPCO in Washington, DC, skipping the state altogether.

PROTECTION OF PUPIL RIGHTS ACT

There are a variety of situations in which the Protection of Pupil Rights Amendment might become especially relevant to mental health personnel working with exceptional children, but one of the most common is when they become involved in class-, school-, or district-wide mental health screenings (e.g., for suicide prevention). See Rapid Reference 9.4.

Parent rights under the PPRA are extensive, and local school boards are required to have policies guaranteeing parents those rights. There have been expensive lawsuits in systems where those rights were not respected. As summarized by FPCO, the Act:

> affords parents certain rights regarding our conduct of surveys, collection and use of information for marketing purposes, and certain physical exams. These include the right to:
>
> Consent before students are required to submit to a survey that concerns one or more of the following protected areas ("protected information survey") if the survey is funded in whole or in part by a program of the U.S. Department of Education (ED)—

1. Political affiliations or beliefs of the student or student's parent;
2. Mental or psychological problems of the student or student's family;
3. Sex behavior or attitudes;
4. Illegal, anti-social, self-incriminating, or demeaning behavior;
5. Critical appraisals of others with whom respondents have close family relationships;
6. Legally recognized privileged relationships, such as with lawyers, doctors, or ministers;
7. Religious practices, affiliations, or beliefs of the student or parents; or
8. Income, other than as required by law to determine program eligibility.

Receive notice and an opportunity to opt a student out of—

1. Any other protected information survey, regardless of funding;
2. Any non-emergency, invasive physical exam or screening required as a condition of attendance, administered by the school or its agent, and not necessary to protect the immediate health and safety of a student, except for hearing, vision,

or scoliosis screenings, or any physical exam or screening permitted or required under State law; and

3. Activities involving collection, disclosure, or use of personal information obtained from students for marketing or to sell or otherwise distribute the information to others.

Inspect, upon request and before administration or use—

1. Protected information surveys of students;
2. Instruments used to collect personal information from students for any of the above marketing, sales, or other distribution purposes; and
3. Instructional material used as part of the educational curriculum. (Family Policy Compliance Office, n.d.)

Standardized Rating Scales and Response to Intervention

A student support team could use behavioral rating scales to measure the effectiveness of behavioral interventions in a multitiered problem-solving process. According to the PPRA, § 1232h(c)(5)(A)(ii) (2002; on CD), if the self-rating survey that you are asking the child to complete is to comply with the provisions of the IDEA 2004 or its implementing regulations, then the PPRA does not apply. However, we still recommend (since student support teams provide regular education support functions, even for children not suspected of a disability) giving parents prior notification and the opportunity to "opt out" before using self-rating scales touching on any of the 8 areas in the context of a multitiered response to intervention process. (None of this would apply to the use of teacher or parent rating forms.)

≋ Rapid Reference 9.4

Any time a school distributes a pupil questionnaire addressing any one of the eight protected areas listed, it must provide parents with a way to inspect the questionnaire before it is given and provide them with an opportunity to "opt out" without penalty to the child.

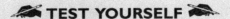 **TEST YOURSELF**

1. **Rights and procedures related to general school records are covered primarily by:**
   (a) IDEA
   (b) ADAAA
   (c) FERPA
   (d) Section 504

2. **Parents or eligible students have the right to request to have an educational record changed and the right to place a statement in their educational record, if they believe it contains inaccurate or misleading information.**
   True or False

3. **Once a school has completed an evaluation of a child, it can legally shred the testing materials to protect the sensitive data contained in them.**
   True or False

4. **FERPA allows a teacher to change a student's grades when:**
   (a) the parent asked the teacher to do so because the child needed a higher grade to get into college.
   (b) the teacher recorded the wrong grade.
   (c) the parent believes that his or her child deserved a better grade.
   (d) the teacher believes that the child must obtain a failing grade in order to remain in special education.

5. **Schools have the right to refuse a parent's request to inspect a test record form (protocol) because revealing the content to a layperson would compromise test security.**
   True or False

Answers: 1. c; 2. True; 3. False; 4. b; 5. False

Appendix A

COMMON ABBREVIATIONS AND ACRONYMS

§	Section (plural §§)
1999 Final Regs.	1999 Final Regulations for the IDEA 97 (34 CFR Parts 300 and 301) (Regulations on CD)
2006 Final Regs.	2006 Final Regulations for the IDEA 2004 (34 CFR Parts 300 and 301) (Regulations on CD)
2008 Final Regs.	2008 Final Regulations for the IDEA 2004 as amended
504	Section 504 of the Rehabilitation Act (on CD)
ADA	Americans with Disabilities Act
ADAAA	Americans with Disabilities Act Amendments Act of 2008
ADD	Attention deficit disorder
ADHD	Attention deficit hyperactivity disorder
ALJ	Administrative Law Judge (in some states, "Hearing Officer")
APA	American Psychological Association
APA	American Psychiatric Association (publisher of the *DSM-IV*)
ASHA	American Speech-Language-Hearing Association
AT	Assistive technology
AYP	Adequate yearly progress
AU	Autistic (IDEA classification)
BIP	Behavior intervention plan
CBA	Curriculum-based assessment
CBM	Curriculum-based measurement
CD	Compact disc

CFR or C.F.R.	Code of Federal Regulations
DD	Developmental delay (IDEA classification if adopted by state)
Cir.	Circuit (court)
DSM	*Diagnostic and Statistical Manual of the American Psychiatric Association*
ED	United States Department of Education
ED	Emotional disturbance (see SED)
EHA	Education for All Handicapped Children Act (now IDEA)
et seq.	and the following (e.g., this *and the following* sections of the regulations) (from Latin *et sequens*, *et sequentes*, or *et sequentia*)
ESEA	Elementary and Secondary Education Act
ESY	Extended school year
FAPE	Free appropriate public education
FBA	Functional behavioral assessment
Fed. Reg.	Federal Register
FERPA	Family Educational Rights and Privacy Act
FOIA	Freedom of Information Act
FPCO	United States Department of Education's Family Policy Compliance Office
FR	Federal Register
GAL	Guardian ad litem (may be either a guy or a gal)
G.E.	Grade equivalent (grade-equivalent score) (not to be confused in some literature with GE, which may refer to general education)
G. M. M.	Guy M. McBride
EHLR	*Education for the Handicapped Law Reporter* (now *Individuals with Disabilities Law Reporter*)
HI	Hearing impaired (IDEA Classification)
H.O. or HO	Hearing officer
IAES	Interim alternative educational setting
ID	Intellectual disability (used in lieu of "mental retardation" in many states and now federally)

IDEA	Individuals with Disabilities Education Act
IDEIA	Individuals with Disabilities Education Improvement Act of 2004
IDELR®	Individuals with Disabilities Education Law Report (LRP Publications)
IEE	Independent educational evaluation
IEP	Individualized education program
IFSP	Individualized family services plan
J. O. W.	John O. Willis
LEA	Local education agency (includes public and charter schools)
LRE	Least restrictive environment
MD	Manifestation determination
MDH/MDT	Manifestation determination hearing/ manifestation determination team
MR	Mental retardation; (replaced by Congress in 2010 with the term "intellectual disability" by Rosa's Law). Various states may use either of those terms or another one.
MD	Multiple disabilities (IDEA classification); also manifestation determination
NASP	National Association of School Psychologists
NCLB	No Child Left Behind
NICHCY	National Dissemination Center for Children with Disabilities (all of NICHCY's publications are copyright free)
NPRM	Notice of proposed rule making
OCR	Office for Civil Rights
OHI	Other health impaired (IDEA classification)
OI	Orthopedic impairment (IDEA classification)
OSERS	Office of Special Education and Rehabilitative Services
OSEP	Office of Special Education Programs
OT	Occupational therapy
PBIS	Positive behavioral intervention strategies

PLOP or PLP	Present levels of performance
PPRA	Protection of Pupil Rights Amendment
PSM	Problem-solving model
PT	Physical therapy
R. P. D.	Ron Dumont
RTI	Response to intervention
SHRO	State Hearing Review Officer
SEA	State education agency
Section 504	Section 504 of the Rehabilitation Act
SED	Serious emotional disturbance (IDEA classification prior to 1999. Changed to ED in the 1999 Federal Regulations with no change in substantive meaning.)
SLD	Specific learning disability (IDEA classification)
SLI	Speech or language impairment (IDEA classification if so designated by the state)
SLP	Speech-language pathologist
sped	Special education (*informal*)
spedlaw	Special education law (*informal*)
SSA	Social Security Administration
SSI	Supplementary Security Income
SST	Student support team (commonly used name for problem-solving teams, but LEAs may use their own names)
TBI	Traumatic brain injury (IDEA classification)
v.	Versus, used in court decisions (e.g., "*Doe v. Withers*, 1992")
VI	Visually impaired (IDEA classification)
VR	Vocational rehabilitation
WPN	Written prior notice

Appendix B

Damages Court Cases

ALJ order Forest Grove 2003
  Background for *Forest Grove v. T.A.* Supreme Court case.

A.W. v. The Jersey City Public Schools (2007)
  Overturned *W.B. v. Matula*, 3rd Circuit, 1995, giving parents the right to sue school administrators under Section 1983.

Baird v. Rose (1999)
  Gave parents right to sue for emotional damages.

Barnes v. Gorman (2001)
  Punitive damages may not be awarded under private lawsuits under ADA and Section 504.

Boring v. Buncombe (1998)
  The right to freedom of speech does not apply to the curriculum.

Burke v. Brookline (2006)
  Money damages are unavailable under IDEA except to recompense parents for expenditures related to FAPE.

C.N. v. Ridgewood (2005)
  Third Circuit rules board did not violate students' rights when it administered pupil survey.

Doe v. Withers (1993)
  Parents sue teacher for failure to implement IEP and win damages; subsequent court rulings subsequent to higher court decisions probably would not reach same outcome today.

Fitzgerald v. Barnstable (2009)
  Supreme Court rules parents can sue school officials for discrimination.

Forest Grove v. T.A. Supreme Court (2008)
Supreme Court rules under some circumstances parents can sue for reimbursement of sped expenditures even if he or she had never received sped from the public school system.

Fox v. Travers City Area Public School Board of Education (2010)
Sixth Circuit rules that teacher's complaints were about conditions of employment and, therefore, did not rise to the level of protected speech.

Lamb v. Boonville (2010)
A United States District Court finds a teacher's speech was about the conditions of her employment, not a matter of public concern, and therefore not protected.

Mark H. v. Hamamoto (2010)
Ninth Circuit allows parents to sue for damages under Section 504 when alleging Hawaii knew that their child was being denied access to a public education and failed to investigate properly.

McGreevy v. Stroup (2005)
Third Circuit holds that school administrators may be individually liable for retaliating against a school nurse who advocated for children with disabilities.

Pickering Supreme Court (1968)
Establishes standard for applying free speech protections.

Polera v. Newburgh (2002)
The Second Circuit found that monetary damages are not available under IDEA because such a remedy would be inconsistent with the statute's purpose.

Settlegoode v. Portland Ninth Circuit (1993)
Teacher wins big bucks after claiming retaliation for speech advocating for special education children.

Sturm v. Rocky Hill (2005)
District Court of Connecticut finds that Section 504 does allow for damages when retaliation is alleged.

Sutton Supreme Court (1999)
Supreme Court determines that eligibility for 504 protection is determined based on limitations after considering

mitigating factors; overturned almost entirely by the ADAAA of 2008.

W.B. v. Matula (Overturned) (1995)

Example of a decision reversed by a subsequent decision (see *A.W. v. The Jersey City School Board* above).

Witte v. Clark (1995)

Fourth Circuit allows parents to seek damages when multiply handicapped child forced to eat regurgitated food.

Deaf Guidance

Deaf Students Education Services

"The Department provides additional guidance about part B of the Individuals with Disabilities Education Act (IDEA) and section 504 of the Rehabilitation Act of 1973 (section 504) as they relate to the provision of appropriate education service to students who are deaf."

OSEP Letter from Guard (7/30/2003) re: ASL

"[A]uxiliary aids and services include qualified interpreters who must be able to interpret effectively, accurately, and impartially, both receptively and expressively, using any necessary specialized vocabulary."

OSEP Letter from Hehir (7/15/1997)

Discusses what must be in an education plan for children with hearing impairments.

OCR Letter from Walker re: Qualified Interpreters (10/12/1996)

Testing Resources (2006)

"This guide provides important information about the professional standards relating to the use of tests for high-stakes purposes, the relevant federal laws that apply to such practices, and references that can help shape educationally sound and legally appropriate practices."

Family Educational Rights and Privacy Act (FERPA)

FERPA and H1N1 (2009)

Discusses how student records should be handled during a flu outbreak.

FERPA Disaster Guidance (2010)
Answers questions about the sharing of personally identifiable information from students' education records to outside parties when responding to emergencies, including natural or man-made disasters.

FERPA HIPPA
Discusses when records are covered by FERPA and when HIPAA would apply.

FERPA Regulations (2004)
These final regulations discuss when electronic consents may be accepted.

FERPA Regulations (2009)
Complete copy of 34 CFR Part 99.

FERPA Regulations Amendments (2008)
These amendments implement a provision of the USA Patriot Act and the Campus Sex Crimes Prevention Act . . . The amendments also implement two U.S. Supreme Court decisions interpreting FERPA and make other necessary changes.

FPCO letter to Matthews (9/13/2005)
Discussed the right of parents to inspect test records.

Gonzaga v. Doe (2002)
Supreme Court held that a student could not in his or her individual capacity sue a university for damages under FERPA.

Letter from Rooker (03/02/2005)
Discussed when education records may be destroyed by school under FERPA; IDEA provides additional rights to parents.

Letter from Rooker to Forgione (3/2/2005)
Schools may not release directory information on specific groups of children because the information they belong to a specific group is protected by FERPA.

Owasso v. Falvo Supreme Court (2002)
Supreme Court says it is okay for teachers to have students exchange papers for grading.

Summary of FERPA Changes (2008)
Official summary of changes made in FERPA in 2008.

IDEA Court Decisions

Sellers v. The School Board of the City of Manassas, VA (1998)
Fourth Circuit dismisses damages lawsuit under IDEA and Section 1983

FAPE Rowley v. Hendrick Hudson (1982)
Landmark case that, paraphrasing, guarantees children in sped a Ford but not the Cadillac.

Florence County v. Carter (1998)
Established that parents need not place their children in state-approved schools for special educational services in order to seek compensation as a result of FAPE being denied.

Garret v. Cedar Rapids Supreme Court (1998)
There is no cost limitation on what a school must provide with respect to related services needed for an otherwise eligible child to receive benefit from his or her IEP.

HISD v. Caius (2000)
Grade equivalents used to document more than trivial benefit.

Honig v. Doe (1998)
Established rights later incorporated into the IDEA for students suspended more than ten days (cumulative or consecutive).

Johnson v. Duneland (1996)
Upheld the right of the schools to its own evaluation; however, parts of the decision (e.g., parent consent not required) are no longer applicable due to subsequent amendments to the IDEA.

Larry P. v. Riles (1984)
Ninth Circuit case banning intelligence tests for African American children in California; no other circuit has reached a similar finding.

Light v. Parkway (1994)
Set formal standards for obtaining a *Honig* injunction.

LRE Sacramento v. Holland (1994)
Parent prevails in lawsuit seeking reimbursement for private school after school denied kindergarten child with 44 IQ opportunity for inclusion.

Pasatiempo v. Aizawa (1996)
Established right of parents seeking evaluations for special education to due process.

Riley v. Ambach (1981)
Early case regarding the criteria used to determine a severe discrepancy for children suspected of SLD.

Schaefer v. Weast (2005)
Party bringing the lawsuit bears burden of proof.

Springer v. Fairfax (1998)
Fourth Circuit applies "social maladjustment" clause to student seeking Emotionally Disturbed classification.

IDEA Regulations and Section 1983

Supplemental Federal Regulations (2008)
Amendments to the 2006 Final Regulations addressing a number of issues including parental consent for sped and related services.

Supplemental Federal Regulations 32CFR160 (2007)
Provides additional leeway for LEAs with respect to accountability issues for students not likely to meet state standards.

Final Federal 1999 Regulations
The Final Regulations for the IDEA '97; for historical reference.

Final 2006 Regulations for IDEA 2004
Federal regulations for 34 CFR Part 300.

Final 1999 Regulations (paginated)
The same as the Final Federal Regulations 1999 above, except with page numbers from the federal register.

IDEA 2004 Statute

Rosas Law (2010)
An act of Congress amending several laws by changing "mental retardation" to "intellectual disability."

Section 1983 Statute (last amended 1996)

Learning Disability Summit (2001) and Yes, Virginia (2001)

OSEP had realized for some time that there is concern over the identification and assessment procedures for LD. The 2001 Washington summit served as follow-up to the 1997 IDEA regulations that called for careful review of research findings, expert opinion, and practical knowledge regarding the evaluation of children suspected of having a specific learning disability and was a first step in fulfilling OSERS' promise to address flaws in the identification of SLD children in the next reauthorization of the IDEA. The executive summaries on the accompanying CD reflect the research that served as a foundation for the changes seen in the IDEA 2004 and the Final Regulations for the IDEA 2004 in 2006.

Early last year, OSEP began developing a process to open a discussion on the identification and assessment of children with learning disabilities. The primary goal is to synthesize and organize the most current and reliable research available on key issues in learning disabilities.

Fletcher Evidence-Based Evaluation
   Classification of Learning Disabilities: An Evidence-Based Evaluation.

Fuchs Final
   Is "Learning Disabilities" Just a Fancy Term for Low Achievement? A Meta-Analysis of Reading Differences between Low Achievers with and without the Label.

Gresham Response to Intervention
   Responsiveness to Intervention: An Alternative Approach to the Identification of Learning Disabilities.

Hallahan History
   Learning Disabilities: Historical Perspectives.

Jenkins Early Identification
   Early Identification and Intervention for Young Children with Reading/Learning Disabilities.

Kavale Discrepancy
   Discrepancy Models in the Identification of Learning Disability.

MacMillan Operational Definition
   Learning Disabilities as Operationally Defined by Schools.

Torgeson Processing Assessment
   Empirical and Theoretical Support for Direct Diagnosis of Learning Disabilities by Assessment of Intrinsic Processing Weaknesses.

Wise Clinical Judgment
   Clinical Judgments in Identifying and Teaching Children with Language-Based Reading Difficulties.

These articles were not part of the Washington Summit: "Yes, Virginia" and the Stakeholders Consensus statement.
The Stakeholders Consensus statement reflects the consensus of ten organizations with a stake in SLD identification practices at a conference sponsored by OSEP in 2002. Participants included:
Association for Higher Education and Disability (AHEAD)
American Speech-Language-Hearing Association (ASHA)
Council for Exceptional Children's Division for Communicative Disabilities and Deafness (DCDD)
Council for Exceptional Children's Division for Learning Disabilities (DLD)
Council for Learning Disabilities (CLD)
Learning Disabilities Association of America (LDA)
International Dyslexia Association (IDA)
International Reading Association (IRA)
National Association of School Psychologists (NASP)
National Center for Learning Disabilities (NCLD)

The meeting at which the Stakeholders Consensus statement was generated was sponsored by OSERS in 2002.

"Yes, Virginia" is an article by the authors of this book in 2001 detailing ways in which eligibility groups could responsibly, ethically, and legally apply discrepancy criteria using clinical judgment.

Stakeholders Consensus Statement (2002)

Yes, Virginia
Authors' 2001 article on the application of ability achievement discrepancy requirements.

OCR Letters
Joint Policy Memorandum on ADD (1991)
OSERS and OCR explain the eligibility rights of children with ADD.

Letter from Lim re: ADD (1993)
OCR explains the obligation of schools to evaluate children with ADD.

Letter from Monroe to Colleague (2007)
Discusses rights of children transitioning to postsecondary institutions.

Letter to Zirkel re: Section 504 FAPE
 Explains OCR's interpretation of schools' obligation to provide
 disabled children with FAPE.

OCR on Section 504

34 CFR 104 Section 504 Regulations
 Complete regulations in pdf format.

ADA Amendment (2008)
 Expanded definition of disabilities; reversed Supreme Court
 decision in Sutton.

ADA and 504 URLs
 Authors' recommended list of on-line references.

Letter to Runkel
 Discussed a variety of grading issues with respect to disabled
 children.

Frequently Asked Questions about Section 504 and the Education of
Children with Disabilities
 This resource document clarifies pertinent requirements of Section
 504; authoritative and highly recommended by the authors.

OCR FAPE 504
 This pamphlet addresses these questions:
 • Who is entitled to a free appropriate public education?
 • How is an appropriate education defined?
 • How is a free education defined?

Student Placement in Elementary and Secondary Schools and Section
504 and Title II of ADA
 Concisely addresses schools responsibility to evaluate and place
 disabled children under Section 504 and the ADA.

Students with Disabilities Preparing for Postsecondary Education
 Addresses the differences students may expect in the rights
 they have under 504 in public school and institutions of higher
 learning.

The Use of Tests in High Stakes
 Addresses the rights of children with disabilities to participate in
 high-stakes testing with appropriate accommodations.

OSEP Letters

Note: While OSERS/OSEP may provide only informal guidance that is not binding on school systems, their opinions nevertheless may be persuasive in a court of law.

Clarification Re: Joint Memorandum (1992)
> Clarifies OSER/OCR Joint Memorandum from 1991 in saying that schools not obligated to test for ADD if they do not suspect a disability; but parents' due process rights would apply.

Cox Revocation of Consent (2009)
> Clarifies schools obligations when parents disagree over revocation of consent.

Letter from Guard to Shuster (2007)
> Explains additional rights to parents granted by IDEA with respect to education records.

Hagar Letter on Reevaluations (2007)
> Explains under what conditions written parental consent is required.

Letter from Guard (2007)
> Discussed differences between federal and other groups definition of SLD.

Letter from Hehir to Assistant Superintendent (1996)
> Discussed the role state agencies may play in defining terms vaguely defined in the federal regulations.

Letter to Hoekstra (2000)
> Provides informal guidance on the appropriateness of school personnel requiring children to be medicated as a condition of service; superseded by federal prohibitions in the IDEA 2004.

Letter to OSEP from Wisconsin (1996)
> Wisconsin's response to OSEP's concerns that it was limiting SLD entitlements to children with "average" intelligence.

Letter to Runkel (2008)
> OSEP's clarification of states' responsibilities when disproportionality is suspected.

Lillie Felton Letter (1994)
> Addresses a number of issues with respect to the factors schools should consider in determining entitlement.

OSEP Search Engine by Quarter
Search by date for OSEP letters.

Posny to Clark (2007)
Interpretation of the phrase "adversely affects educational performance" especially with respect to SLI children.

Recording IEP Meeting (2003)
OSEP's position on the use of tape recorders or videotapes at team meetings.

Riley to Redacted (2000)
Addresses, among other things, parent complaints that LEAs were not advising parents of their rights to a free evaluation at district expense.

Search OSEP Letters by Topic Links
Office search engine of OSEP letters by topic.

SLD Eligibility (2008)
OSEP opines that once a child is found eligible as SLD in one area, he or she need not be found eligible in other areas if he or she needs sped in those areas in order to receive FAPE.

OCR, Title VI, and Title IX

Archived High-Stakes Testing
OCR study of legal and ethical standards applicable to the assessment of LEP and deaf or hearing impaired children.

Federal Regulations for Title VI
Regulations prohibiting discrimination based on race, color, or national origin.

Letter from Ali (2010)
Guidelines and standards for determining what is simple bullying and what rises to the level of discrimination.

OCR Questions and Answers on the Rights of Limited English Learners
Brief Q and A on the basic rights of children with limited English in public schools.

OCR re: Identification of Discriminations and the Denial of Services on the Basis of National Origin
"The purpose of this memorandum is to clarify D/HEW policy on issues concerning the responsibility of school districts to provide

equal educational opportunity to national origin-minority group children deficient in English language skills."

OCR re: The Provision of an Equal Education Opportunity to Limited
Similar to the above, provides historical background and guidance to schools with respect to Limited English Proficient students.

Part 106 Nondiscrimination on the Basis of Sex
1975 regulations prohibiting "discrimination on the basis of sex in any education program or activity receiving Federal financial assistance, whether or not such program or activity is offered or sponsored by an educational institution as defined in this part."

Plyler v. Doe (1982)
Landmark Supreme Court decision giving children, regardless of their national origin, a right to a public school education.

Racial Incidents and Harassment against Students
"[I]nvestigative guidance, under title VI of the Civil Rights Act of 1964, that has been provided to the Office for Civil Rights (OCR) Regional Directors on the procedures and analysis that OCR staff will follow when investigating issues of racial incidents and harassment against students at educational institutions."

Sex Harassment (2008)
OCR guidance on addressing sexual harassment in public schools.

Sex Harassment (2006)
OCR guidance on addressing sexual harassment in public schools (historical document).

Sexual Harassment (1998)
OCR guidance on addressing sexual harassment in public schools (historical document).

Sexual Harassment Guidance (2001)
OCR guidance on addressing sexual harassment in public schools (historical document).

OSERS OSEP Guidance

ADHD Topic Brief
> Archived document summarizing OSEP's positions on ADD
> assessment and eligibility.

Alignment with NCLB
> One of the goals of Congress in 2004 was to bring the IDEA more
> into alignment with No Child Left Behind (formerly the ESEA);
> this summarizes the changes made to meet that goal.

Changes in Evaluation and Reevaluation (2006)
> Summarizes the changes in the IDEA 2004 Final Regulations
> (2006) regarding schools' assessment responsibilities.

Children with Disabilities Enrolled by their Parents in Private Schools
> "This document addresses significant changes from preexisting
> regulations to the final regulatory requirements regarding children
> enrolled by their parents in private schools."

Discipline Q and A (2009)
> A Q and A on OSEP's most current interpretation of its own
> regulations regarding discipline; supersedes the next documents.

Discipline (2006)
> Another in the OSEP series of documents bringing together the
> regulatory changes regarding specific topics; superceded by 2009
> Q and A on discipline.

Disproportionality and Overidentification
> Guidelines for the states in addressing disparate impact
> (disproportionality) in special education on minority populations.

Disproportionality Questions and Answers (2007)
> A Q and A on the burdens imposed on public school systems when
> disparate impact is found in special education programs.

Early Intervening Services
> Addresses the regulatory requirements regarding the use of federal
> special education funds for early intervening services.

Guidance for Visually Impaired and Blind
> Official guidance on the requirements imposed by the federal
> regulations for the IDEA as reported in the 2000 Federal Register.

History of IDEA
An archived OSEP document detailing this history of federal special education law through the IDEA 97.

Identification of SLD (2006)
Summarizes the federal regulatory requirements regarding the assessment of SLD.

IEP Questions and Answers (2010)
Interpretation of the 2006 Final Regulations Regarding IEPs in a Q-and-A format.

IEP (2006)
A handy-dandy handout summarizing the federal regulatory requirements for an IEP in the 2006 Final Regulations

IEP Team and Changes to the IEP (2006)
Summarizes regulatory changes from 1999 to 2006 in IEP development; superseded by the next Q and A.

Mediation Questions and Answers
OSEP Memorandum "Questions and Answers on Mediation" (11/30/00) included for historical reference only.

Model Form Compendium
Congress in the IDEA 2004 required the U.S. Department of Education to develop model forms including a notice of procedural safeguards, prior written notice, and the IEP. These forms were provided in response to that requirement. Readers should are cautioned that these forms may not address all their state requirements.

OSERS Transportation (2009)
Informal guidance on IDEA 2004 regulations regarding transportation as a related service

OSEP Topic Briefs Due Process Hearings
Addresses changes in requirements that took place in 2005; it does not address any regulatory changes that might have occurred in 2006.

OSEP Topic Briefs Highly Qualified Teachers
Addresses changes made in statutory requirements effective in 2005.

OSEP Topic Briefs Statewide Assessments
Addresses changes made by the IDEA 2004 that were effective on
July 1, 2005.

OSERS Letter on Reevaluations (2007)
Letter from Hagar answering questions on reevaluations in a
Q-and-A format.

Pasternack PowerPoint® 2002
A presentation by Robert Pasternack, assistant secretary for
OSERS, at NASP in 2002; provided an early warning regarding
OSERS opinion regarding "The Demise of IQ Test for Children
with Learning Disabilities."

Procedural Safeguards Mediation
Addresses changes made in 2006 Final Regulations regarding the
use of mediation in dispute resolution.

Procedural Safeguards Resolution Meeting and Due Process Hearings
"This document addresses the final regulatory requirements
regarding resolution meetings and significant changes from
preexisting [pre-2006] regulatory requirements regarding due
process hearings."

Procedural Safeguards Surrogates Notice and Consent
"This document primarily addresses significant changes to the
preexisting regulatory requirements regarding surrogate parents,
notice and parental consent."

Procedural Safeguards Questions and Answers
"Questions and Answers on Procedural Safeguards and Due
Process Procedures for Parents and Children with Disabilities"; this
June 2009 document supercedes all previous Q and As on this topic.

Questions and Answers re: Private Schools
A topic brief on the rights of children placed by their parents in
private school settings.

Questions and Answers on Mediation
Same content as in Mediation overheads above, but in handout
format

Secondary Transition
"This document addresses significant changes from preexisting regulations to the final [2006] regulatory requirements regarding secondary transition."

Special Education and Homelessness
Provides "information to assist with implementation of the requirements of the Individuals with Disabilities Education Act (IDEA) and its implementing regulations and the McKinney-Vento Homeless Assistance Act (McKinney-Vento Act)."

State Complaint Procedures
"This document addresses significant changes from preexisting regulations to the final regulatory requirements [2006] regarding state complaint procedures."

Part C References and Links
Code of Federal Regulations
34CFR303, "Early Intervention Program for Infants and Toddlers with Disabilties" (1999); OSERS has issued no implementing regulations since publication of the IDEA 2004.

Growing Up Naturally
Sample state guidance from North Carolina; not legally binding anywhere.

Letter from Guard to Ingram re: Consent (2009)
Is a parent signature required for any change to a child's Part C program?

Letter from Posny to Foreman (2007)
Transition from Part C to Part B and "stay put."

Letter from Posny to Kane (2010)
A service provider asks whether the term "peer-reviewed research" applies just to interventions or to the frequency and intensity of those interventions.

Links to State Regulations for Part C

OSERS IDEA Changes in Part C
A summary of the statutory changes affecting state obligations under Part C.

PPRA

Protection of Pupil Rights
> Statutory excerpts from Title 20 U.S.C. Section 1232h Protection of pupil rights.

FPCO Letter to School Superintendents (2009)
> Letter from Paul Gammill, Family Policy Compliance Office (FPCO), to chief school executive officers regarding the application of the PPRA to public schools.

Model Notification
> The PPRA requires parents to be notified of their rights under that act; this is FPCO's model notification.

PPRA-FERPA Letter to Superintendents
> Similar to the model notification above but also includes sample FERPA notification.

PPRA for Parents
> A very brief explanation of parent rights under the PPRA provided by FPCO.

State and Federal Links and Book Reference

The remaining documents on the CD include reference links to government agencies, state codes, and references with links for the reader's convenience.

References

Aaron, P. G. (1997). The impending demise of the discrepancy formula. *Review of Educational Research, 67*(4), 461–502.

A.E. v. Independent Sch. Dist. No. 25, of Adair Co., OK, 936 F.2d 472, 476 (17 IDELR 950, 952) (10th Cir. 1991).

Alexandra R. v. Brookline School District, U.S. Dist. Civil No. 06-cv-0215-JL, Opinion No. 2009 DNH 136 (2009). Retrieved from http:// media. nashuatelegraph.com/assets/Brooklinelawsuit.pdf

Alfonso, V. C., Johnson, A., Patinella, L., & Rader, D. E. (1998). Common WISC-III examiner errors: Evidence from graduate students in training. *Psychology in the Schools, 35*, 119–125.

American Educational Research Association, American Psychological Association, & National Council on Measurement in Education. (1999). *Standards for educational and psychological testing.* Washington, DC: American Psychological Association.

American Psychiatric Association. (2000). *Diagnostic and statistical manual of mental disorders* (4th ed., Text Revision) (*DSM-IV-TR*). Washington, DC: Author.

American Psychological Association. (2010). Ethical principles of psychologists and code of conduct, 2010 amendments. Retrieved from http://www.apa.org/ethics/code/index.aspx

American Speech-Language-Hearing Association. (1997–2011). Cognitive referencing. Retrieved from www.asha.org/slp/schools/prof-consult/cog-ref.htm

Assistance to States for the Education of Children with Disabilities and the Early Intervention Program for Infants and Toddlers with Disabilities. 34 CFR, Part 300 (1999, March 12).

Assistance to States for the Education of Children with Disabilities and Preschool Grants for Children with Disabilities; Final Rule, 34 CFR, Parts 300 and 301 (2006, August 14). Retrieved from http://idea.ed.gov/download/finalregulations.pdf

Associated Press. (2004, December 8). Girl with digestive disease denied Communion: 8-year-old cannot consume wheat wafers. Retrieved from www.msnbc.msn.com/id/5762478/

A.W. v. Jersey City Public Schools, United States Court of Appeals, 486 F.3d 791, No. 05–2553 (3rd Cir. 2007). Retrieved from http:// scholar.google.com/scholar_case?case=3649144988016233003&hl=en&as_sdt=2&as_vis=1&oi=scholarr

Babb v. Knox County School System, 965 F.2d 104, 107 (6th Cir. 1992).

Baird v. Rose, 192 F.3d 462, (4th Cir. 1999). Retrieved from http://wrightslaw.com/law/caselaw/4th_Baird_Rose_9910.htm

Barnes v. Gorman, 536 U.S. 181 (2002). Retrieved from www.law.cornell.edu/supct/pdf/01-682P.ZS and www.law.cornell.edu/supct/html/01-682.ZS.html

Bierce, A. (1911/1958). *The devil's dictionary.* New York, NY: Dover.

Bijou, S. W. (1942). The psychometric pattern approach as an aid to clinical assessment—A review. *American Journal of Mental Deficiency, 46,* 354–362.

Boring v. Buncombe County Bd of Educ., 136 F.3d 364 (4th Cir. 1998). Retrieved from http://scholar.google.com/scholar_case?case=14862244195086718285&hl=en&as_sdt=2&as_vis=1&oi=scholarr

Bradley, R., Danielson, L., & Hallahan, D. P. (Eds.). (2002). *Identification of learning disabilities: Research to practice.* Mahway, NJ: Erlbaum.

Brody v. Dare County Public Schools. State Hearing Review, North Carolina, 1997. Retrieved from www.wrightslaw.com/law/caselaw/case_Brody_RO_decision.html. See also www.wrightslaw.com/advoc/articles/ltr_to_stranger_brody.html

Brody, L., & Brody, Z. (1996). *Letter to a stranger.* Retrieved from www.wrightslaw.com/advoc/articles/ltr_to_stranger_brody.html

Brosig, A. D. (2010, March 16). Board quashes report alleging teachers falsified records. *Mexia News,* p. 1. Retrieved from www.mexiadailynews.com/index.asp?Story=2203.

Brown-Chidsey, R., & Steege, M. W. (2005). *Response to intervention: Principles and strategies for effective practice.* New York, NY: Guilford Press.

Burke & Rolfhamre v. Brookline School District, U.S. App. LEXIS 28865; 257 Fed. Appx. 335, No. 07–1645 (1st Cir. 2007). Retrieved from www.lexisone.com/lx1/caselaw/freecaselaw?action=OCLGetCaseDetail&format=FULL&sourceID=gdif&searchTerm=eSCU.egfa.UYGY.dcaT&searchFlag=y&l1loc=FCLOW

Burke v. Brookline Sch. Dist., U.S. Supreme Court, 07–1175 U.S. LEXIS 4983, certiori denied (2008). Retrieved from http://supreme.lp.findlaw.com/supreme_court/orders/2007/061608pzor.pdf

Buros Center for Testing. (n.d.). *Mental measurements yearbooks.* Retrieved from www.unl.edu/buros/; and http:// buros.unl.edu/buros/jsp/search.jsp

Canter, A. (2001a). Test protocols, Part I: Right to review and copy. *Communiqué, 29*(7). Retrieved from www.nasponline.org/publications/cq/cq297protocols1.aspx

Canter, A. (2001b). Test protocols, Part II: Storage and disposal. *Communiqué, 30*(1). Retrieved from www.nasponline.org/publications/cq/cq301protocolsII.aspx

Canter, A. (2002). Copying protocols to parents: Clarification of FERPA requirements. *Communiqué, 31*(1). Retrieved from www.nasponline.org/publications/cq/cq311protocols.aspx

Canter, A. (2005). Test protocols and parents rights—to copies? *Communiqué, 34*(1). Retrieved from www.nasponline.org/publications/cq/cq341protocols.aspx

Caroline T. v. Hudson School District, 915 F.2d 752, No. 90–1245 (1st Cir. 1990). Retrieved from http://ftp.resource.org/courts.gov/c/F2/915/915.F2d.752.90–1245.html

Carroll, L. (1865/1962). *Alice's adventures in wonderland.* London, UK: Macmillan.

Carter v. Florence Cty, U.S. Dist. Court, South Carolina, Florence Division, 17 EHLR 452, 1991. Retrieved from www.wrightslaw.com/law/caselaw/case_carter_usdist_sc.htm

Cedar Rapids v. Garret F., 526 U.S. 66 (1999). Retrieved from www.wrightslaw.com/law/caselaw/case_Cedar_Rapids_SupCt_990303.htm and www.law.cornell.edu/supct/html/96–1793.ZS.html

Civil Rights Act. Civil action for deprivation of rights. 42 USC § 1983. Retrieved from www.law.cornell.edu/uscode/42/1983.html

Community Alliance for Special Education & Protection and Advocacy, Inc. (2005). *Special education rights and responsibilities* (9th ed.). San Francisco, CA: Author. Retrieved from www.pai-ca.org/pubs/504501.htm

Condon, R. J. (2006, July 6). Letter to Hon. Joel I. Klein, Chancellor, New York City Public Schools. Retrieved from www.nycsci.org/reports/08–06%20Lovenheim%20letter%20to%20klein.pdf

Conejo Valley Unified Sch. Dist., 1985–86 EHLR DEC. 507:213, 214 (SEA Cal. 1985).

Corpus Christi Independent Sch. Dist., 18 IDELR 1281, 1282 (SEA Tex. 1992).

Cronbach, L. J. (1957). The two disciplines of scientific psychology. *American Psychologist, 12*, 671–684.

Crouse, S. L. (1990). Do not be consumed by differing LD discrepancy formulas. *Communiqué,* Newsletter, *18*(6), 14.

Cummins, J. (1979). Cognitive/academic language proficiency, linguistic interdependence, the optimum age question and some other matters. *Working Papers on Bilingualism, 19*, 121–129.

Dallas Sch. Dist. v. Richard C., 24 IDELR 241, 244–45 (Pa. Commw. Ct. 1996).

Dehn, M. J. (2006). *Essentials of processing assessment.* Hoboken, NJ: Wiley.

Dickson, P. (1978). *The official rules.* New York, NY: Delacorte Press.

Dixon, S. G., Eusebio, E. C., Turton, W. J., Wright, P. W. D., & Hale, J. B. (2010). *Forest Grove School District v. T.A.* Supreme Court case: Implications for school psychology practice. *Journal of Psychoeducational Assessment.* Published online before print November 28, 2010, doi: 10.1177/0734282910388598.

Doctors not needed to diagnose attention deficit disorder, ED says. (1992). *Education of the Handicapped, 18*(11), 5.

Doe v. Bd of Educ. of the State of Connecticut, 753 F. Supp. 65, 17 EHLR 37, 39 (D. Conn. 1990).

Doe v. Sequoia Union High School District, 1987–88 EHLR DEC. 559:133, 135 (N.D. Cal. 1987).

Doe v. Withers, West Virginia Circuit Court (20 IDELR 422) (1992). Retrieved from www.faculty.piercelaw.edu/redfield/library/case-doe.v.withers.htm. See also www.wrightslaw.com/law/caselaw/case_Doe_Withers_Juryorder.html

Dumont, R., Willis, J. O., & McBride, G. M. (2001). Yes, Virginia, there is a severe discrepancy clause, but is it too much ado about something? *School Psychologist, 55* (1), 1, 4–13, 15. Retrieved from www.indiana.edu/~div16/the_school_psychologist.pdf

Educational Testing Service Office of Disability Policy. (2007). *Policy statement for documentation of a learning disability in adolescents and adults* (2nd ed.). Princeton, NJ: Author. Retrieved from www.ets.org/disabilities/documentation/documenting_learning_disabilities/

Educational Testing Service. (n.d.). Disability documentation policy statements and forms. Retrieved from www.ets.org/disabilities/documentation/

Elliott, C. D. (2007). An outline of the Rasch Model. In C. D. Elliott, *Differential ability scales (2nd ed.). Introductory and technical handbook* (pp. 265–272). San Antonio, TX: Psychological Corporation.

Embretson, S. E., & Hershberger, S. L. (Eds.) (1999). *The new rules of measurement: What every psychologist and educator should know.* Mahwah, NJ: Erlbaum.

Embretson, S. E., & Reise, S. P. (2000). *Item response theory for psychologists.* Mahwah, NJ: Erlbaum.

Emery Unified Sch. Dist., 22 IDELR 1071, 1072 (SEA Cal. 1995).

Encarta® World English Dictionary [North American Edition]. (2009). Developed for Microsoft by Bloomsbury Publishing Plc. Retrieved from http://encarta.msn.com/dictionary_/pervasive.html

Errol B. v. Houston ISD, Texas Section 504 Hearing (1995, October 26).

Exceptional Children Division, Public Schools of North Carolina. (n.d.). Screening and evaluation for serious emotional disability. Guidance issued by the Division. Retrieved from www.ncpublicschools.org/ec/supportprograms/resources/screening/

Exceptional Children Division, Public Schools of North Carolina. (2006, September 19). Guidelines for Speech-Language Pathology Services in Schools. Retrieved from www.ncpublicschools.org/

Fairfax County Pub. Sch., 22 IDELR 998, 999 (SEA Va. 1995).

Family Educational Rights and Privacy Act. (2004, April 21). Regulations Final Rule, Part V, 34 CFR, Part 99. Retrieved from www2.ed.gov/legislation/FedRegister/finrule/2004–2/042104a.pdf (see also www2.ed.gov/policy/gen/guid/fpco/pdf/ferparegs.pdf)

Family Educational Rights and Privacy Act. (2008, December 9). Regulations Final Rule, Part II, 34 CFR, Part 99. Retrieved from www.nacua.org/documents/FERPA_FinalRule.pdf

Family Policy Compliance Office. (n.d.). Model notification of rights under the Protection of Pupil Rights Amendment (PPRA). Washington, DC: U.S. Department of Education. Retrieved from www2.ed.gov/policy/gen/guid/fpco/pdf/modelnotification.pdf

Family Policy Compliance Office. (2002, July 18). Letter from Rooker to Anonymous. Retrieved from www.pattan.net/files/OSEP/CY2002–3qu/Anonymous3.pdf

Family Policy Compliance Office. (2005, March 2). Letter to Austin Independent School District (TX) re: Disclosure of special education records under Open Records Law. FERPA Online Library. Retrieved from www2.ed.gov/policy/gen/guid/fpco/ferpa/library/tx030205.html

Family Policy Compliance Office. (2005, September 13). Letter from Rooker to Matthews. Retrieved from www2.ed.gov/policy/gen/guid/fpco/ferpa/library/carrollisd091305.html

Fauquier County Pub. Sch., 20 IDELR 579, 583 (SEA Va. 1993).

Fitzgerald v. Barnstable School Committee, 129 S. Ct. 788 (2009). Retrieved from 0 http://scholar.google.com/scholar_case?case=18375651420170098873&q=fitzgerald+v.+barnstable+school+committee&hl=en&as_sdt=4000000002&as_vis=1. See also www.law.cornell.edu/supct/html/07–1125.ZS.html

Fletcher, J. M., Denton, C., & Francis, D. J. (2005). Validity of alternative approaches for the identification of LD: Operationalizing unexpected underachievement. *Journal of Learning Disabilities, 38*, 545–552.

Fletcher, J. M., Francis, D., Rourke, B., Shaywitz, S. & Shaywitz, B. (1992). The validity of discrepancy-based definitions of reading disabilities. *Journal of Learning Disabilities, 25*, 555–561.

Florence County School Dist. Four v. Carter, Supreme Court of the United States, 510 US 7 (1993). Retrieved from http://scholar.google.com/scholar_cas e?case=5947486327700586383&q=carter+v.+florence+cty&hl=en&as_ sdt=4000000002&as_vis=1

Forest Grove v. T.A., 08–305, 557 U. S. _____ (2009). Retrieved from http:// www.law.cornell.edu/supct/html/08-305.ZS.html and http:// supreme.justia. com/us/557/08-305/opinion.html

Fox v. Traverse City Area Pub. Sch. Bd of Educ., 605 F.3d 345 (6th Cir. 2010). Retrieved from http://scholar.google.com/scholar_case?case=17161771016834 675556&q=fox+v.+traverse&hl=en&as_sdt=4000000002&as_vis=1

Geisinger, K. F., Spies, R. A., Carlson, J. F., & Plake, B. S. (Eds.). (2007). *The seventeenth mental measurements yearbook.* Lincoln, NB: University of Nebraska Press.

Goleta Union Elementary School District v. Ordway, 248 F. Supp. 2d 936 (C.D. Cal. 2002). Retrieved from www.wrightslaw.com/law/caselaw/2003/ca.goleta. ordway.damages.pdf

Gonzaga Univ. v. Doe, 536 U.S. 273 (2002). Retrieved from www.law.cornell.edu/ supct/html/01–679.ZS.html

Hale, J. B., Alfonso, V., Berninger, V., Bracken, B., Christo, C., Clark, M., et al. (2010). Critical issues in response-to-intervention, comprehensive evaluation, and specific learning disabilities identification and intervention: An expert white paper consensus. *Learning Disabilities Quarterly, 33,* 223–236.

Hall v. Vance County Board of Education, 774 F.2d 629 (4th Cir. 1985). Retrieved from www.wrightslaw.com/law/caselaw/NC_Hall_Vance_4th_851010.pdf

Harris Interactive Market Research. (2004, March 10). Evaluating attitudes toward the threat of legal challenges in public schools, final report. Report conducted for Common Good. Retrieved from www.educationworld.com/a_admin/ admin/admin371.shtml

Harris, L. (2001, November 15) Letter to directors, Exceptional Children. North Carolina Exceptional Children Division.

Heartland Area Education Agency 11. (2007–2008). *Heartland special educator procedures: Module four: Decision making practices.* Retrieved from www.aea11.k12. ia.us/spedresources/ModuleFour.pdf

Hendrick Hudson District Bd of Ed. v. Rowley, 458 U.S. 176 (1982). Retrieved from http://supreme.justia.com/us/458/176/

Henry County Bd of Educ., 22 IDELR 761, 763 (SEA Ala. 1995).

Honig v. Doe, 484 U.S. 305 (1988). Retrieved from http://supreme.justia.com/ us/484/305/

Houston Independent School District (HISD) v. Bobby R., Joyce R., & Caius R., 200 F.3d 341 No. 98–20546 (5th Cir. 2000).

In re Morgan Hill Unified Sch. Dist., 19 IDELR 557, 564–65 (SEA, Cal. 1992).

In re Pflugerville Indep. Sch. Dist., 21 IDELR 309, 311 (SEA Tex. 1994).

International Reading Association. (1982, January). Misuse of grade equivalents: Resolution passed by the delegates' assembly of the International Reading Association, April 1981. *Reading Teacher*, 464.

Jaffe, L. E. (2009). *Development, interpretation, and application of the W score and the Relative Proficiency Index* (Woodcock-Johnson III Assessment Service Bulletin No. 11). Rolling Meadows, IL: Riverside. Retrieved from www.riverpub.com/products/wjIIIComplete/pdf/WJ3_ASB_11.pdf

Kavale, K. A. (2001, August). *Discrepancy models in the identification of learning disability*. Paper presented at U.S. Office of Special Education Programs Learning Disabilities Summit: Building a Foundation for the Future, Washington, DC. Executive Summary retrieved from http://ldsummit.air.org/download/Kavale%20Final%2008–10–01.pdf

Kavale, K. A. (2002). Discrepancy models in the identification of learning disabilities. In R. Bradley, L. Danielson, & D. P. Hallahan (Eds.), *Identification of learning disabilities: Research to practice* (pp. 370–371). Mahwah, NJ: Erlbaum.

Kavale, K. A., Kaufman, A. S., Naglieri, J. A., & Hale, J. B. (2005). Changing procedures for identifying learning disabilities: The danger of poorly supported ideas. *School Psychologist, 59*(1), 16–25.

Lamb v. Booneville School District, Dist. Court, N.D. Mississippi, Eastern Div., Civil Action No. 1:08CV254-SA-JAD (2010). Retrieved from http://scholar.google.com/scholar_case?case=16539814423984622329&hl=en&as_sdt=2&as_vis=1&oi=scholarr

Lapides v. Coto, 1987–88 EHLR DEC. 559:387, 390 (N.D. Cal. 1988).

Lassen Elementary v. Parents. California Office of Administrative Hearings Case No. 2010050797 (2010). Retrieved from www.documents.dgs.ca.gov/oah/seho_decisions/2010050797.pdf

Lee, C. J. (2004). Referring and evaluating limited English proficient (LEP) students for programs and services for children with special needs. North Carolina School Psychology Association. Retrieved from http:// ncschoolpsy.org/NCSPALEPProfessionalPracticePaper.pdf

Light v. Parkway C-2 School Dist., 41 F.3d 1223, No. 94–2333 (8th Cir. 1994). Retrieved from www.loislaw.com/livepublish8923/doclink.htp?alias=F8CASE&cite=41+F.3d+1223

Lyons v. Smith, 20 IDELR 164, 167 fn. 11 (D.C.D.C., 1993).

Mark H. v. Hamamoto, No. 09–15754 H., D.C. No.1:00-cv-00282- MLR-LEK (9th Cir. 2010). Retrieved from www.ca9.uscourts.gov/datastore/opinions/2010/08/26/09–15754.pdf

Mather, N., & Healey, W. C. (1990). Deposing the aptitude-achievement discrepancy as the imperial criterion for learning disabilities. *Learning Disabilities: A Multidisciplinary Journal 1*(2), 40–48.

McBride, G. M., Dumont, R., & Willis, J. O. (2004). Response to response to intervention legislation: The future for school psychologists. *School Psychologist, 58*, 3, 86–91, 93.

McGreevy v. Stroup, 413 F.3d 359 (3rd Cir. 2005). Retrieved from http://cases.justia.com/us-court-of-appeals/F3/413/359/616867/

McKinnon, J. A., & Burge, S. (2008, July 3). Safety checkpoints put illegal immigrants in line to lose cars, sometimes more. *Press-Enterprise*. Retrieved from www.pe.com/localnews/immigration/stories/PE_News_Local_S_checkpoint03.44350fa.html

Merrillville Community Schools, Northwest Indiana Special Education Cooperative, 37 IDELR 108 (SEA Ind. 2002).

Mobile County Bd of Educ., 23 IDELR 594, 599 (SEA Ala. 1995).

M.R. v. Lincolnwood Bd of Educ., 843 F. Supp. 1236, 20 IDELR 1323 (N.D. Ill. 1994).

National Association of School Psychologists. (2000). *Professional conduct manual: Principles for professional ethics; guidelines for the provision of school psychological services.* Bethesda, MD: Author. Retrieved from www.nasponline.org/standards/ProfessionalCond.pdf

National Association of School Psychologists. (2010). *Professional conduct manual: Principles for professional ethics 2010.* Bethesda, MD: Author. Retrieved from www.nasponline.org/standards/2010standards/1_%20Ethical%20Principles.pdf

Newport-Mesa Unified v. State of Cal. Dept. of Ed., Dist. Court, CD California, Southern Div. 371 F. Supp. 2d 1170 (2005). Retrieved from http://scholar.google.com/scholar_case?case=7234139377035154397&q=Newport+Mesa+v.+California+Depart+of+Education&hl=en&as_sdt=4000000002&as_vis=1

New York City Sch. Dist. Bd of Educ., 18 IDELR 1326, 1328 (SEA N.Y. 1992).

New York State Education Department. (2010). New York State Law, Regulations and Policy Not Required by Federal Law/Regulation/Policy—Revised January 2010. Retrieved from www.emsc.nysed.gov/specialed/policy/partB/analysis-lawsregs2010.htm

Nondiscrimination on the Basis of Handicap in Programs or Activities Receiving Federal Financial Assistance, 34 CFR, Subtitle B, Chapter 1, pt. 104. Retrieved from www2.ed.gov/policy/rights/reg/ocr/edlite-34cfr104.html

Oakland Unified Sch. Dist., 1985–86 EHLR DEC. 507:191 (SEA Cal., 1985).

Office for Civil Rights. (n.d.) Overview of the agency. Retrieved from www2.ed.gov/about/offices/list/ocr/index.html

Office for Civil Rights. (1984). In re Tri-County, Illinois.

Office for Civil Rights. (1990). St. Charles Community School District, 17 EHLR 18, 1990.

Office for Civil Rights. (1991, July). *Placement of school children with acquired immune deficiency syndrome (AIDS).* Washington, DC: U.S. Department of Education. Retrieved from www2.ed.gov/about/offices/list/ocr/docs/hq53e9.html

Office for Civil Rights. (1992, August 13). Senior Staff Memo, 19 IDELR 894.

Office for Civil Rights. (1996, December 13). Letter to McKethan, 25 IDELR 295, 296.

Office for Civil Rights. (1996, September 30). Dunbar letter to Runkel (25 IDELR 387).

Office for Civil Rights. (2000a). The provision of an equal education opportunity to limited-English proficient students. Retrieved from www.ed.gov/about/offices/list/ocr/eeolep/index.html

Office for Civil Rights. (2000b). The use of tests as part of high-stakes decision-making for students: A resource guide for educators and policy-makers. Retrieved from www2.ed.gov/offices/OCR/archives/pdf/TestingResource.pdf

Office for Civil Rights. (2007). Transition of students with disabilities to postsecondary education: A guide for high school educators. Retrieved from www2.ed.gov/about/offices/list/ocr/transitionguide.html

Office for Civil Rights. (2010). Letter to Colleague from Russyln Ali. Retrieved from www2.ed.gov/about/offices/list/ocr/letters/colleague-201010.pdf

Office of Special Education and Rehabilitative Services. (n.d. a).Welcome to OSERS! Retrieved from www2.ed.gov/about/offices/list/osers/index.html

Office of Special Education and Rehabilitative Services. (n.d. b). IDEA—Reauthorized Statute, Part C Amendments in IDEA 2004. Retrieved from www.nectac.org/~pdfs/calls/2007/vulnerablepops/tb-partc-ammend.pdf

Office of Special Education and Rehabilitative Services. (1980, May 30). Letter from Martin to Dublinske. Retrieved from www.asha.org/uploadedFiles/OSERS-Letter-Policy-Interpretation.pdf

Office of Special Education and Rehabilitative Services. (1991, September 16). Joint policy memorandum. Retrieved from www.wrightslaw.com/law/code_regs/OSEP_Memorandum_ADD_1991.html

Office of Special Education Programs. (formerly Bureau of Education of the Handicapped) (1979). Letter from Irvin to Hafner. EHLR 211:181.

Office of Special Education Programs. (1981). Inquiry of Hill, EHLR 211:259.

Office of Special Education Programs. (1981, April 28). Smith letter to Murphy.

Office of Special Education Programs. (1989, April 28). Smith letter to Murphy.

Office of Special Education Programs. (1990, June 29). Schrag letter to Kennedy.

Office of Special Education Programs. (1994, March 14). Letter to Michel Williams (21 IDELR 73).

Office of Special Education Programs. (1994, May 10). Letter to Lillie/Felton. Digest retrieved from www.dueprocessillinois.org/LillieFelton.html

Office of Special Education Programs. (1996, September 12). Hehir letter to Cole.

Office of Special Education Programs. (1997, January 24). Hehir letter to Matthew.

Office of Special Education Programs. (2007, February 9). Posny letter to Christiansen.

Office of Special Education Programs. (2000, June 3). Riley letter to redacted.

Office of Special Education Programs. (2007, March 8). Posny letter to Clarke. Retrieved from www.pattan.net/files/OSEP/CY2007/Clarke01.pdf

Office of Special Education Programs. (2007, June 29). Letter to Clarke.

Office of Special Education Programs. (2007, August 7). Letter from Guard to Schuster.

Office of Special Education Programs. (2008, June 3). Letter to Anonymous. Retrieved from www.pattan.net/files/OSEP/CY2008/Redactedb060308.pdf

Office of Special Education Programs. (n.d.). *Improving Child Find*. Retrieved from www.childfindidea.org/stages.htm

Owasso Independent School Dist. v. Falvo, 534 U.S. 426 (2002). Retrieved from http://scholar.google.com/scholar_case?case=3859044527801586319&q=Owasso+v.+Falvo&hl=en&as_sdt=4000000002&as_vis=1

Pasatiempo v. Aizawa, 103 F.3d 796, 115 Ed. Law Rep. 314, 19 A.D.D. 826, 96 Cal. Daily Op. Serv. 9216, 96 Daily Journal D.A.R. 15, 203 (9th Cir. 1996). Retrieved from http://ftp.resource.org/courts.gov/c/F3/103/103.F3d.796.94—17092.html

Pasternack, R. H. (2002, March 1). The demise of IQ testing for children with learning disabilities. PowerPoint presentation, National Association of School Psychologists Annual Conference, Chicago, IL. *Communiqué, 30*(7), 41. Adaptation by W. A. Coulter retrieved from http://www.ritap.org/ritap/content/iq.ppt

Pawlisch, J. S. (1996, April 1). Letter to Dr. Thomas Hehir, Director, Office of Special Education Programs.

Peterson, K. M. H., & Shinn, M. R. (2002). Severe discrepancy models: Which best explains school identification practices for learning disabilities? *School Psychology Review, 31*, 459–476.

Pickering v. Board of Ed. of Township High School Dist., 205, Will Cty., 391 US 563 (1968). Retrieved from http://scholar.google.com/scholar_case?case=16997195768089298466&q=pickering+v.+the+board+of+education&hl=en&as_sdt=4000000002&as_vis=1

Plyler v. Doe, 457 U.S. 202 (1982). Retrieved from www.law.cornell.edu/supct/html/historics/USSC_CR_0457_0202_ZO.html

Polera v. Newburgh, 01–7400, 01–7439 (2nd Cir. 2002). Retrieved from www.wrightslaw.com/law/caselaw/2002/2nd.polera.newburgh.504.exhaust.htm

Protection of Pupil Rights Amendment (20 U.S.C. § 1232h; 34 CFR Part 98), as amended by NCLB in 2002. Retrieved from www.gpo.gov/fdsys/pkg/USCODE-2008-title20/html/USCODE-2008-title20-chap31.htm

Rancho Palos Verdes v. Abrams, 544 U.S. 113 (2005). Retrieved from www.law.cornell.edu/supct/pdf/03-1601P.ZS and www.law.cornell.edu/supct/html/03-1601.ZS.html

Reschly, D. J., & Tilly, W. D. (1999). Reform trends and system design alternatives. In D. J. Reschly, W. D. Tilly III, and J. P. Grimes (Eds.), *Special education in transition: Functional assessment and noncategorical programming* (pp. 19–48). Longmont, CO: Sopris West.

Riley v. Ambach, 668 F.2d 635, 80–7600 (2d Cir, July 31, 1981). Retrieved from http://ftp.resource.org/courts.gov/c/F2/668/668.F2d.635.80-7600.465.html

Rogers, C. (2006, August 31). D. A. will charge P.S. 276 psychologist for forgery, falsifying school records. *Canarsie Courier*. Retrieved from www.canarsiecourier.com/news/2006–08–31/TopStories/013.html

Rosenfeld, S. J. (2010, June 8). Must school districts provide test protocols to parents? *Communiqué, 38*. Retrieved from www.nasponline.org/publications/cq/mocq388testprotocols.aspx

Sacramento City School Dist. v. Rachel H., 14 F.3d 1398 (9th Cir. 1994). Retrieved from http:// cases.justia.com/us-court-of-appeals/F3/14/1398/613232/

Sattler, J. M. (2008). *Assessment of children: Cognitive foundations* (5th ed.). San Diego, CA: Author.

Sattler, J. M., & Hoge, R. (2006). *Assessment of children: Behavioral, social and clinical foundations* (5th ed.) San Diego, CA: Author.

School Board of Nassau County v. Arline, 480 U. S. 273 (1987). Retrieved from http://supreme.justia.com/us/480/273/case.html

Sellers v. Manassas, 141 F.3d 524, No. 97–1762 (4th Cir. 1998). Retrieved from
http:// scholar.google.com/scholar_case?case=11755800013565816646&hl=en
&as_sdt=2&as_vis=1&oi=scholarr

Settlegoode v. Portland School District, 02–35260. No. CV-00–00313-ST, (9th Cir.
2004). Retrieved from http://caselaw.findlaw.com/us-9th-circuit/1054316.html

Shinn, M. R. (2002). Best practices in curriculum-based measurement and its use
in a problem-solving model. In A. Thomas & J. Grimes (Eds.), *Best practices in
school psychology IV* (pp. 671–698). Bethesda, MD: National Association of School
Psychologists.

Siegel, L. S. (1998). The discrepancy formula: Its use and abuse. In B. K. Shapiro,
P. J. Accardo, & A. J. Capute (Eds.), *Specific reading disability: A view of the spectrum*
(pp. 123–135). Timonium, MD: York Press.

Slenkovich, J. (1983). *P.L. 94–142 as applied to DSM-III diagnoses: An analysis of
DSM-III diagnoses vis-à-vis special education law.* Cupertino, CA: Kinghorn Press.

Smith, M., III (2009). *The Hippocratic oath and grade equivalents* (Metametrics Position
Paper 1330L). Retrieved from www.lexile.com/m/uploads/grade-equivalents/
HippocraticOathGradeEquivalents.pdf

Springer v. Fairfax County School Board, 134 F.3d 659, 664, 27 IDELR 367 (4th Cir.
1998). Retrieved from http://scholar.google.com/scholar_case?case=51967163
07127639252&hl=en&as_sdt=2&as_vis=1&oi=scholarr

Stanovich, K. E. (1986). Matthew effects in reading: Some consequences of
individual differences in the acquisition of literacy. *Reading Research Quarterly, 21,*
360–407.

Stanovich, K. E. (1993). The construct validity of discrepancy definitions of
reading disability. In G. R. Lyon, D. Gray, J. Kavanagh, N. Krasnegor (Eds.),
*Better understanding learning disabilities: New views from research and their implications for
education and public policies.* (pp. 273–308). Baltimore, MD: Paul H. Brookes.

State of New Jersey. (2006). New Jersey Administrative Code, Title 6a, Education,
Chapter 14, Special Education. Retrieved from www.state.nj.us/education/
code/current/title6a/chap14.pdf

Sturm v. Rocky Hill Board of Education, District Court, D. Connecticut, Case No.
3:03CV666 (AWT) (2005).

Sutton v. United Air Lines, Inc., 527 U.S. 471 (1999). Retrieved from www.law.
cornell.edu/supct/html/97–1943.ZS.html

T.A. v. Forest Grove School District, OAH Case No. 20031306, Oregon
Department of Education Case No. 03-113 (2003, January 26). Retrieved from
http://oah.state.or.us/decisions/Department_of_Education/T_A_Special_
Education_of_FO_03.DOC

Torgeson, J. K. (2002). Empirical and theoretical support for direct diagnosis of
learning disabilities by assessment of intrinsic processing weaknesses. Paper
presented at U.S. Office of Special Education Programs Learning Disabilities
Summit, Building a Foundation for the Future, Washington, DC. Executive
Summary retrieved from www.aea11.k12.ia.us/spedresearch/res1102/
research-ldsummit_article.html

U.S. Department of Health and Human Services & U.S. Department of Education.
(2008, November). Joint guidance on the application of the Family Educational

Rights and Privacy Act (FERPA) and the Health Insurance Portability and Accountability Act of 1996 (HIPAA) to student health records. Retrieved from www2.ed.gov/policy/gen/guid/fpco/doc/ferpa-hipaa-guidance.pdf

VanDerHeyden, A. M., & Burns, M. K. (2010). *Essentials of response to intervention.* Hoboken, NJ: Wiley.

Vitello, P. (2009, October 9). Another landlord worry: Is the elevator kosher? *New York Times.* Retrieved from www.nytimes.com/2009/10/10/nyregion/10elevator.html

Vock, D. (2007, August 24). Tighter license rules hit illegal immigrants. Stateline.org. Retrieved from www.stateline.org/live/details/story?contentId=234828

W.B. v. Matula, United States Court of Appeals, 3rd Circuit No. 95–5033, 67 F.3d. 484 (3rd Cir. 1995). Retrieved from www.wrightslaw.com/law/caselaw/3rd.wb.matula.pdf and ftp.resource.org/courts.gov/c/F3/67/67.F3d.484.95-5033.html

Watkins, M. W. (2009). Errors in diagnostic decision making and clinical judgment. In T. B. Gutkin & C. R. Reynolds (Eds.), *Handbook of school psychology* (4th ed.) (pp. 210–229). Hoboken, NJ: Wiley.

Webster's encyclopedic unabridged dictionary of the English language. (1996). New York, NY: Random House.

Weems v. North Franklin School District, Court of Appeals of Washington, Division 3, Panel Six 19024-2-III. (2002). Retrieved from http://caselaw.findlaw.com/wa-court-of-appeals/1297078.html

Wendling, B. J., & Mather, N. (2009). *Essentials of evidence-based academic interventions.* Hoboken, NJ: Wiley.

West Chester Area Sch. Dist., 18 IDELR 802 (SEA Pa. 1992).

Willis, J. O. (2001). Scoring errors necessitate double-checking protocols. *Today's School Psychologist, 4*(5), 7.

Willis, J. O., & Dumont, R. (n.d.). Mnemonics for five issues in the identification of learning disabilities taken from the three synoptic gospels of the New Testament of the King James Version of the Bible first by Keith Stanovich and later, in imitation, by John Willis and Ron Dumont. Retrieved from http://alpha.fdu.edu/~dumont/psychology/mnemonics_for_five_issues.htm

Wise, B. W., & Snyder, L. (2002). *Judgments in identifying and teaching children with language-based reading difficulties.* Paper presented at the LD Summit, Building a Foundation for the Future, Washington, DC, August 27–28, 2001.

Witte v. Clark County School District, 197 F.3d 1271 (9th Cir. 1999).

Wright, P. W. D. (2003). *Judge finds school official liable for denial of special ed — parents gain tool in fight to force schools meet kids' educational needs.* Retrieved from www.wrightslaw.com/news/2003/ca.goleta.ordway.damages.htm

Wright, P. W. D. (2009, March 31). Damages against teacher who refused to implement iep: Doe v. Withers. Wrightslaw Special Education Law and Advocacy. Retrieved from www.wrightslaw.com/advoc/ltrs/Why_doe_withers.html

Zirkel, P. A., & Thomas, L. B. (2010). State laws for RTI: An updated snapshot. *Teaching Exceptional Children, 42*(3), 56–63. Retrieved from framewelder.com-cache.s3.amazonaws.com/extras/10/pattan_rtii/handouts/Zirkel%20RTI%20Article%20June%202014.pdf and from http:// findarticles.com /p/articles/mi_7749/is_201001/ai_n49422401/pg_5/?tag=content;col1

Annotated Bibliography

American Educational Research Association, American Psychological Association, & National Council on Measurement in Education. (1999). *Standards for educational and psychological testing*. Washington, DC: American Psychological Association.

According to the authors, the 1999 Standards reflected changes in federal law and measurement trends affecting validity, testing individuals with disabilities or different linguistic backgrounds, and new types of tests as well as new uses of existing tests. The Standards, written for the professional and the educated layperson, address professional and technical issues of test development and use in education, psychology, and employment. They were a standard reference used by the Office for Civil Rights in reviewing appropriate testing procedures from a scientific and ethical perspective. (See Office for Civil Rights, 2000.) A revision is in preparation.

American Speech-Language-Hearing Association. (1997–2010). *Cognitive referencing.* Retrieved from: www.asha.org/slp/schools/prof-consult/cog-ref.htm

This publication discusses the problems in cognitive referencing when considering language remediation, provides an update on the literature showing that children can profit from language remediation even when there is no discrepancy between ability and achievement, and recommends that speech-language pathologists not use cognitive referencing as a case management tool.

Dumont, R., Willis, J., & McBride, G. (2001). Yes, Virginia, there is a severe discrepancy clause, but is it too much ado about something? *School Psychologist, 55* (1), 1, 4–13, 15. Retrieved from: www.indiana.edu/~div16/the_school_psychologist.pdf

Although somewhat dated, this article is still relevant for practitioners in states allowing the use of the historical achievement/ability discrepancy methodology and not imposing a rigid formulaic approach to determining eligibility.

Exceptional Children Division, Public Schools of North Carolina. (n.d.). *Screening and evaluation for serious emotional disability.* Guidance issued by the division. http://www.ncpublicschools.org/ec/supportprograms/resources/screening/

This guidance is officially applicable to North Carolina, but it presents a thoughtful and helpful discussion of, and some useful historical insights regarding the thorny issue of identification of emotional disturbance under IDEA regulations, including the especially vexing question of social maladjustment. We recommend it to all team members who participate in the identification of emotional disturbance.

International Reading Association. (1982). Misuse of grade equivalents: Resolution passed by the Delegates Assembly of the International Reading Association, April 1981. *Reading Teacher* (January), 464.

This resolution very succinctly reviews some of the problems with the use of grade-equivalent scores and concludes bluntly that evaluators should simply "abandon the practice of using

grade equivalents to report performance." The Delegates Assembly further "Resolved, that the president or executive director of the Association write to test publishers urging them to eliminate grade equivalents from their tests." This document provides an authoritative opinion that might be useful to evaluators and teams, so it would be worth tracking down and copying. See also http://alpha.fdu.edu/~dumont/psychology/oat_cereal.htm. [NB: This discussion refers to grade-equivalent scores (e.g., "Johnny's score on the reading comprehension test was grade 5.7"), not to grade-based norms versus age-based norms (e.g., "Guy scored in the 93rd percentile by norms for his grade but only the 75th percentile by norms for his age") or readability designations of reading passages (e.g., Ronny easily and accurately read the fifth-grade passage, struggled with the sixth-grade passage, and was unable to read the seventh-grade passage"). Those are entirely different issues.]

Kavale, K. A. (2002). Discrepancy models in the identification of learning disabilities. In R. Bradley, L. Danielson, & D. P. Hallahan (Eds.), *Identification of learning disabilities: Research to practice* (pp. 369–464). Mahwah, NJ: Erlbaum.

There are in the literature many good discussions of the myriad problems with the use of statistical discrepancy models for identification of specific learning disabilities. This is one that we have found particularly helpful.

Lee, C. J. (2004). Referring and evaluating Limited English Proficient (LEP) students for programs and services for children with special needs. North Carolina School Psychology Association. http://www.ncschoolpsy.org/NCSPALEPProfessionalPracticePaper.pdf

The evaluation of Limited English Proficient students poses special challenges for the school evaluator. This relatively brief document, prepared as a Best Practices paper for the North Carolina Exceptional Children Division, summarizes the problems and recommends defensible practices designed to protect children's civil rights. Sample forms that can be adapted locally to standardize the prereferral information gathering process are also provided.

McBride, G. M., Dumont, R., & Willis, J. O. (2004). Response to response to intervention legislation: The future for school psychologists. *School Psychologist, 58*, 3, 86–91, 93. Retrieved from: www.indiana.edu/~div16/publications/school_psychologist_summer_2004.pdf

This article was written during, not after, the 2004 reauthorization of IDEA and discusses some of the probable changes in the roles of school psychologists as state regulations begin to encourage or to require response to intervention as a means or the means of identifying specific learning disabilities.

National Association of School Psychologists. (2010). *Professional conduct manual: Principles for professional ethics 2010.* Bethesda, MD: Author. Retrieved from: www.nasponline.org/standards/2010standards/1_%20Ethical%20Principles.pdf

School psychologists and other professionals involved with special education sometimes find themselves in apparent conflicts between laws, professional ethics, and the demands of supervisors. (Tip: Laws prevail.) Just as we urge readers to download and save copies of federal and state regulations, we also recommend maintaining copies of the current ethical requirements and guidelines of professional organizations to which we belong, such as NASP, APA (www.apa.org/ethics/code/index.aspx), and ASHA (www.asha.org/docs/html/ET2010-00309.html). *There is no substitute for being able to confirm for ourselves precisely what laws, regulations, and standards actually say. Professional organizations amend and revise the codes of ethics, so it is important to check for changes.*

Office for Civil Rights. (2000). *The use of tests as part of high-stakes decision-making for students: A resource guide for educators and policy-makers.* Retrieved from: www2.ed.gov/offices/OCR/archives/pdf/TestingResource.pdf

By way of preface, Norma Cantu, writing for OCR in December 2000, says: ". . . federal civil rights laws affirm good test use practices. Thus, an understanding of the measurement principles related to the use of tests for high-stakes purposes is an essential foundation to better understanding the federal legal standards that are significantly informed by those measurement principles." The document is divided into two major parts; Chapter 1 addresses measurement principles as they apply to the assessment of LEP students and students who are deaf; Chapter 2 summarizes the legal principles that apply and includes a liberal amount of relevant case law from various landmark cases. This guide remains relevant and valuable but does not reflect changes in the law since 2000.

Office for Civil Rights. (2009). *Frequently asked questions about Section 504 and the education of children with disabilities.* Retrieved from: www2.ed.gov/about/offices/list/ocr/504faq.html

This is a revision of a FAQ originally produced by the Chicago office of the Office for Civil Rights and it incorporates changes, particularly changes in the definition of a disability, from the amendments to the Americans with Disabilities Act in 2008. Those amendments specifically required changes in how Section 504 of the Rehabilitation Act of 1973 was applied in determining eligibility. (The definition of "disability" was broadened.)

Office for Civil Rights. (2010). Dear colleague letter. Retrieved from: www2.ed.gov/about/offices/list/ocr/letters/colleague-201010.html

This three-page letter updating OCR's sexual harassment policies is particularly germane because, while lawsuits under Title IX are still relatively rare, they can be very costly for school employees and administrators. This memorandum clarifies, among other things, the difference between bullying (a school disciplinary problem) and harassment rising to the level of a civil rights violation requiring immediate administrative action.

Pasternack, R. H. (2002). The demise of IQ testing for children with learning disabilities. PowerPoint presentation at the National Association of School Psychologists Annual Conference, Chicago, IL, March 1, 2002. Retrieved from http://www.ritap.org/ritap/content/iq.ppt

Pasternack's original PowerPoint appears to be unavailable. The link cited here is to a presentation by W. Alan Coulter, "The demise of IQ testing for children with learning disabilities in Rhode Island: We can be functional," which is "based on" the original presentation by Pasternack, who was at the time Assistant Secretary, Office of Special Education and Rehabilitive Services. In his influential presentation, Pasternack argues very strongly for the elimination of IQ testing from the identification of learning disabilities.

Torgeson, J. K. (2002). Empirical and theoretical support for direct diagnosis of learning disabilities by assessment of intrinsic processing weaknesses. Paper presented at U.S. Office of Special Education Programs Learning Disabilities

Summit: *Building a Foundation for the Future*, Washington, DC. Executive summary retrieved from: www.aea11.k12.ia.us/spedresearch/res1102/research-ldsummit_article.html

Torgeson's executive summary of his paper for the 2001 OSEP Learning Disabilities Summit cites a number of possible advantages to a processing deficit model but notes two difficulties in implementing such a model: (1) we still do not completely understand what psychological processing capabilities are needed to attain good learning outcomes; and (2) it is not always possible to determine with assurance that the "processing deficits" we see identified on processing tests are truly intrinsic to the child and not the result of a lack of appropriate instruction. For those reasons, Torgeson did not recommend that a processing model be adopted in the next reauthorization.

Wright, P. W., & Wright, P. D. (2005). Wrightslaw: IDEA 2004, Parts A & B; with commentary, strategies, cross-references. Hartfield, VA: Harbor House Law Press.

Designed for parents, teachers, advocates, and related service providers, this book offers the full text of parts A and B of the Individuals with Disabilities Education Improvement Act of 2004, along with analysis, commentary, resources, and cross-references.

Wright, P. W., & Wright, P. D. (2007). *Wrightslaw: Special education law, 2nd ed.* Hartfield, VA: Harbor House Law Press.

This second edition of the Wrights' Wrightslaw: Special Education Law is an invaluable resource for parents, advocates, educators, and attorneys. It includes very helpful commentary on, and the actual text of, IDEA 2004, the 2006 IDEA Regulations, Section 504, NCLB 2001, FERPA, and McKinney-Vento. There are also two chapters on important case law, a chapter explaining various aspects of special education law, a chapter on the history of special education law, and an annotated list of resources and references. The book is designed to provide clear guidance to the laws and how they can be used to get better services for all children with disabilities.

Zirkel, P. A., & Thomas, L. B. (2010). State laws for RTI: An updated snapshot. *Teaching Exceptional Children, 42*(3), 56–63.

This article provides organized and current information on a rapidly evolving and important aspect of special education law.

Zirkel, P. A. (2005). Section 504, student issues, legal requirements, and practical recommendations. Phi Delta Kappa Educational Foundation.
Or try: http://tinyurl.com/6hapx4z

This short guide is designed to be a practical primer on the interrelated federal civil rights laws concerning disability discrimination, namely, Section 504 of the Rehabilitation Act of 1973 and the Americans with Disabilities Act (ADA) of 1990. This book specifically explores student issues in K–12 public education as they are affected by the requirements of Section 504 and ADA.

Author Index

Subject Index

About the Authors

Guy M. McBride, Ph.D., is a school psychologist and licensed practicing psychologist from Hickory, North Carolina. He served two years in the Peace Corps and taught sixth grade before going to George Peabody College in Nashville, Tennessee in 1968. Interning in Long Beach, New York, he served the next 38 years as a school psychologist in New York and then North Carolina. He retired from the public school system in 2009.

Ron Dumont, Ed.D., NCSP, is a school psychology trainer, professor, and chair of the psychology department at Fairleigh Dickinson University in New Jersey. He was a practicing school psychologist for over 20 years in Massachusetts, New Hampshire, and New York. He began his involvement with special education in 1971 when he was a VISTA volunteer and worked as a teacher in an alternative school. Since then he has continued to work in the special education field as a teacher, administrator, school psychologist, trainer, and expert witness.

John O. Willis, Ed.D., is a certified special education teacher who works as a Specialist in Assessment of Intellectual Functioning (SAIF) for the Regional Services and Education Center in Amherst, New Hampshire. He is Senior Lecturer in Assessment at Rivier College, Nashua, New Hampshire, where he is the instructor for the SAIF Certification Program. He became involved in special education as a volunteer in 1962 and has worked as a teacher, administrator, evaluator, and/or author since 1969. He has been an expert witness for parents and school districts in due process hearings and court cases.

About the CD-ROM

INTRODUCTION

This appendix provides you with information on the contents of the CD that accompanies this book. For the latest information, please refer to the ReadMe file located at the root of the CD.

System Requirements

A computer with a processor running at 120 Mhz or faster

- At least 32 MB of total RAM installed on your computer; for best performance, we recommend at least 64 MB
- A CD-ROM drive

  NOTE: Many popular word processing programs are capable of reading Microsoft Word files. However, users should be aware that a slight amount of formatting might be lost when using a program other than Microsoft Word.

Using the CD with Windows

To install the items from the CD to your hard drive, follow these steps:
1. Insert the CD into your computer's CD-ROM drive. The license agreement appears (for Windows 7, select Start.exe from the AutoPlay window or follow the same steps for Windows Vista).

   The interface won't launch if you have autorun disabled. In that case, click Start➤Run (for Windows Vista and Windows 7, click Start➤All Programs➤Accessories➤Run). In the dialog box that appears, type **D:\Start.exe.** (Replace *D* with the proper letter if your CD drive uses a different letter. If you don't know the letter of your CD drive, see how it is listed under My Computer.) Click OK.

2. Read through the license agreement, and then click the Accept button if you want to use the CD.

3. The CD interface displays. Select the lesson video you want to view.

USING THE CD WITH A MAC

1. Insert the CD into your computer's CD-ROM drive.

2. The CD-ROM icon appears on your desktop, double-click the icon.

3. Double-click the Start icon.

4. The CD-ROM interface will appear. The interface provides a simple point-and-click way to explore the contents of the CD.

Note for Mac users: the content menus may not function as expected in newer versions of Safari and Firefox; however, the documents are available by navigating to the Contents folder.

What's on the CD

The following sections provide a summary of the software and other materials you'll find on the CD.

Content

The companion CD-Rom contains PDF and Word files of key landmark cases and judicial decisions, including those having bearing on the interpretation of the IDEA and Section 504; as well as supplemental material including final regulations for the IDEA, Section 504, and FERPA, and a collection of federal agency memorandums and letters interpreting those and other federal regulations.

Applications

The following applications are on the CD:

Adobe Reader

Adobe Reader is a freeware application for viewing files in the Adobe Portable Document format.

OpenOffice.org

OpenOffice.org is a free multi-platform office productivity suite. It is similar to Microsoft Office or Lotus SmartSuite, but OpenOffice.org is absolutely free. It includes word processing, spreadsheet, presentation, and drawing applications that enable you to create professional documents, newsletters, reports, and presentations. It supports most file formats of other office software. You should be able to edit and view any files created with other office solutions.

Shareware programs are fully functional, trial versions of copyrighted programs. If you like particular programs, register with their authors for a nominal fee and receive licenses, enhanced versions, and technical support.

Freeware programs are copyrighted games, applications, and utilities that are free for personal use. Unlike shareware, these programs do not require a fee or provide technical support.

GNU software is governed by its own license, which is included inside the folder of the GNU product. See the GNU license for more details.

Trial, demo, or evaluation versions are usually limited either by time or functionality (such as being unable to save projects). Some trial versions are very sensitive to system date changes. If you alter your computer's date, the programs will "time out" and no longer be functional.

Customer Care

If you have trouble with the CD-ROM, please call the Wiley Product Technical Support phone number at (800) 762-2974. Outside the United States, call 1 (317) 572-3994. You can also contact Wiley Product Technical Support at **http://support.wiley.com.** John Wiley & Sons will provide technical support only for installation and other general quality control items. For technical support on the applications themselves, consult the program's vendor or author.

To place additional orders or to request information about other Wiley products, please call (877) 762-2974.

CUSTOMER NOTE: IF THIS BOOK IS ACCOMPANIED BY SOFTWARE, PLEASE READ THE FOLLOWING BEFORE OPENING THE PACKAGE.